CW00531335

LIVE FROM F*CKING

LOCATION

DATE

ADAM KATZ SINDING

teNeues | MENDO

YOU KNOW ADAM LIKE I KNOW ADAM.
FROM EVERY SHOW, FROM EVERY CAPITAL,
FROM SEEMINGLY EVERY CORNER OF THE
(UN)KNOWN WORLD.
      FROM THE INTERNET. SOMETIMES
      ADAM IS SO UBIQUITOUS THAT I
      HAVE TO WONDER IF HE'S EVEN REAL.
MAYBE HE'S ACTUALLY SOME KIND OF
NANO-MACHINE CONJURED UP FROM THE
ENDLESSLY EVERTING OBSERVATIONS
OF THE SMARTPHONE PANOPTICON. THE
FINAL BRIDGE BETWEEN OUR INDIVIDUAL
HUMANITY AND A SOON-TO-BE FORMED,
NETWORK-ENABLED GLOBAL META-
CONSCIOUSNESS.

BUT HE'S REAL.

—Errolson Hugh,
Co-founder of *ACRONYM*
and designer of *Stone
Island Shadow Project*

It's telling that his copious digital output is fuelled by simple repetitive physical activity. That sweat makes the pixels possible. That his visual capture of the highly aesthetic needs its opposite to enable it. That the necessarily social dynamics of subject and object, transmission and observation, can only occur because the person initiating them spends time pushing pedals (often) alone.

This is the "non-geo" now that we're all living in. Our contemporary atemporality. Time agnostic. Location agnostic. Platform agnostic. Always on. Always ephemeral. Forever a finger on the shutter release.

I used to think I traveled a lot. That was until I started following Adam on Instagram and realized I don't travel at all. I'll go to Fashion Week in Milan for Stone Island, and I'll do Paris once every two years or so. And to be honest, after four days of being in Paris I'm absolutely exhausted. Every time I'm completely oversaturated and trying not to see anybody for at least a week after. But Adam goes to every single one. He's traveling 300 days a year, and you have to respect that. People who don't travel for work have this kind of romantic idea of what it is. And, as you'll see in this book, it is an amazing thing. But to have to do this on a day to day basis: living in airports, living out of a suitcase, and in the same clothes for ages. It's an endurance game. It's Adam's game.

I met Adam for the first time in Milan, in 2015. It was outside of the Missoni show. I didn't get in, which was quite funny, because my friend Stephen Mann was doing the styling. Adam got in though, obviously, and we spoke after the show. I had known him before that through Instagram, of course, and since that summer in 2015, Adam and I have been friends. I don't see him that much, because, as you might understand, he's difficult to catch up with, but he's definitely a friend. We've never directly worked together either, but if you check out his wardrobe, you'd think that we have.

I DON'T THINK YOU CAN BE REALLY GOOD AT ANYTHING UNLESS YOU ARE OBSESSED TO THE DEGREE THAT YOU'RE WILLING TO MAKE OTHER PEOPLE UNCOM- FORTABLE.
—Errolson Hugh

Actually I'm pretty sure that in the first photo I saw of Adam, he was wearing the first ever ACG jacket that we had designed for NikeLab. When I saw him wearing our stuff, it struck me that he's actually our perfect proof of concept. He's out there at Fashion Week, in the fashion capitals of the world, but he's *outside*, shifting locations I don't even know how many times a day, traveling with all different sorts of transportation, carrying around all his equipment, while still needing to move fast and handle quickly. While doing this, he also has to feel good and look cool. So he's this edge case. He's the prototypical user. When we design clothes, we don't design them to have a specific end use. Instead, we try to have a horizontal approach in which the widest possible spectrum of activities is taken into consideration with one single garment. I think that most companies have one person in mind around which they make a concept for a product. If we would, Adam would be the perfect guy.

In that respect, I'm always following him. What is he doing? Where is he? What is he wearing, and how is he wearing it? He's ended up acquiring a great number of items we've designed, and it's always interesting to see how he uses them. You can see that he actually needs these things to do what he does. Fashion, and more in particular, apparel, is interesting because it functions at the intersection of utility and identity. While you do want it to work, just as much (or maybe even more) you want it to say something about who you are—your position in the world, your perspective, and your outlook. Adam is obviously in the field, doing what he needs to do, but he's also a sophisticated person who wants to express who he is.

Adam is not your simple, everyday customer though. But that's exactly the point. The stuff that we make is like an interface. You can systematically put your wallet here, your phone and passport there, and your flight tickets in this pocket. In this way, your jacket becomes an extension of who you are. Which is good for anyone like Adam who is constantly on the move, and always outside—even during the miserable winters.

One of the things I remember from when we first met was that he said something like: "Discovering your work was a big revelation for me because of the work that my mother had done." I was like, "Oh, that's cool," not really processing what that was about. It took me a few months to realize that Adam's mother designed outerwear. And not just random stuff, but actually iconic items like the original Jordan Flight Suit, and the Nike Windrunner. I remember texting him later: "Holy shit! Your Mom made this?" Diane Katz is a legend. In some sense, we kind of have the same background. He was in the Pacific Northwest, in that type of weather, which was quite similar to the Canadian climate that I grew up in. Now I'm in Berlin and he's in Copenhagen, both of which are probably less shit, but they're still shit. You just have a different way of approaching apparel when you absolutely need to wear it. And because you rarely find things that work, when you finally find something that actually does, it's a revelation. And you won't give it up easily either.

That's how I know that he understands what we do, on multiple levels. Over the years that I've been following him, I've noticed how he's built up this physical process. The amount of physical activities and sports that he engages in wherever he goes has been steadily increasing. I haven't spoken to him about it, but I can only imagine that he does this to keep himself sane. It's hardcore to perpetually transition through different environments in rapid succession. So Adam is running 15K, cycling from Paris to Amsterdam, or doing 100 pushups before he goes to sleep. These are all tools to help deal with the traveling. To have groundedness, to be physically in your body, to achieve an almost meditative state. That's the way to stay balanced despite the frenzy.

I'M TYPING THIS GOING 939 KM PER HOUR, AT AN ALTITUDE OF 11,886 METERS, AND I CAN'T HELP BUT FEEL CONNECTED TO ADAM.
—Errolson Hugh

He also has a really good balance of seriousness and lightheartedness. I like the total respect he has for his work. The precision that he applies to it and how committed he is to doing what he does. But then I also really like that he's constantly goofing off. I think that's an incredibly healthy thing when you do something that's super intense. You have to balance it all out and he's a perfect example of that.

Some might say that he's demanding, but I've never seen him as such. I don't think you can be really good at anything unless you're obsessed to the degree that you're willing to make other people uncomfortable. If you're worried about what everybody else is going to think, you're not going to do very good work. But if you believe in what you're doing, then that's going to happen. It's almost a prerequisite to being good at things. Adam is a great guy, and I've only had positive experiences with him, but yeah, let the man get his shot!

There is this quote from science fiction writer William Gibson. In *Mona Lisa Overdrive* he uses the phrase: *"It's moving so fast it's standing still."* I always think of Adam when I read or hear that phrase. He has this frenetic pace, but then also this sort of monk-like approach to everything he does. The work he makes, the running, the cycling, the traveling—and I'm sure that his drinking is on that level, too. Adam is an iconoclast. He thinks for himself and he completely does his own thing. When I see someone like that wearing our stuff, making it part of their daily lives, then I know that we're doing the right thing. It's proof that it works.

I'm typing this going 939 km per hour, at an altitude of 11,886 meters, and I can't help but feel connected to Adam. I wonder if this is the end of an era. Is he the last of his kind? As the oceans rise and the climate breaks down, will air travel become an unthinkable artifact of the past? Will we look back at all of this and wonder at the pace and the distance, and shake our heads at the frenetic fashion calendar that it enabled? Or will we all, like Adam, cut out meat and dairy, and start to pace ourselves? Walk more, cycle more; incrementally build a new world of possibility and harmony together. Who knows? I think it's the latter. And when we do, I bet we'll all still be watching, and Adam—Adam will still be live from fucking everywhere.—

FASHION PHOTOGRAPHER ADAM KATZ SINDING TRAVELS AT LEAST 300 DAYS A YEAR. EVERY YEAR, HE GOES TO THE MOST IMPORTANT FASHION WEEKS IN THE WORLD TO CAPTURE THE ZEITGEIST AND THE NEW WAVE. WHEN HE'S NOT WORKING, HE'S RUNNING, CYCLING, WALKING, SHARING, OR STILL WORKING. ADAM KATZ SINDING HAS FIVE FULL-TIME JOBS, AND HE DOES THEM WITH IRON DISCIPLINE AT AN INCREDIBLE PACE. THIS IS HOW, KIND OF.

MIKEL   Your first book opened with a photo taken at an Off-White show of a neon sign that read: "You're obviously in the wrong place." It always kind of struck me as a reminder to yourself.

ADAM   I guess you could see it like that. It obviously is a way of questioning the people who come to these shows. With this new influx of people within fashion in the last ten years, you see a lot of faces sitting at the front rows who do not necessarily belong there. And I'm definitely a part of that. I was sitting front row at Off-White FW19 and French *Vogue* editors were sitting behind me. I would be so pissed off if I were one of those people. It doesn't make any sense.

M   But you, personally, do you feel like the fashion world is your world?

A   My perspective has always been from the outside looking in. I've always felt more comfortable not really being a part of it. I'm not turning down an opportunity to sit front row at such an amazing fashion show, of course, that would be stupid. But frankly, I feel like I don't feel like I need to be attending any fashion show. I'm super happy when they grant me backstage access, though. But that's my work. Every season I feel like I'm less and less interested in what's being worn. It remains interesting to photograph, and the fashion is an essential part of what I do—it would be a lot less intriguing if there wasn't such novelty and aesthetics involved. But if it wasn't for brands like Acronym, I would have had a lot more difficulties with it. Balenciaga can make a t-shirt for $500 with just a logo on it; that's just a scam. Errolson doesn't make stuff that doesn't make sense.

M   Do you?

A   Well, a lot of what I do doesn't make sense. So maybe I do belong in fashion. But what I like about Acronym is that the price matches the product. That is something that is quite rare in fashion. I don't really care that much about what these other brands do. I can see something I like, but I never feel the urge to buy it. I'm trying to limit my buying habits anyways.

M   Does that also involve your "buying Acronym jackets" habit?

A   I said I was trying. I have around 20, 21 Acronym jackets. Do I really need 22? Maybe. I'm undoubtedly a consumer, but I'm more interested in experiences than in having things. I know that some people are going to roll their eyes at me for saying that. I love having things, don't get me wrong, but oftentimes I like tracking my package before it arrives more than actually having the package.

M   I understand that. The anticipation is often more valuable than the actual thing.

A   Yes. It can be something simple as walking along a different route, or cycling through a new city. Experiences like these are super rewarding, they make me happier person. In the end, all of this is a way of finding happiness and fulfillment. I definitely think that buying new things is the wrong way of getting to that destination.

M   Traveling was (and is) a byproduct of your work, but what you're saying actually makes it seem like it is the most valuable aspect of your work.

A   My mom traveled a lot for work when I was growing up, so I think it always was part of my life as if it was a normal thing. Traveling is incredible, but obviously I do it at an obsessive level. I do it up to a point where I almost numb myself. I wish I traveled less, or stayed in places a little bit longer in order to actually experience them. I've been to Paris at least four times each year in the last decade, and I haven't been to a single museum. The only times I've visited art galleries was when there was another fashion event going on. Every single one of them was filled with the

Adam's Fashion Week Backstage Passes

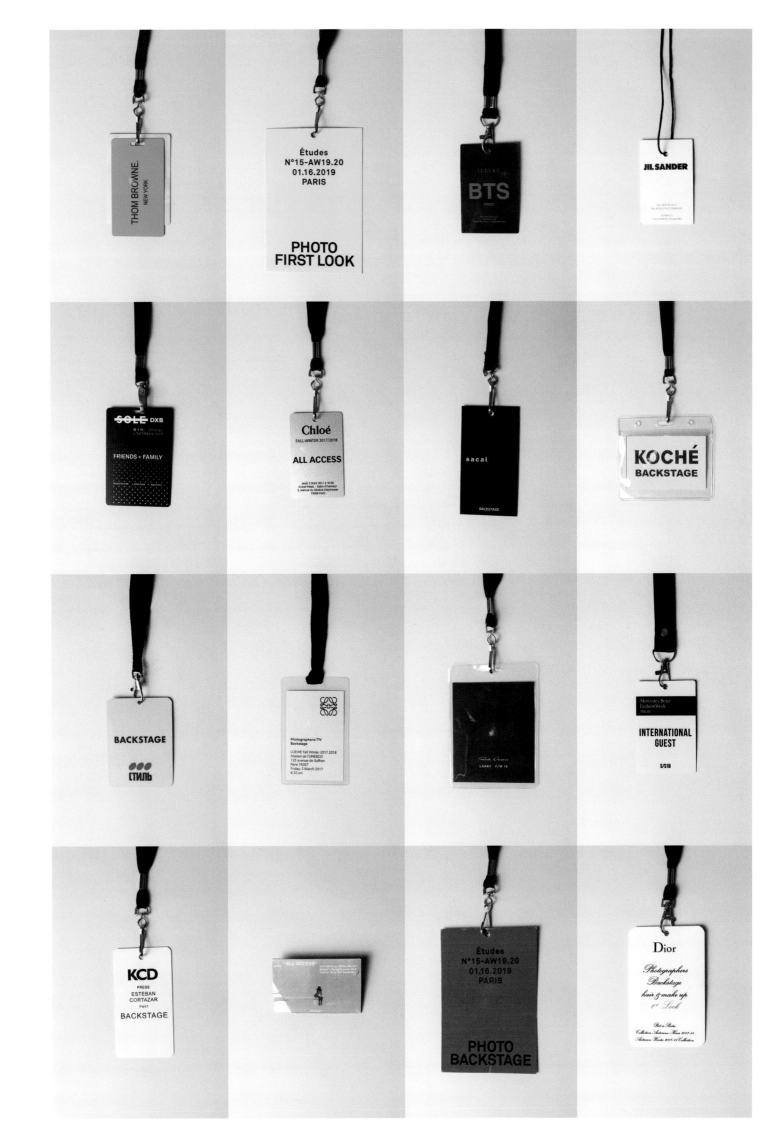

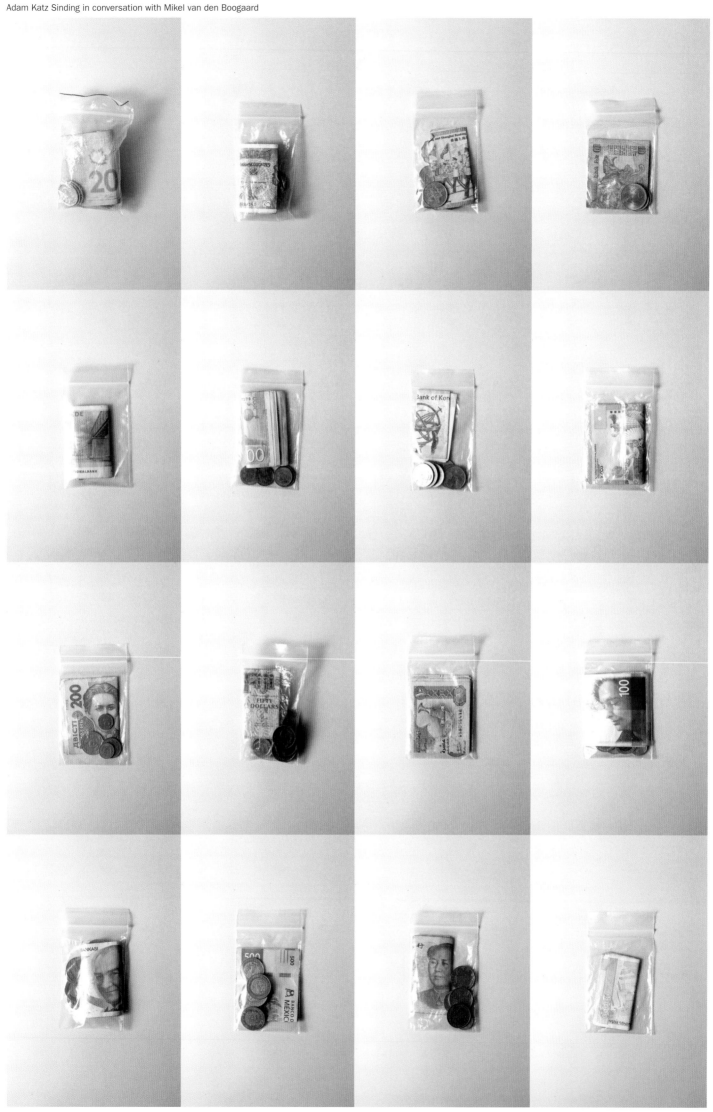

same people, and most of them weren't even Parisian.

M So the photos in these books are a way of escaping that?

A I love my job, don't get me wrong, but it can get very superficial. That's why I try make these photos while I walk through cities. It's a way of cataloging my experiences and to see something that's off the normal path that I usually take. I see these places over and over, so these photos make me feel like I've done something else while I'm there.

M I actually feel like you're always doing something wherever you are. I was just about to ask how many hours you have in one day.

A These photos were mostly made while commuting. For example, in Milan, the subway system sucks, the shared bikes are too small, and their Ubers are expensive, so I'd rather walk. In these big cities during Fashion Week, half the time it only takes marginally more to walk to places. And I'd rather be late and calm, and see something of the city along the way.

M So these photos were made during these walks?

A I carry my camera with me at all times. So whenever I have to kill some time, or have a walk, I like to snap some photos. Some of these were made during holidays, but most of the time, it's just these dead moments in between.

M What I'm wondering is, between all the shooting, traveling, running, cycling, editing, emailing, moving, and Instagramming, do you have time to relax?

A Not really. Even during my vacations I'm always busy. I'm a bit under the weather right now, and my bike was three days delayed, so I'm doing a lot of chilling, but not by my own choice. I'm just not really good at relaxing, I like to be occupied. Even when I'm at home in Copenhagen I use my down time to go for walks or for a run. And running for me is relaxing. A lot of people ask me where I find the energy to run at the end of the day, but that's where I get my energy. I get so many endorphins from running.

M How many hours do you sleep?

A I think around six hours a day, during Fashion Week.

M That's not that bad.

A It used to be a lot worse. But that probably also has to do with the exercising.

M You're from Tacoma, Washington. What was it like growing up there?

A My mom is a designer. She was Helly Hansen's ski-wear designer, and she was involved in Nike Sportswear when it was still Blue Ribbon Sports. She would take trips to

I FEEL LIKE I'M GETTING A WATERED-DOWN VERSION OF WHAT I WOULD HAVE GOTTEN 20 YEARS AGO.

Hong Kong quite often because there was no such thing as internet back then, and I came along on a few of those trips. I did pretty well at school, even though my mom would probably argue that. When I was 15, I had my first job at a mountain bike shop. I've washed dishes. I went to the University of Washington and worked at a hotel during the weekends. It wasn't that interesting, to be honest. I didn't really start to travel myself until 2012, when I went to London Fashion Week. It all went crazy after that.

M In what way has all this traveling changed your perspective on the world?

A Obviously it has, but I never really quantified that. The world became a lot smaller, especially when I just started. With social media everyone is connected with everyone anyways, but it's so interesting to meet people from around the world. I think it was more interesting 20 years ago, maybe even ten years ago. I feel like, due to social media and the internet, in general, culture is diminishing. Everyone wants to live like Americans or Western Europeans, which is great for a traveler like me because you won't experience a huge culture shock. But on the other side, isn't that what I want when I'm visiting another country? The first meal I had when I was in Tbilisi was McDonald's, and my first meal in

Korea was Shake Shack. I can get Starbucks literally everywhere in the world—that's pretty depressing. Of course, different languages, different faces, different food—that's great. But I feel like I'm getting a watered-down version of what I would have gotten 20 years ago.

M I've read this article that said that there aren't really local trends| anymore, because they get picked up all over the world so quickly. You must experience that as well. Everything kind of becomes the same, wherever you go.

A I was in Reykjavík, and they had a Big Lebowski bar. It was horrible. I remember driving nine hours up north, to this tiny obscure hot spring close to the north coast of Iceland. I got to the pool, and there were only two people in there. I was like "yes, only locals!" But then I noticed they were speaking French. There's no escaping it anymore, even though I'm aware that I'm equally guilty of all this stuff. To get back to your question, I'm sure that all this has enriched my life greatly. But I feel like everything has become a tourist attraction in a way, and I definitely try to avoid that. That's one of the reasons why I couldn't live in Amsterdam anymore. It's just too many tourists. I can't exist in that environment in which everyone has to document the fact that they were there, too. Sometimes I'm wondering what the hell is wrong with people. Okay, I understand there are things you want to see when you're in a certain city. But I try to find and appreciate the places you don't see when you open a tourist guide. Everyone who doesn't have the opportunity to travel as much as I do would probably read this and be like "look at this cocky son of a bitch," but I do realize it. I'm just wondering in which way I'm seeing the things that I'm seeing. That is why I try to stay beyond the normal Fashion Week dates as much as possible. To have a chance to walk around, and maybe eat at a place that serves authentic local food.

M How long have you been living in Europe now?

A I moved to Amsterdam in October 2015. So, almost four years now.

M Do you still see yourself as an American?

A Unfortunately. No, I miss being home, for sure. I don't miss New York, but I do miss the West Coast. When I hear people speaking with my accent, I get nostalgic. I was having a dinner with a group of Americans from the West coast and it was amazing. The language, the slang—it's just so nice to be around people who act the same as you. It's hard to be a foreigner. I've tried learning Danish, but it's so difficult. Also, in the Netherlands and Denmark

Adam's collection of change from various countries.

TBILISI HAS BECOME ONE OF MY FAVORITE PLACES IN THE WORLD.

A   To be distracted.

M   It seems like escapism. Are you afraid of something?

A   I have to talk with my therapist about that.

M   Maybe you should.

A   Look, if someone called you up today and said: "Hey, do you want to go to Kazakhstan for a week? We'll pay for everything." Of course you'll say yes. How many people do you know who've been to Kazakhstan? I've never been to Kazakhstan, and I'll probably only meet a handful of people who have been there. And I don't have to pay for it? Alright. Even though they're quick and fashion related, these experiences are unique. Tbilisi has become one of my favorite places in the world. The people are amazing, the food is amazing, it looks incredible, and it's cheap as hell there. I'll happily come back every time. I don't have this with all these places, more often it's shit and I just want to be home. But at least I've had the experience.

M   Home being...?

A   Copenhagen, in this case. But that's the thing. When I'm in Copenhagen, I want to be in Tacoma with my mom, when I'm in Tacoma, I want to be in Europe. It's so bizarre. When I was on vacation in Greece, somebody posted something and all I could think was "I wish I was there." I was in a house on the hillside, looking out over the sea, and I thought, "What the fuck is wrong with me?"

M   We're always looking for the next best thing.

A   It's quite depressing. I'm never satisfied with where I'm at.

M   Does that maybe have to do with the fact that you're always online?

A   Oh, definitely. But aren't we all?

M   Are we?

A   Well, I've toned it down a lot. Especially Instagram. It does not make you happier.

M   Do you ever get concerned about your privacy? You tend to share a lot.

A   I do. But that's also why I share less now. And who really cares? The first week of the year I didn't post any stories at all, and only two people said something. I was like: "Holy shit, nobody cares!" That's such a sobering thought. You have this idea of self-importance through social media which is totally fake. Maybe if I was a hot babe people would care if I stopped posting, but you know, I'm not really that.

M   You might have some followers for your looks though.

A   I don't think so.

M   I've seen you wearing some tight cycling outfits.

A   Somehow that's only appealing to Italian and Greek dudes. The people who slide in my DMs are often not the kind you'd hope for. Thank you? I don't know.

M   Where is your absolute favorite place to be in this world?

A   That's a hard question. I guess Copenhagen in the summertime. Or Tacoma or Seattle. But they're all kind of similar. It's just great to have a mild summer day with the sun going down at 11 p.m.

M   While being there, what would an ideal day look like for you?

A   Wake up, get coffee, go for a run or a bike ride (without running flat), then go home, have dinner with my friends, and that's it. Not too much actually. Bizarre, because it's the opposite of my normal day.

M   When do you think you'll have enough of this lifestyle?

A   I want to see as much as I can. Maybe not for Fashion Week, but I think that anybody who has the opportunity to see as much of the world as possible, should do it. I would want to travel less frequently, and probably stay a little longer, but, frankly, I don't see myself ever stopping doing this.—

everybody speaks English so well that they always speak English back to me. I feel so guilty about this. I'm sure they don't even care, but when I'm going to the bathroom and come back to hear them switching from Danish to speaking English again, I feel guilty. I'm in your house, it's so weird that you're adapting to me. We Americans are so entitled. English is the language, right? I'm definitely American, and I'm sure that it's obvious because of the things I say or do, the volume I speak with, or my lack of manners, but whenever I see Americans during my travels I'm always like "ugh." It's so embarrassing.

M   Are you ashamed to be American?

A   Well, I'm a proud American, but at the same time it can be difficult. Especially in the current political climate. I feel like we've had better moments in our history.

M   I would agree. You just said that it's hard to be a foreigner. You are a foreigner for at least 300 days a year, right?

A   Yes, but that's different. When I'm traveling, I'm visiting. People are happy to have visitors as long as they're leaving. But in Copenhagen, I sometimes feel like I'm imposing in a way. When I'm traveling for fashion, everyone's happy to have me. There's much less the sense of imposing.

M   Why do you do all this?

Adam's running and cycling heatmaps.

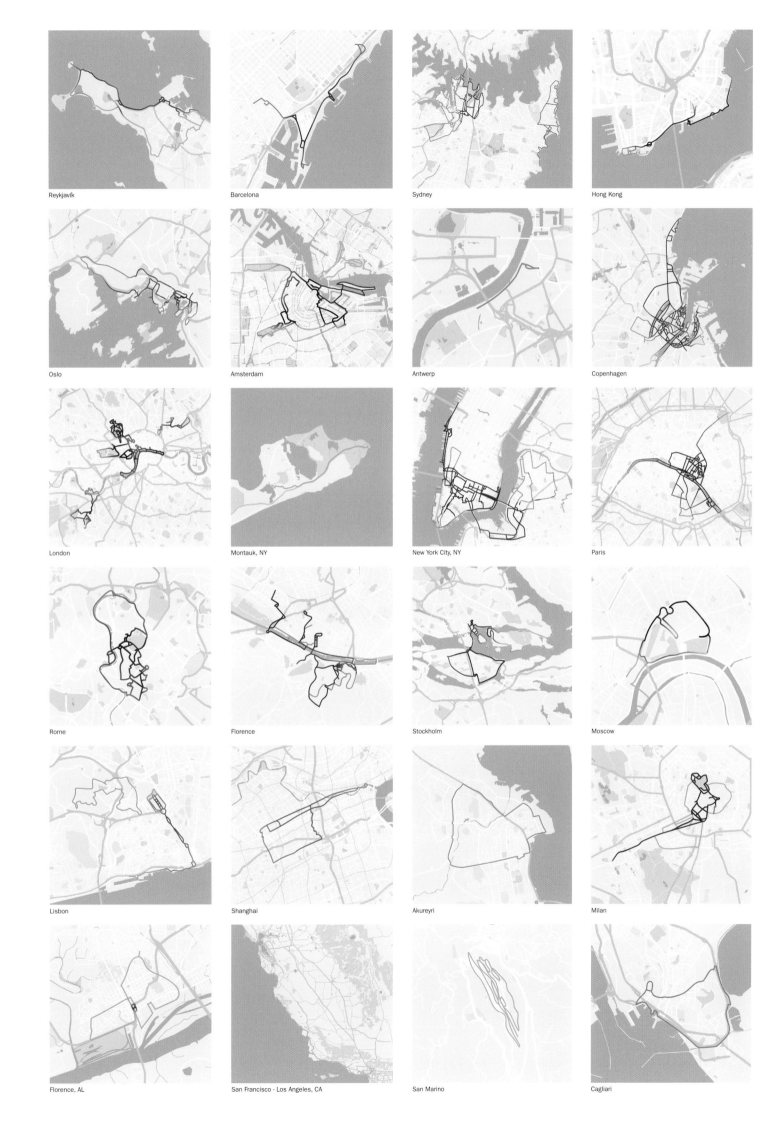

Reykjavík

Barcelona

Sydney

Hong Kong

Oslo

Amsterdam

Antwerp

Copenhagen

London

Montauk, NY

New York City, NY

Paris

Rome

Florence

Stockholm

Moscow

Lisbon

Shanghai

Akureyri

Milan

Florence, AL

San Francisco - Los Angeles, CA

San Marino

Cagliari

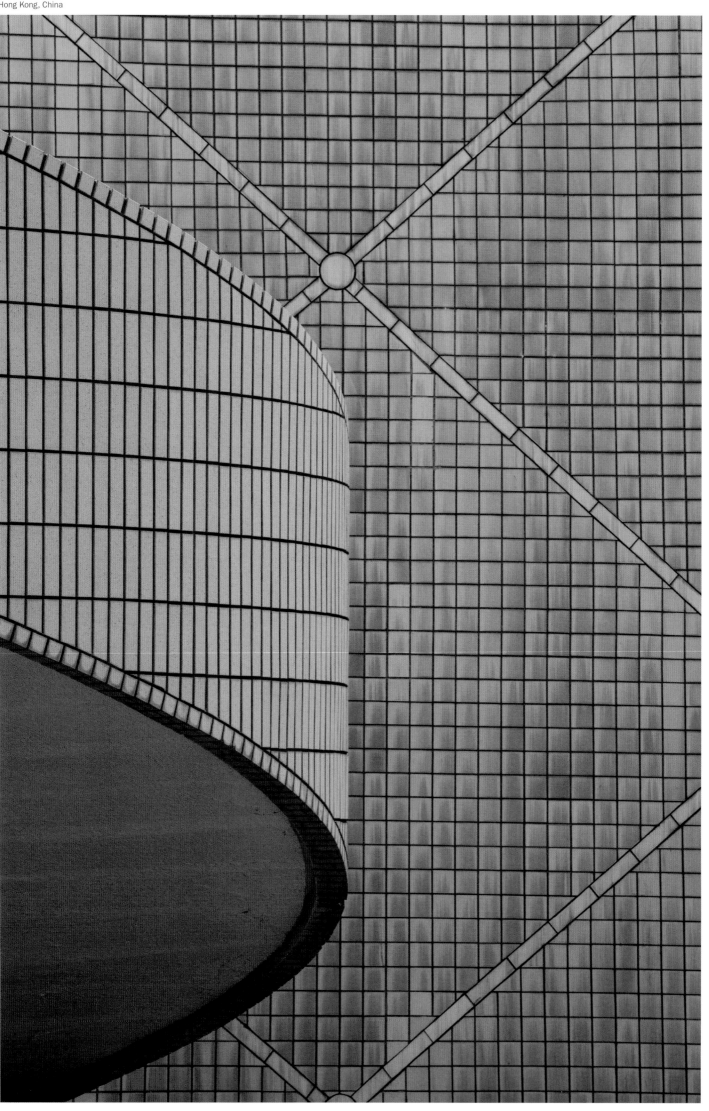

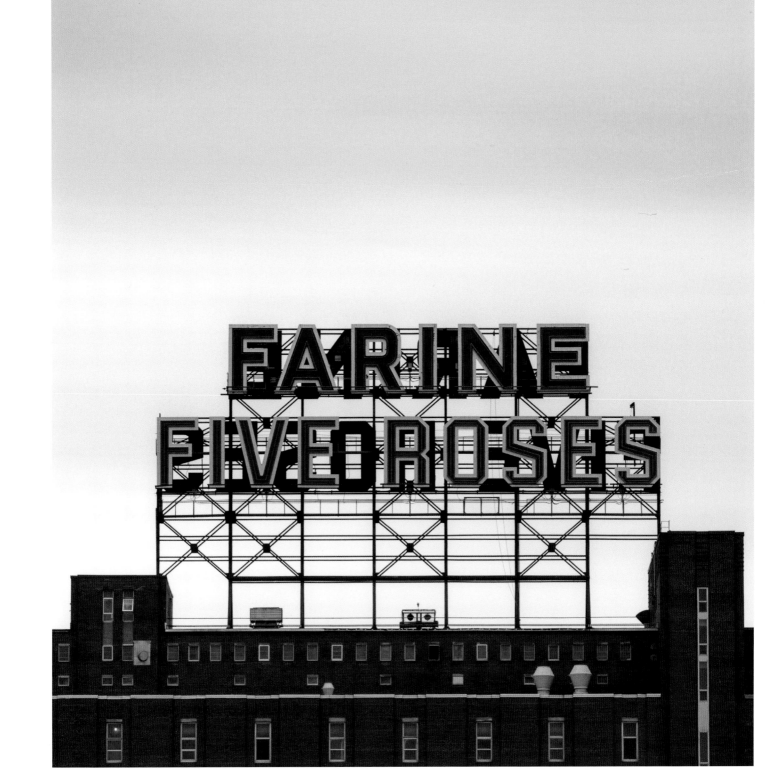

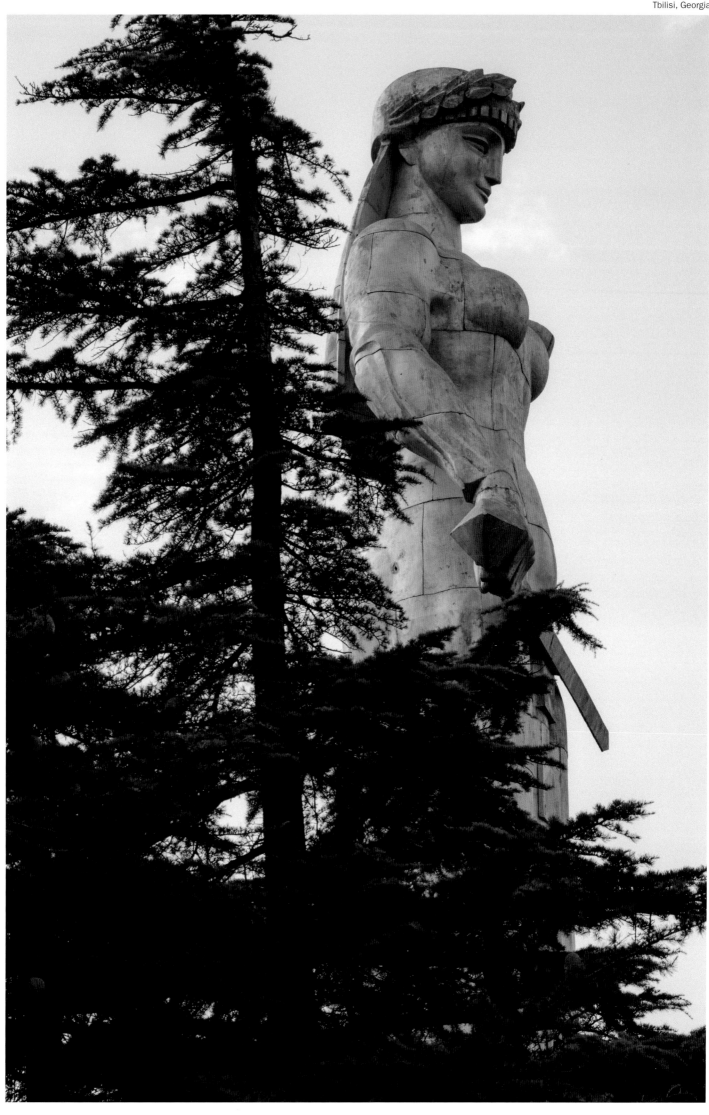

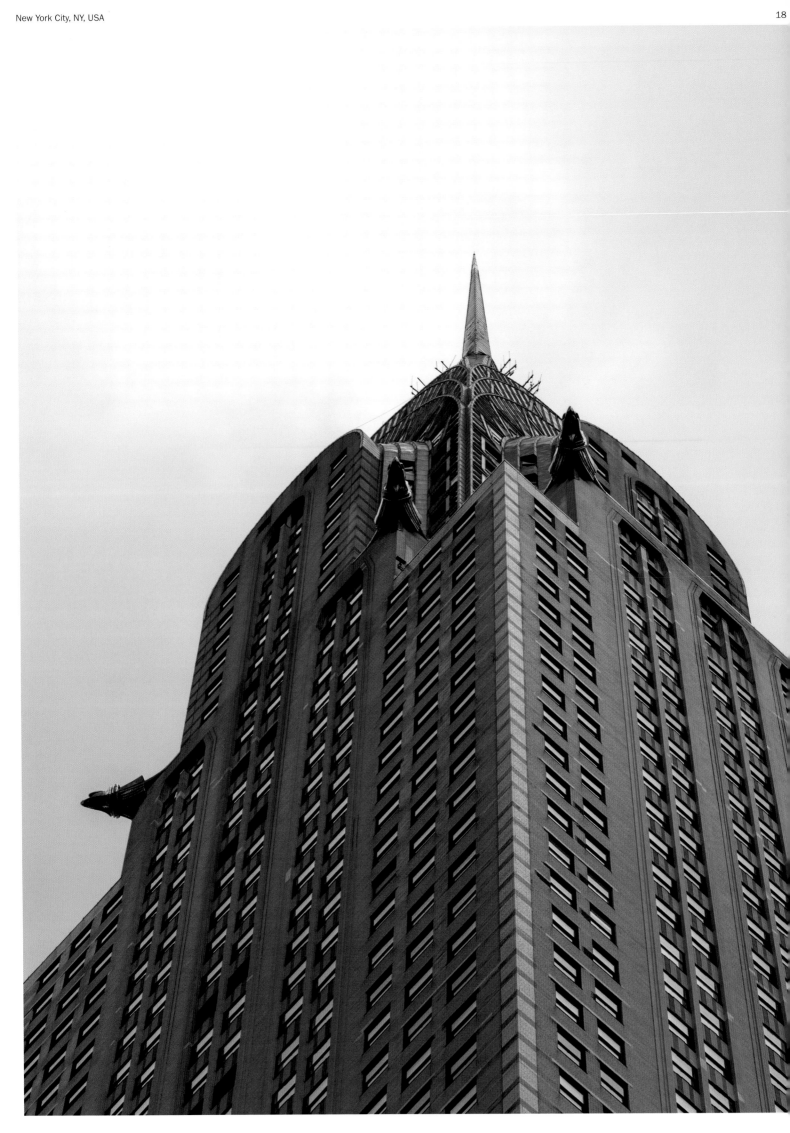

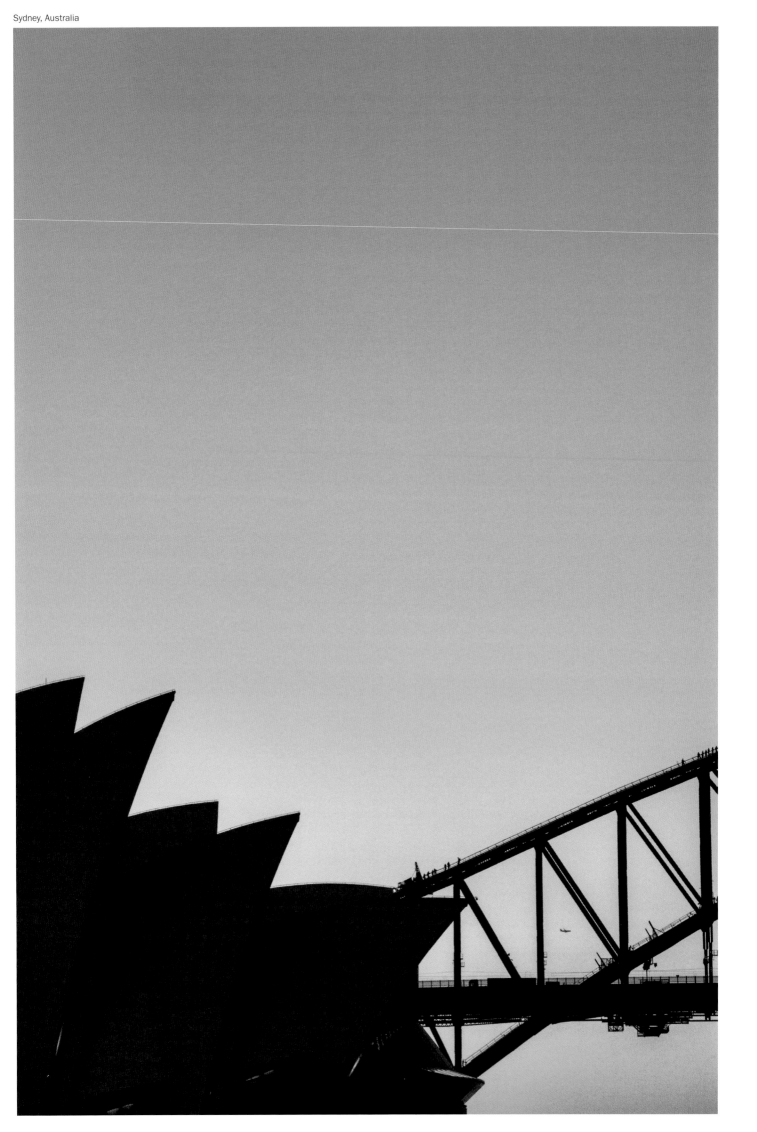

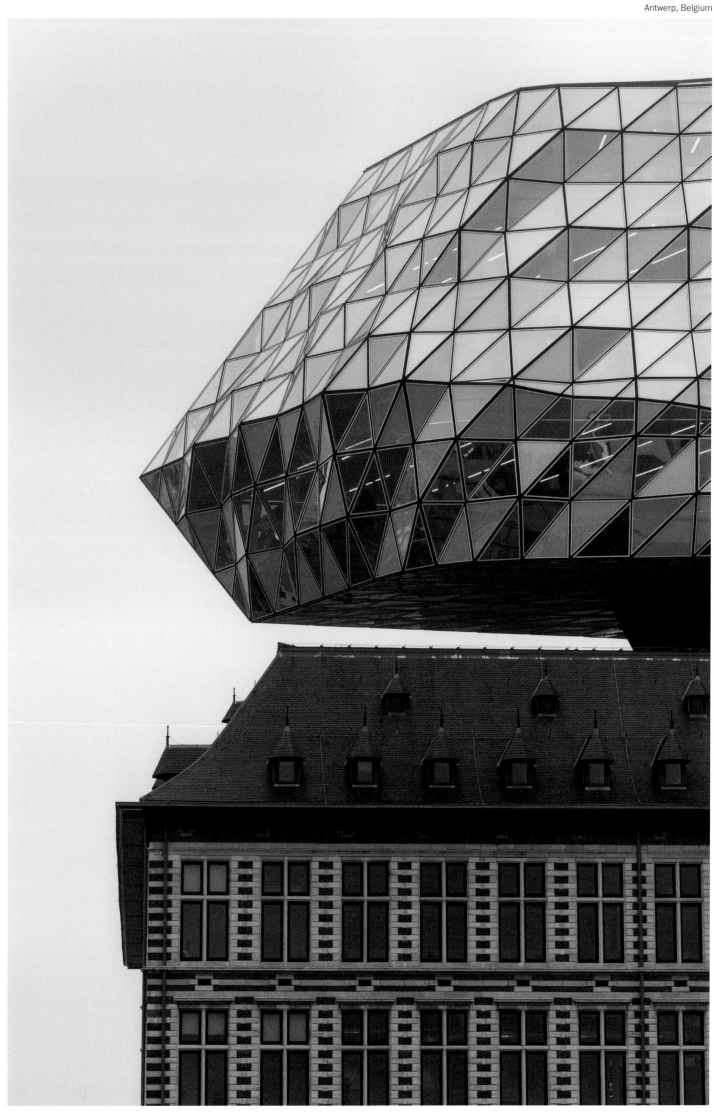

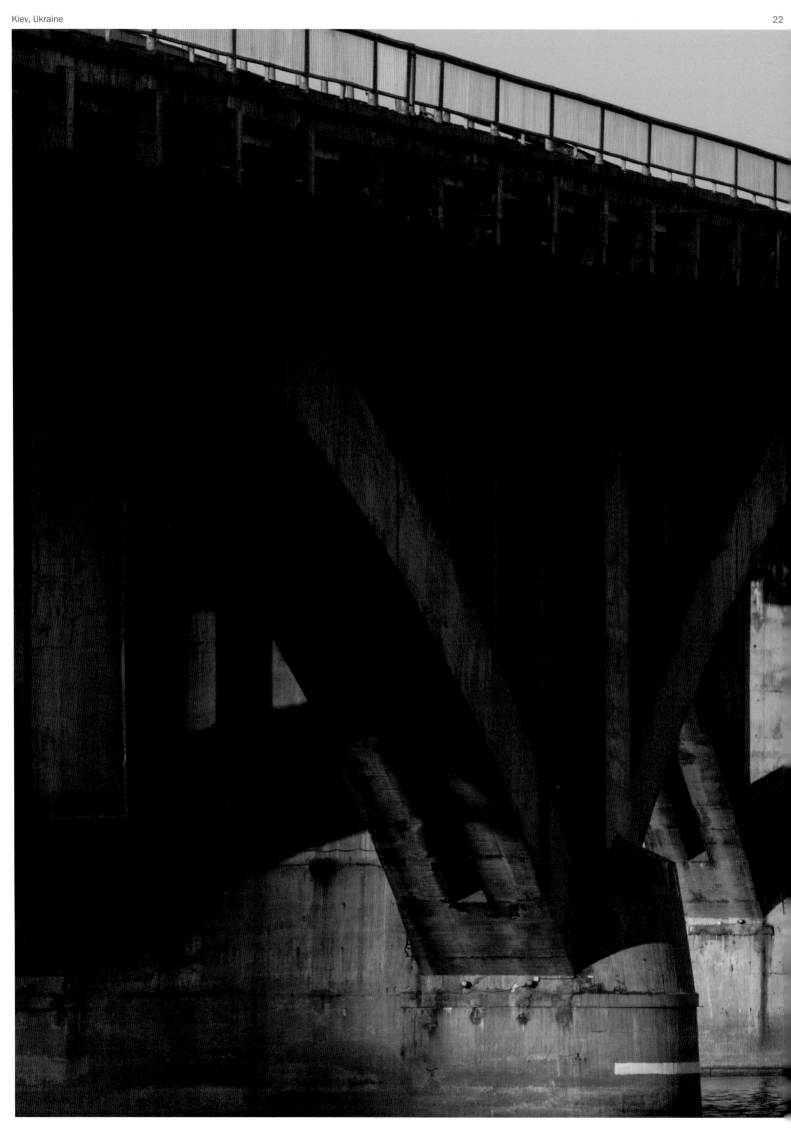

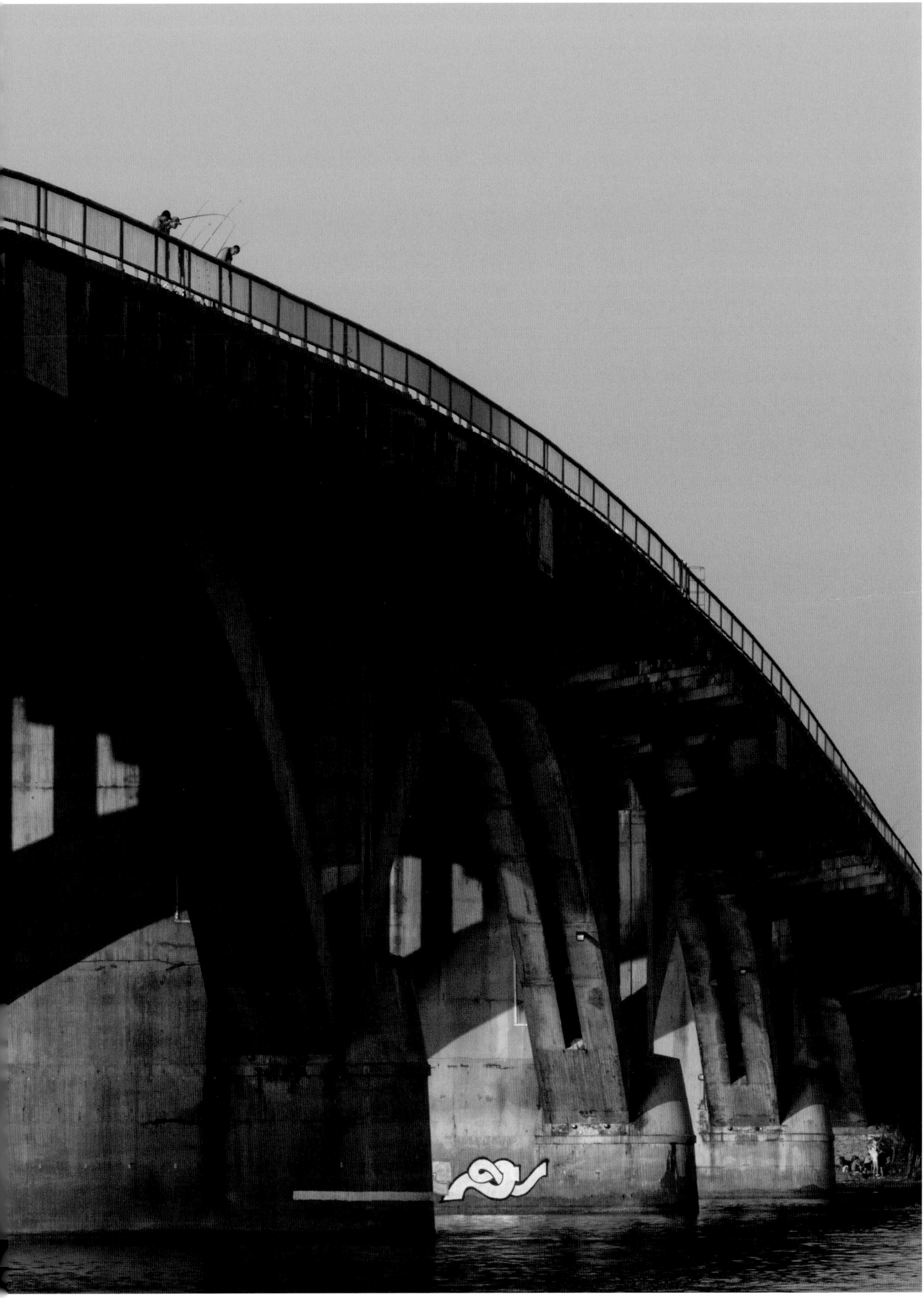

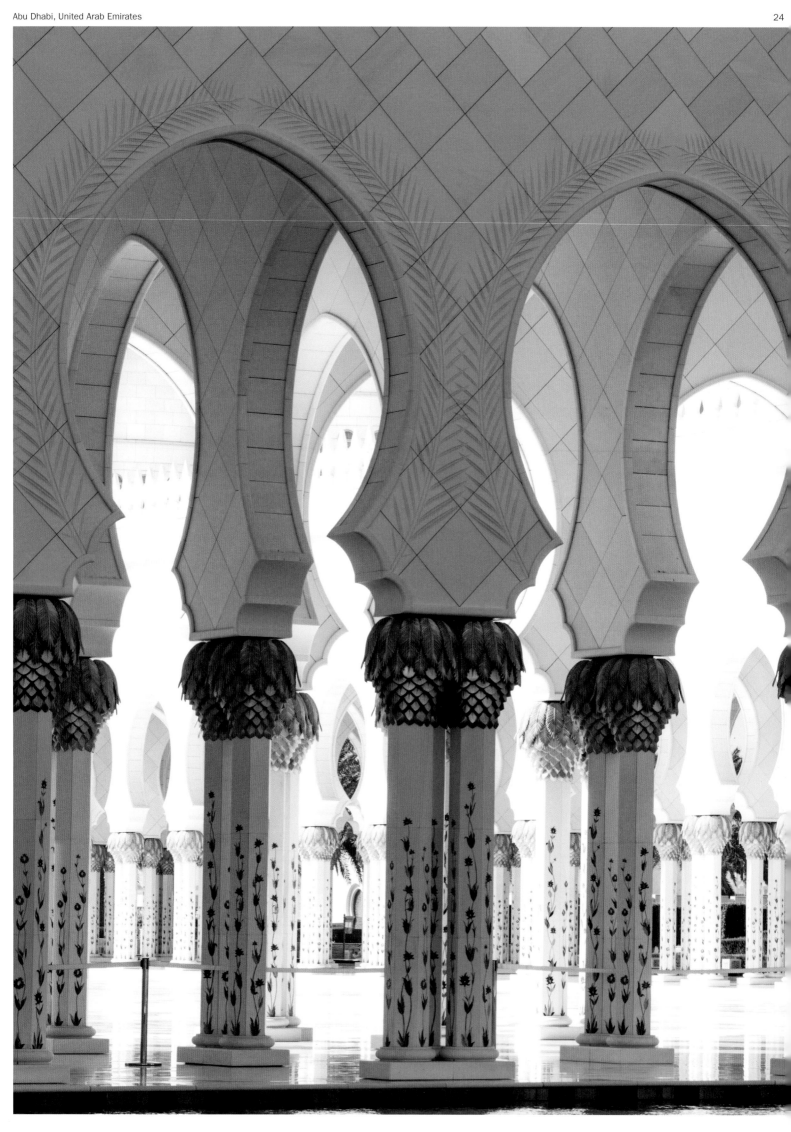

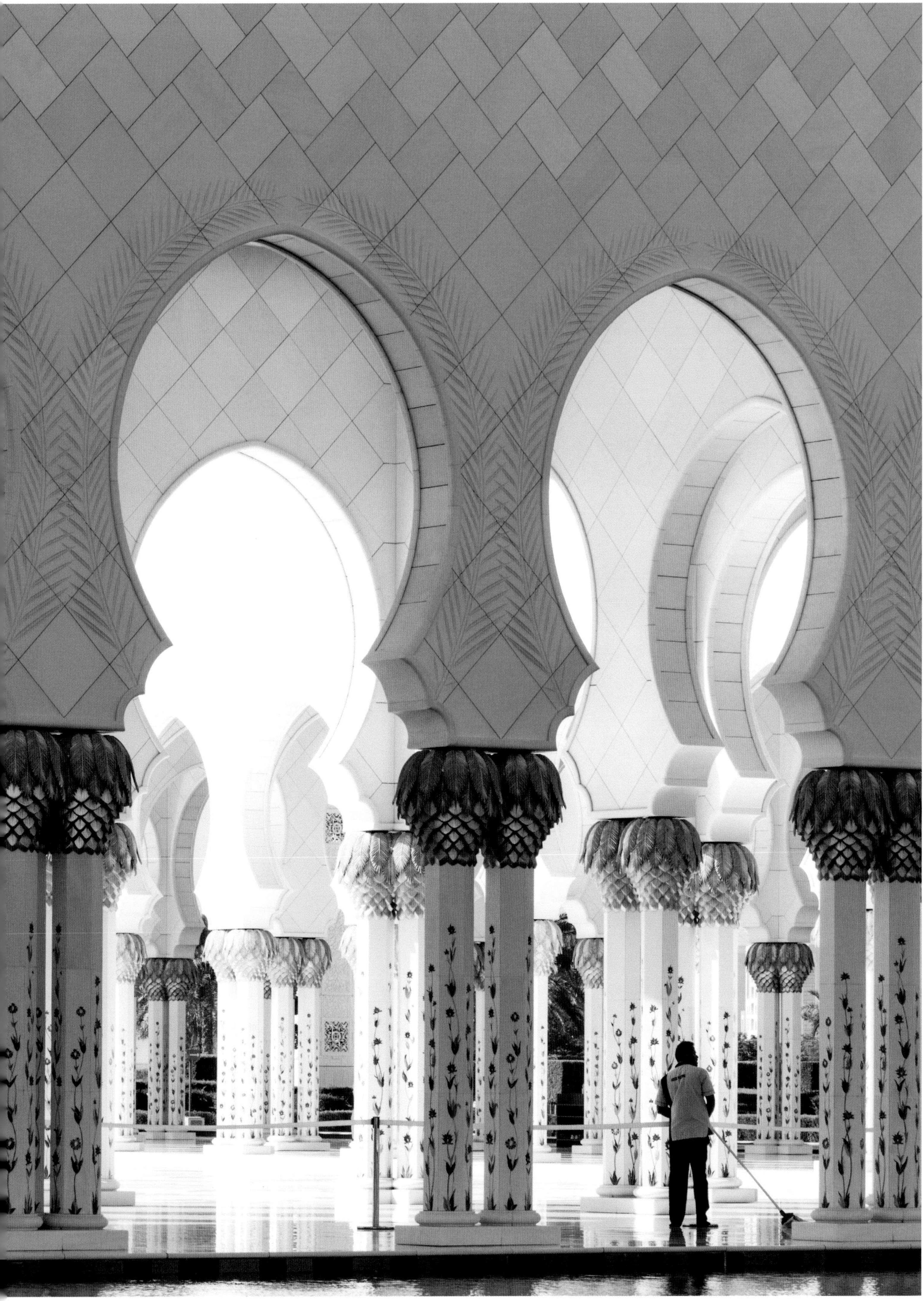

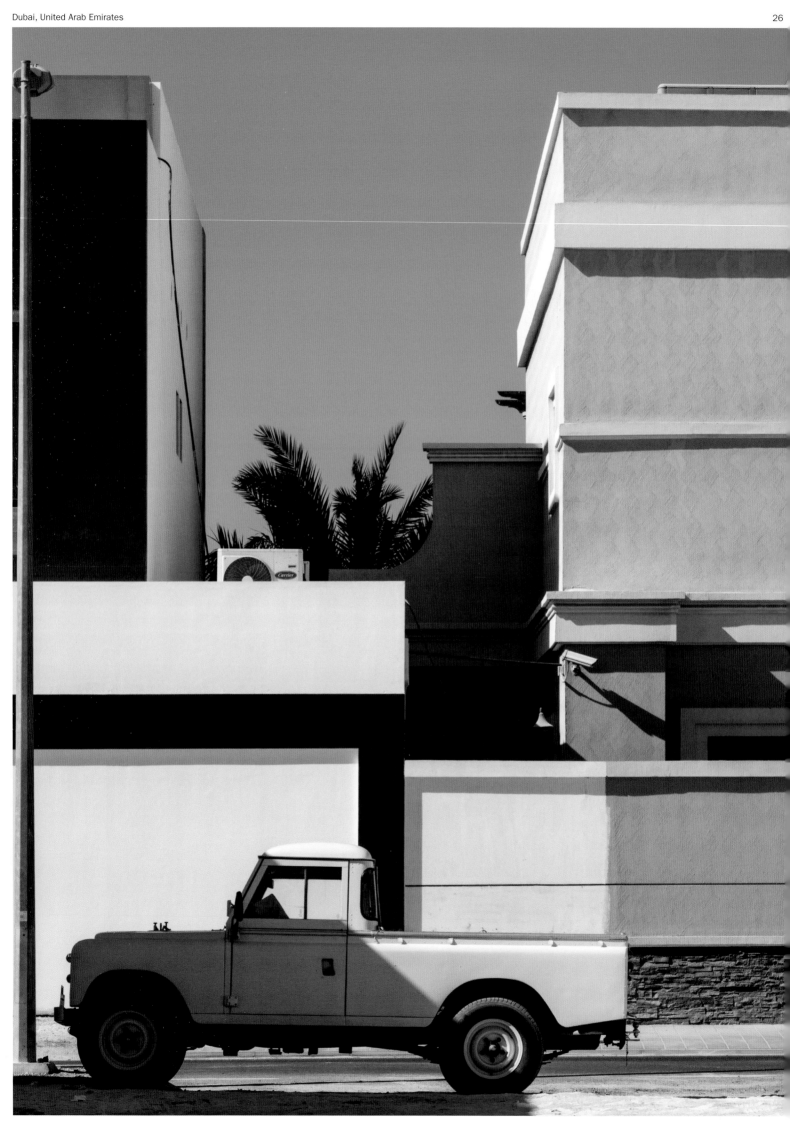

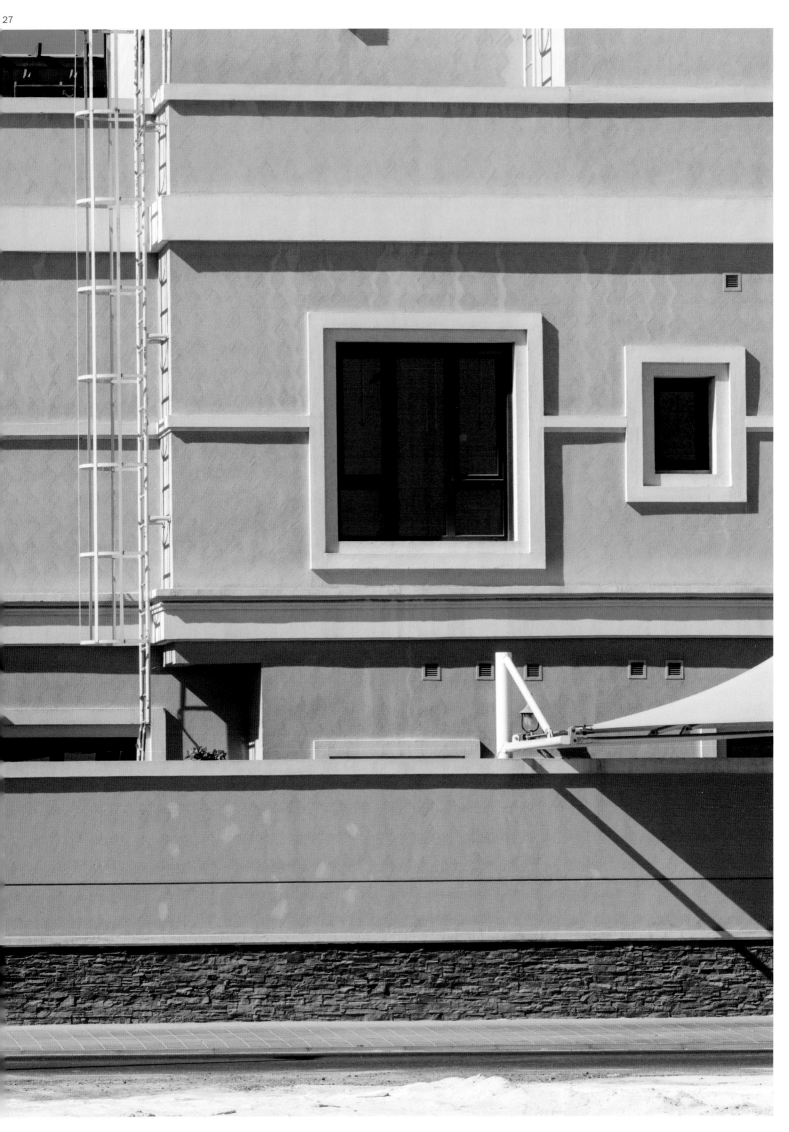

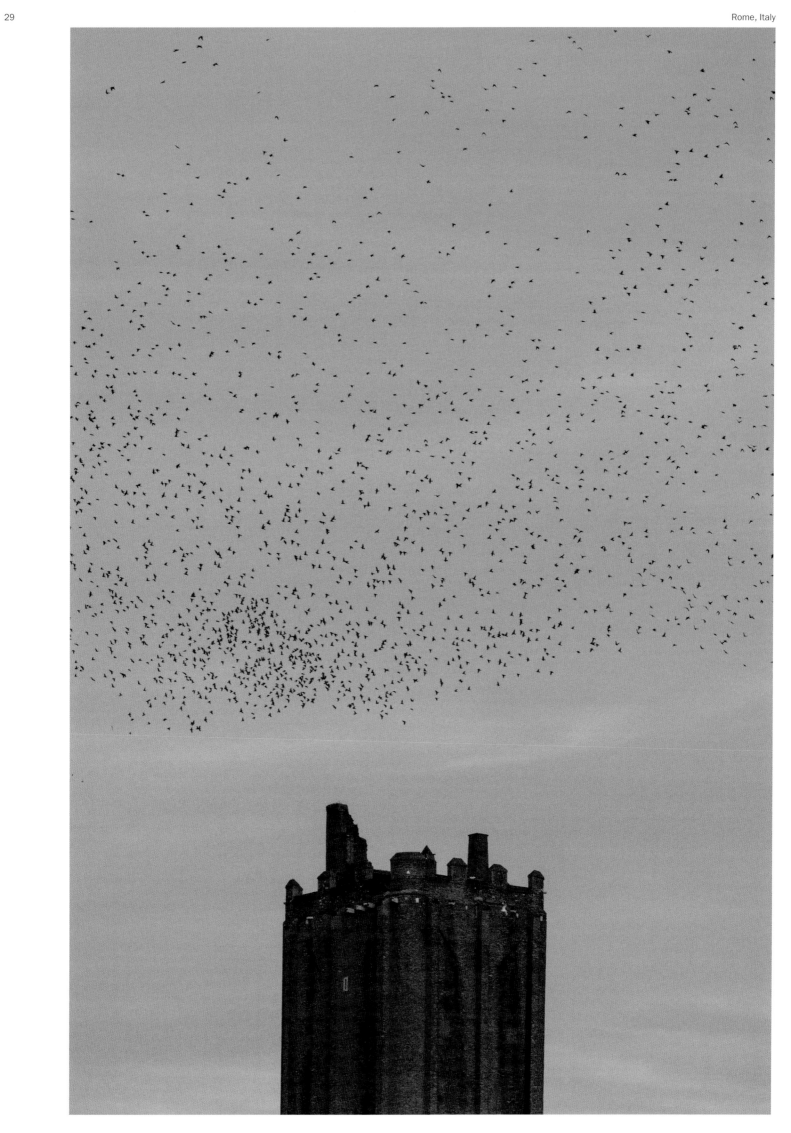

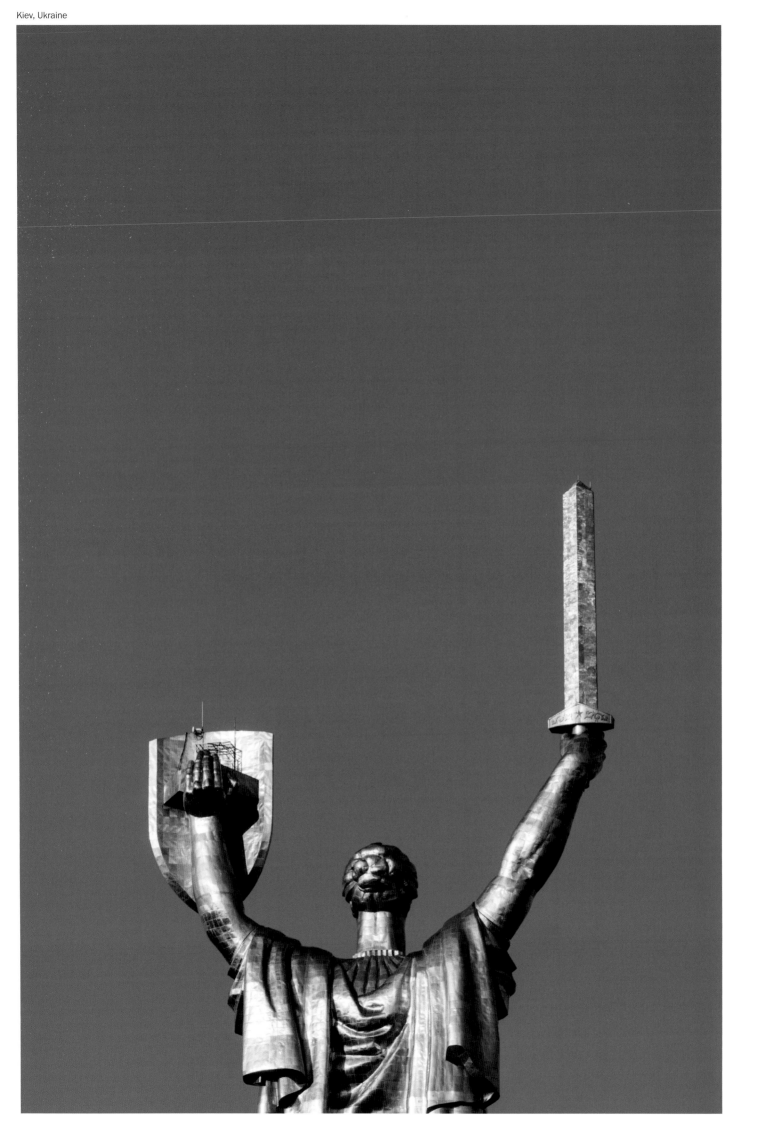

230

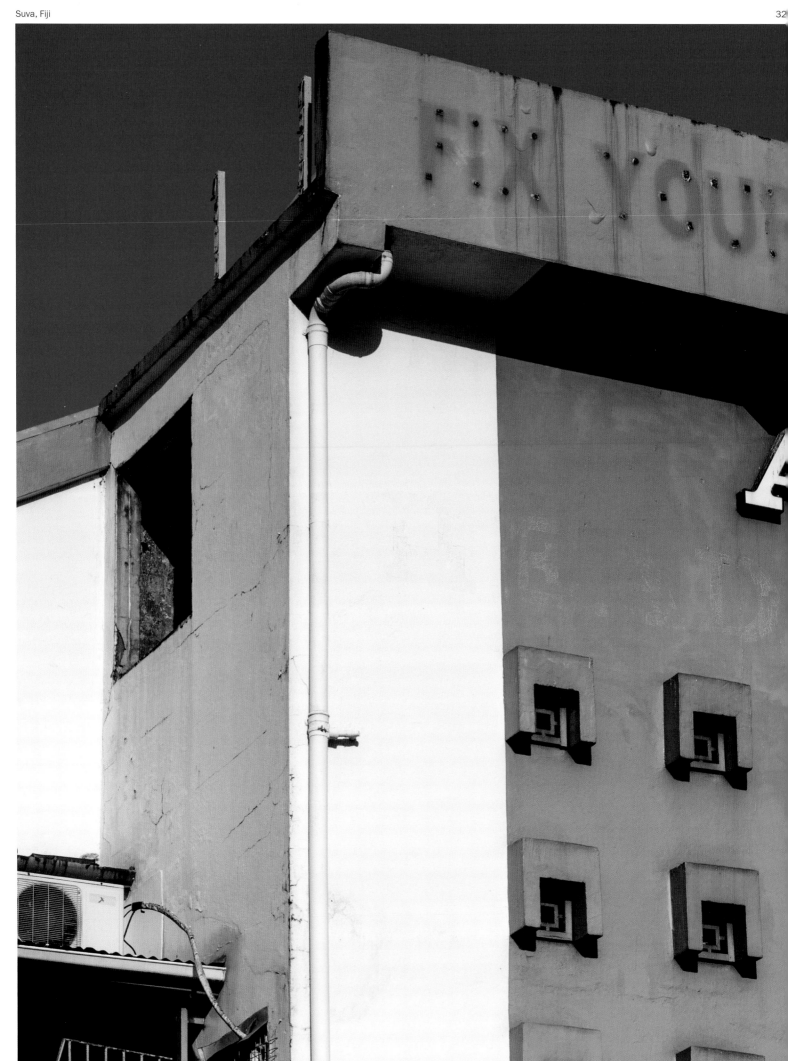

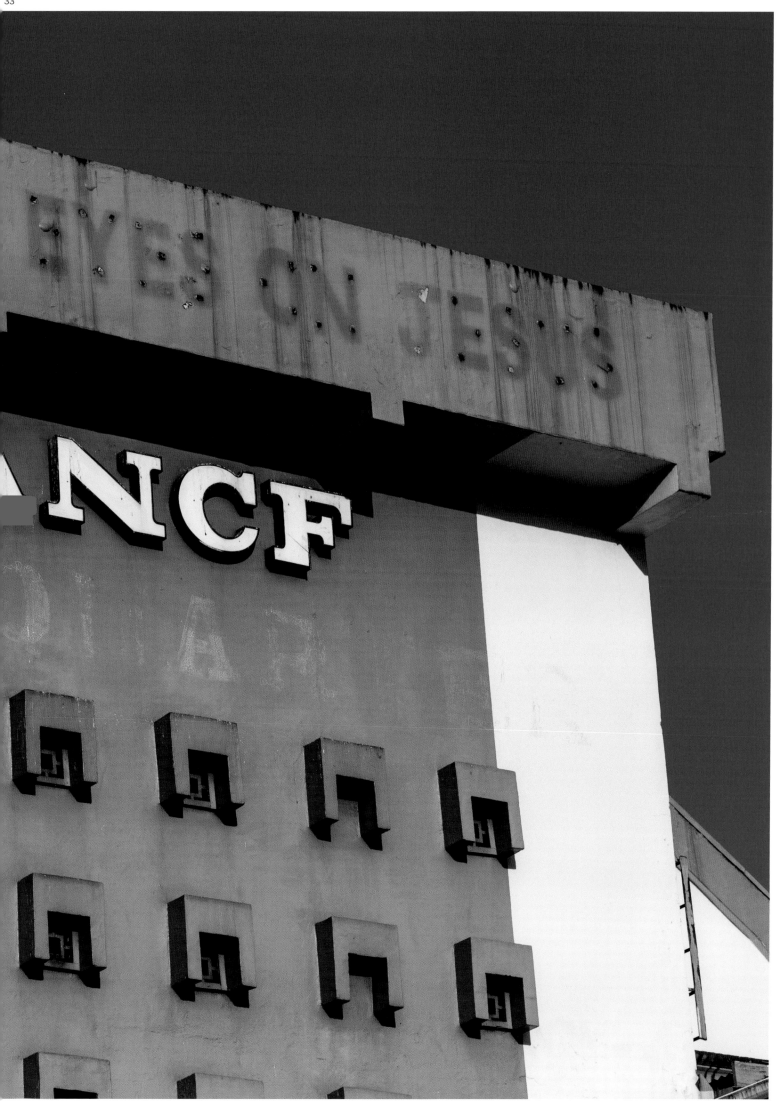

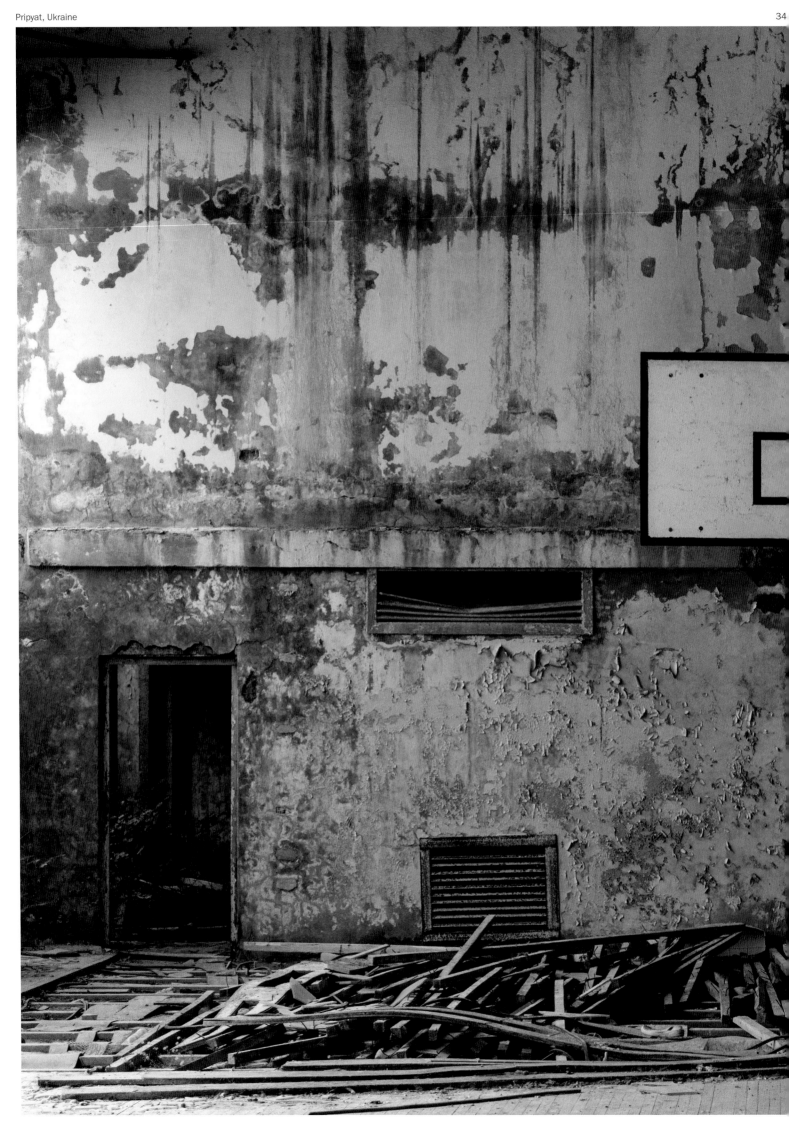

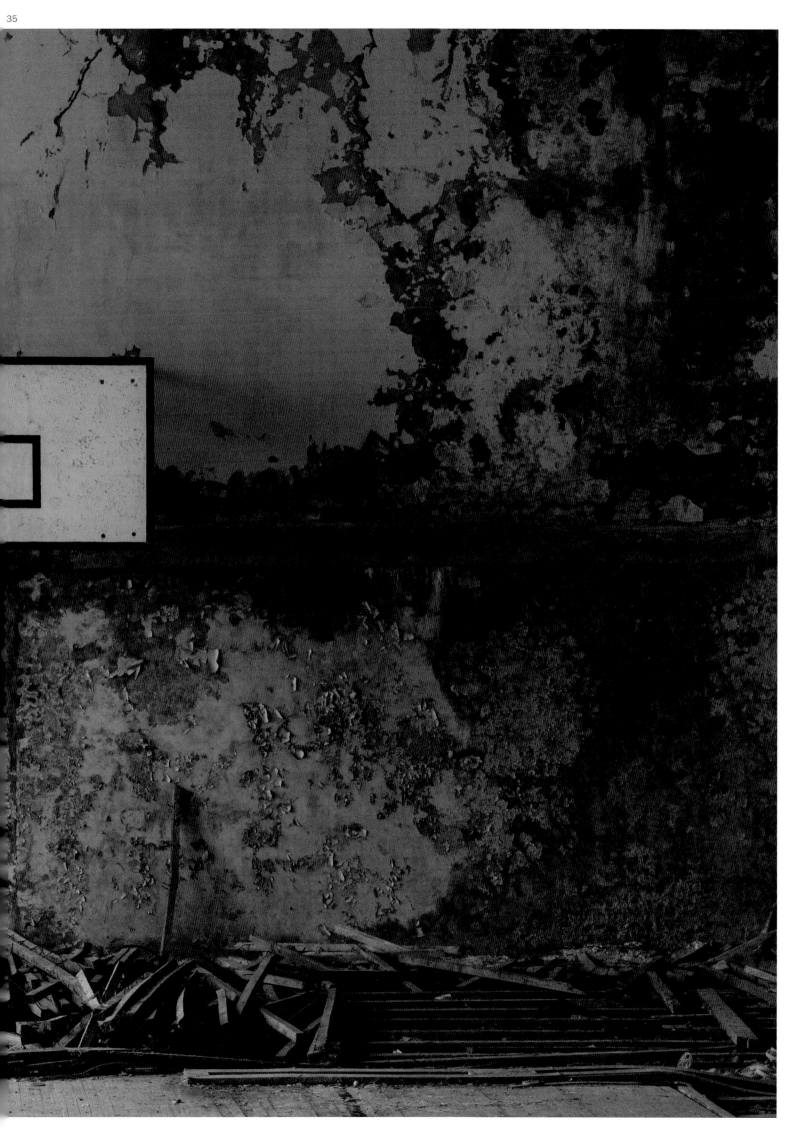

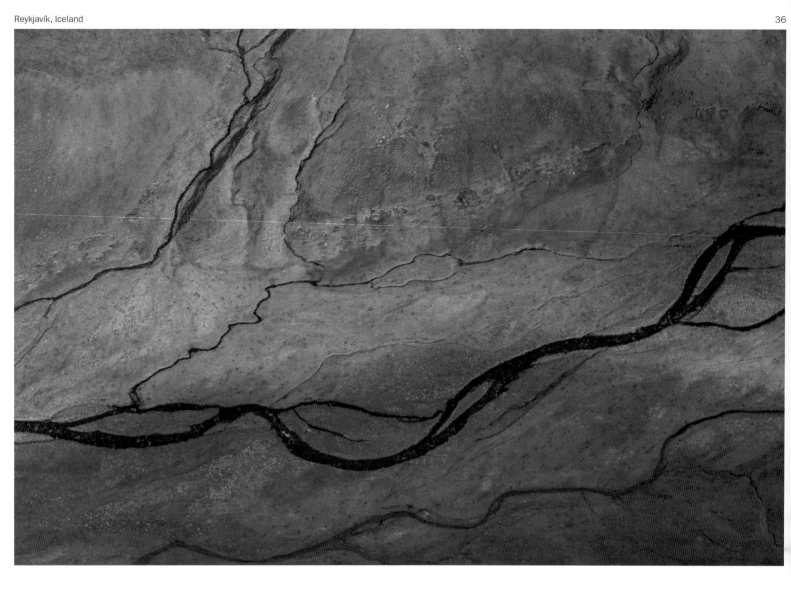

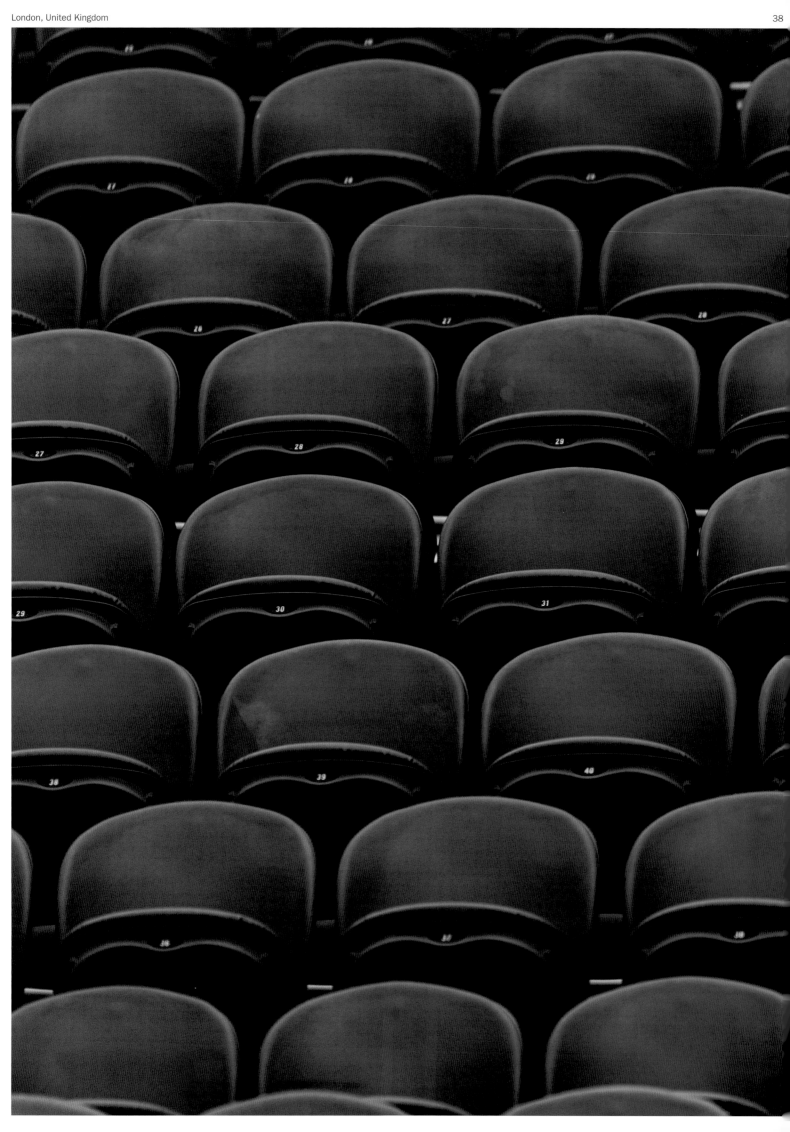

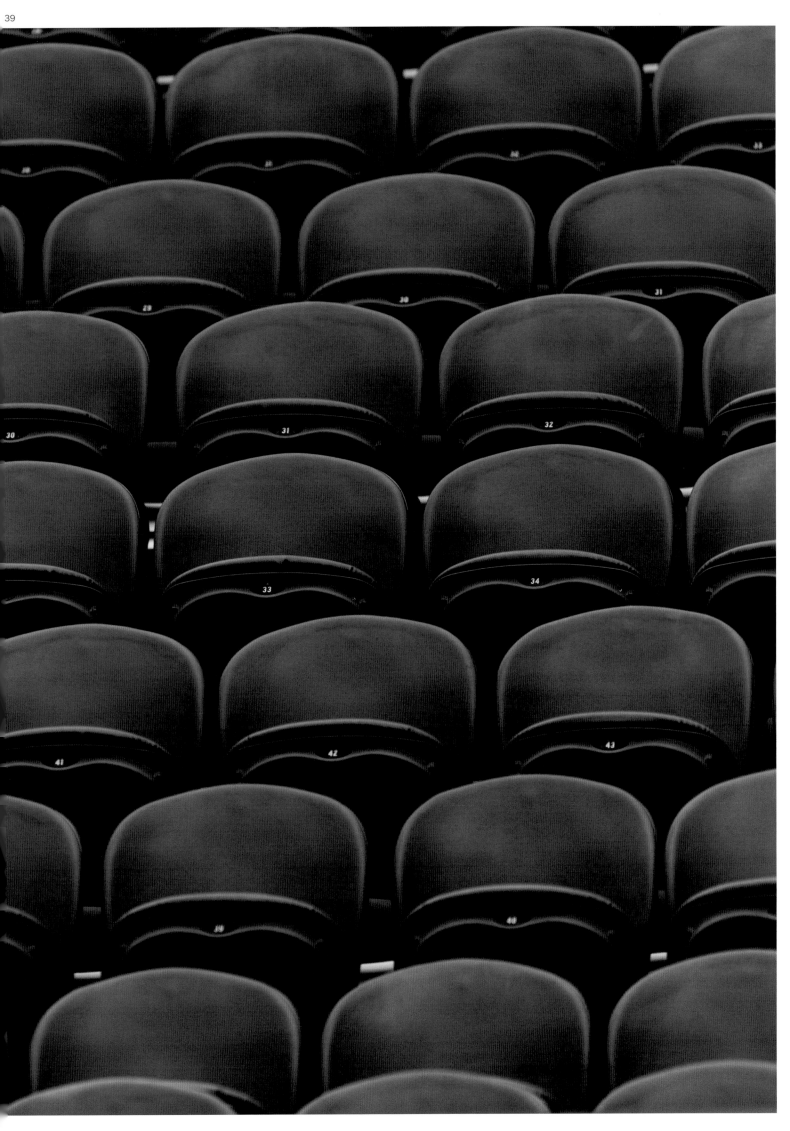

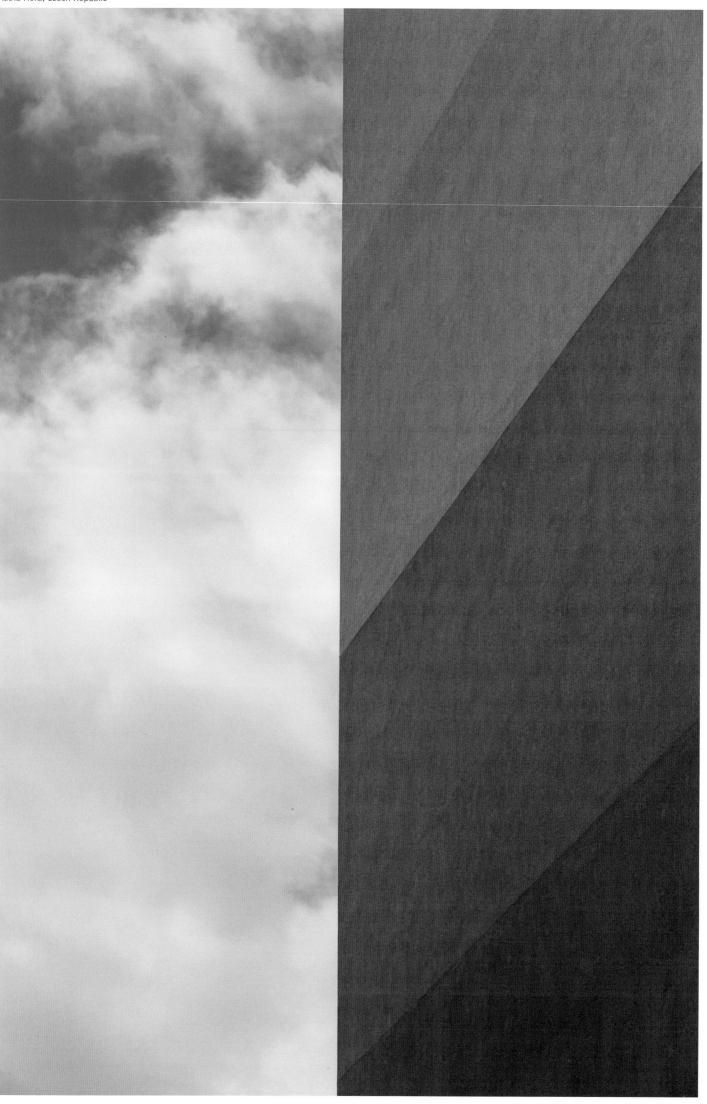

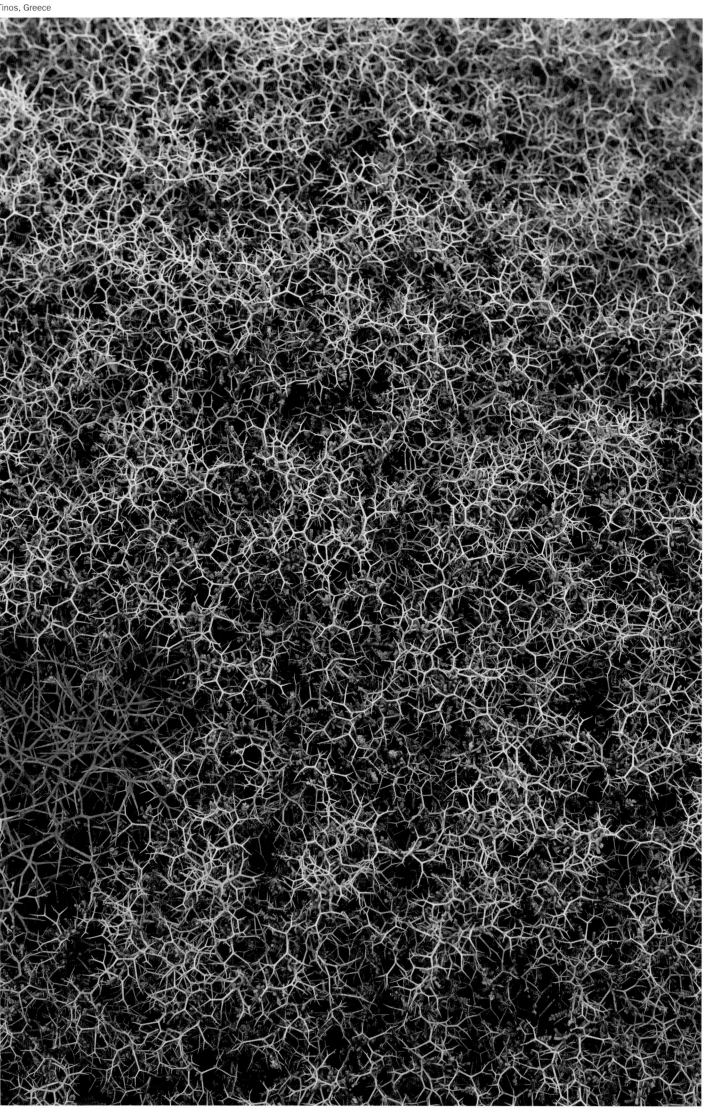

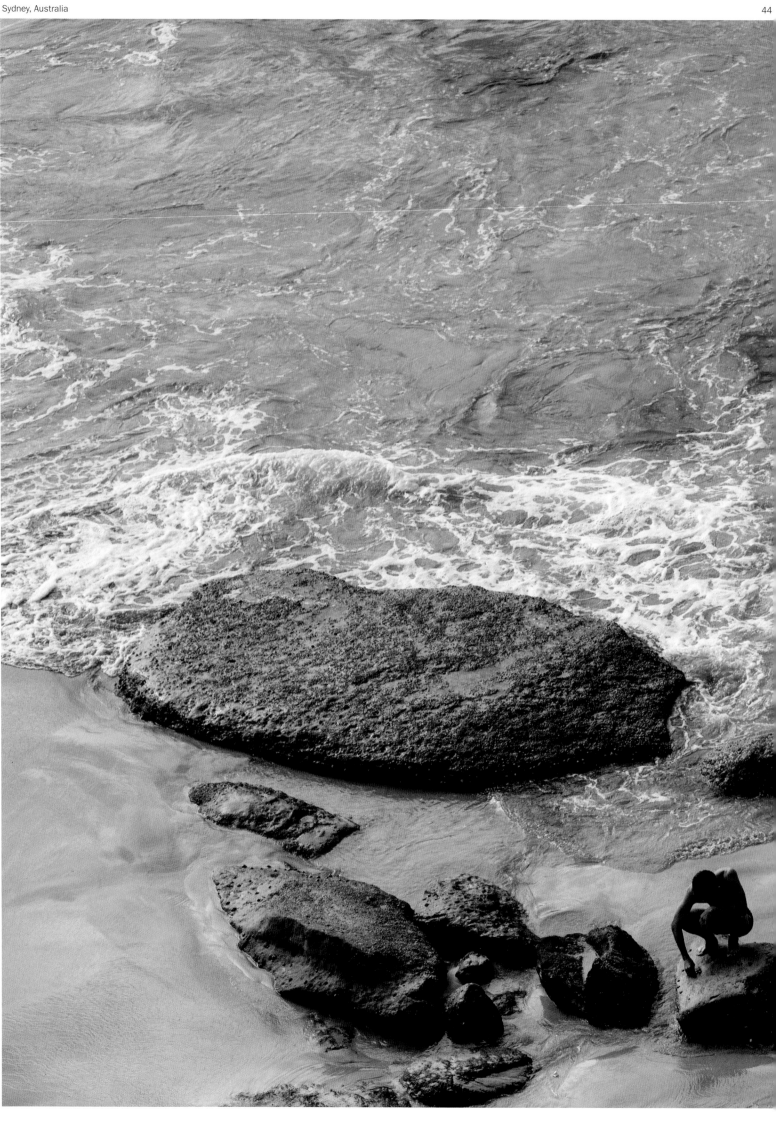

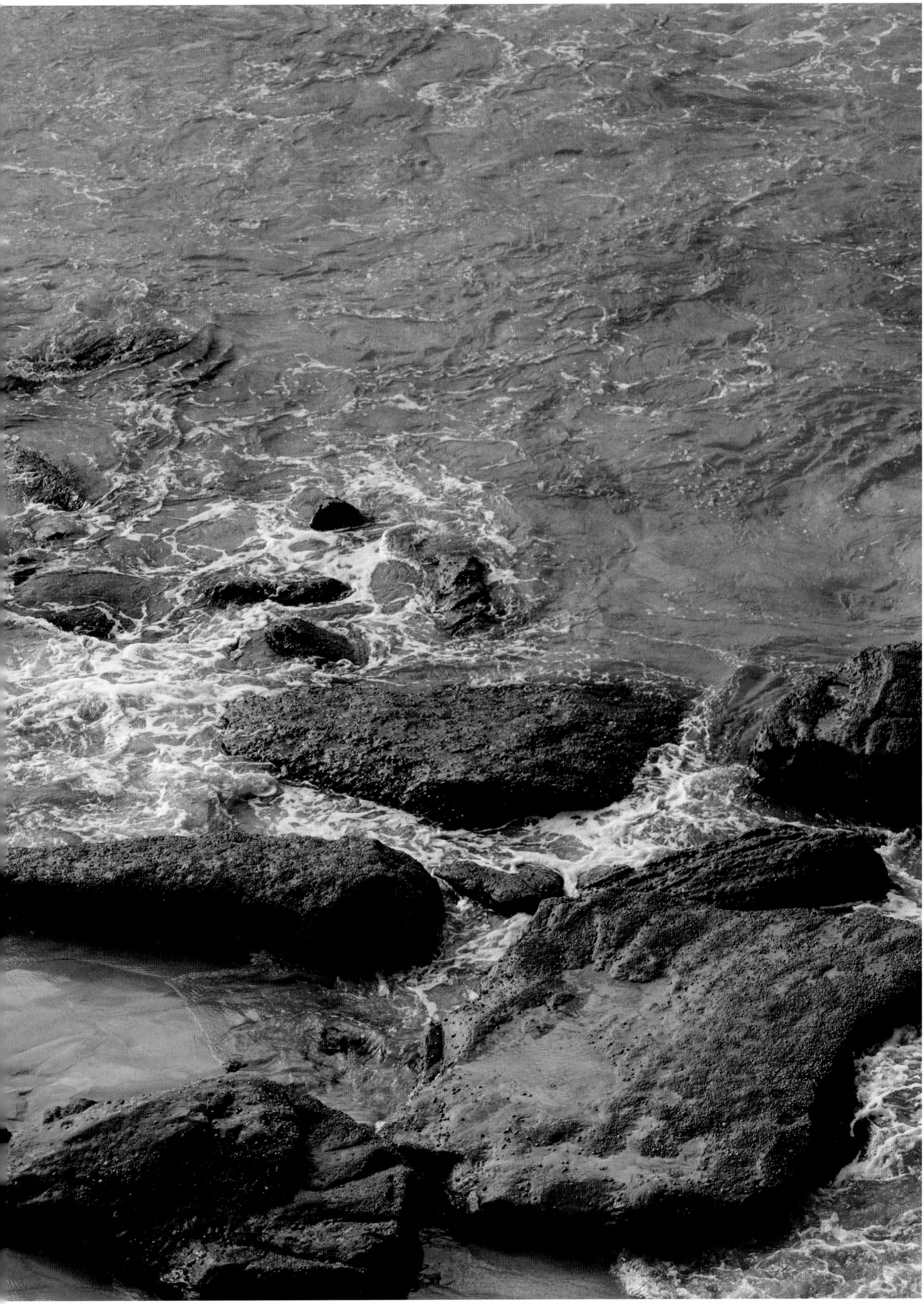

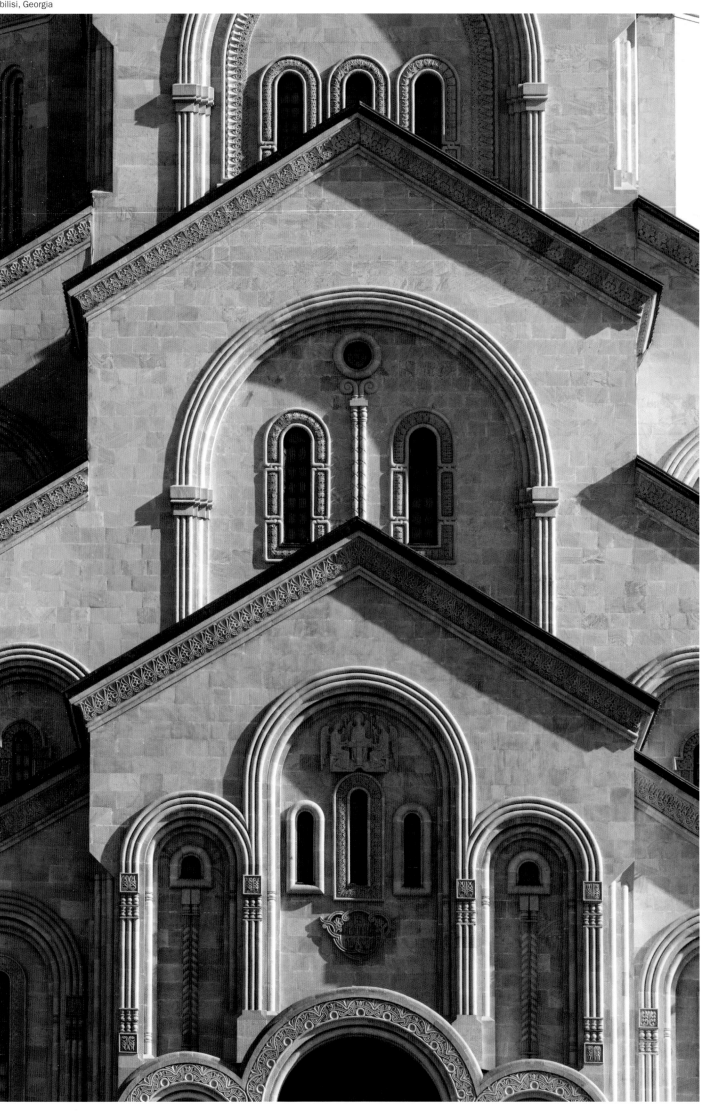

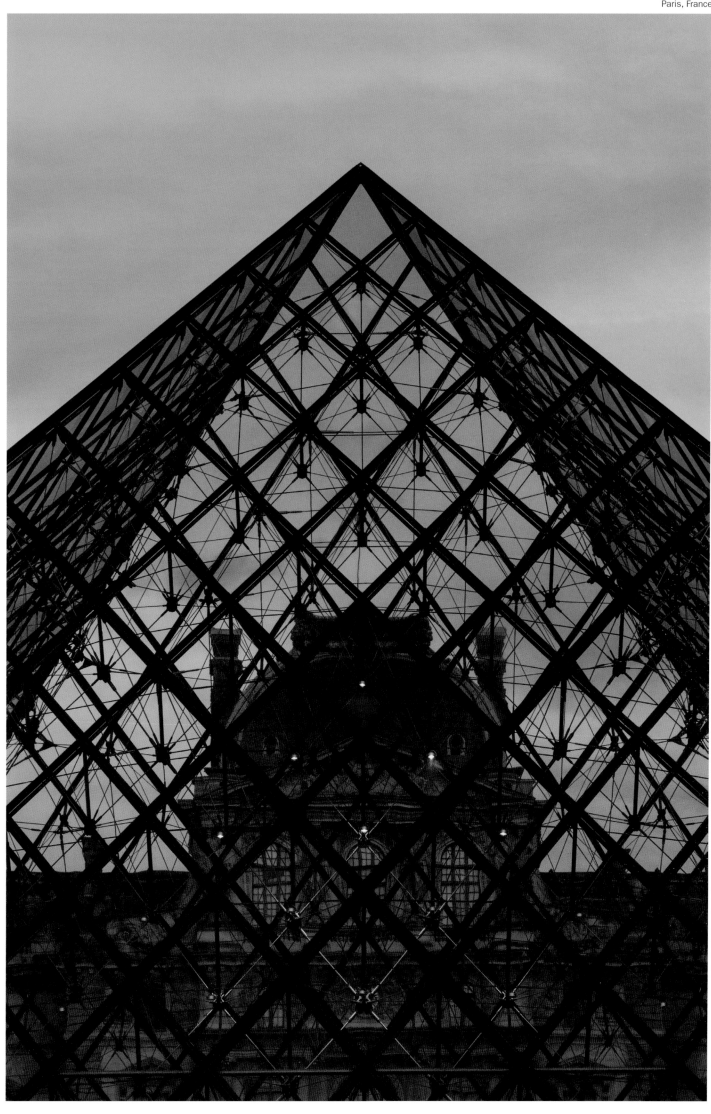

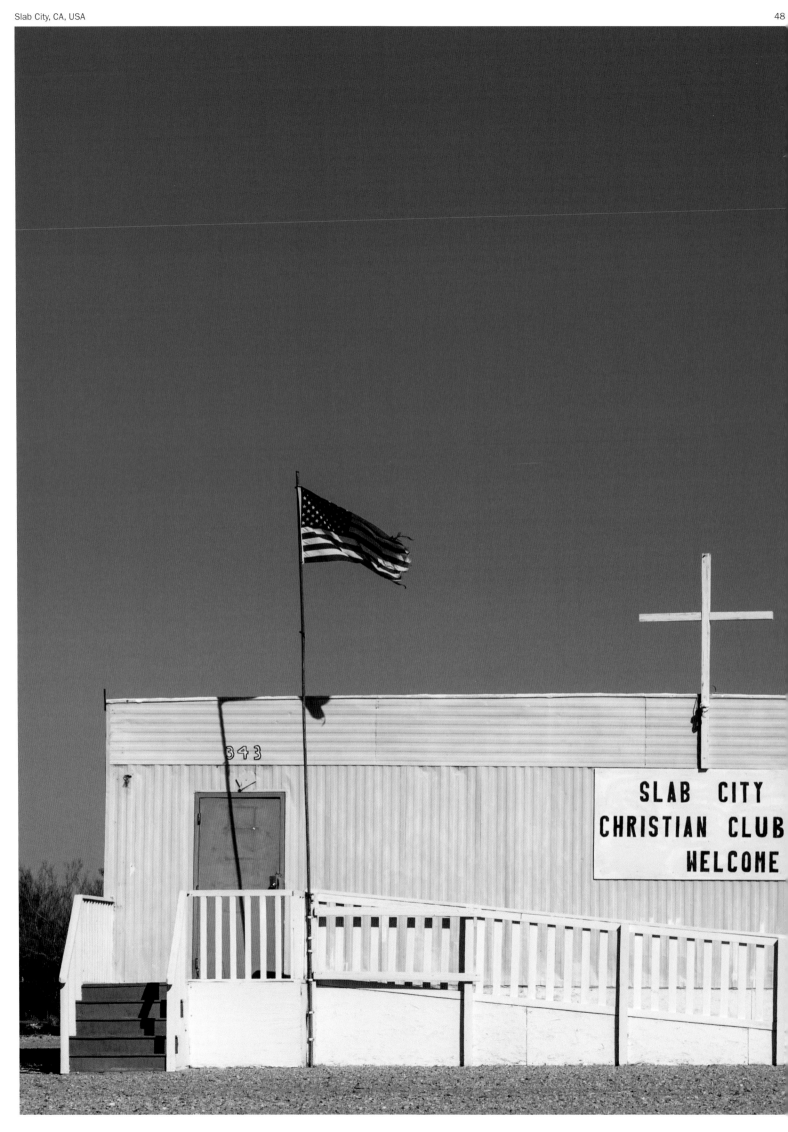

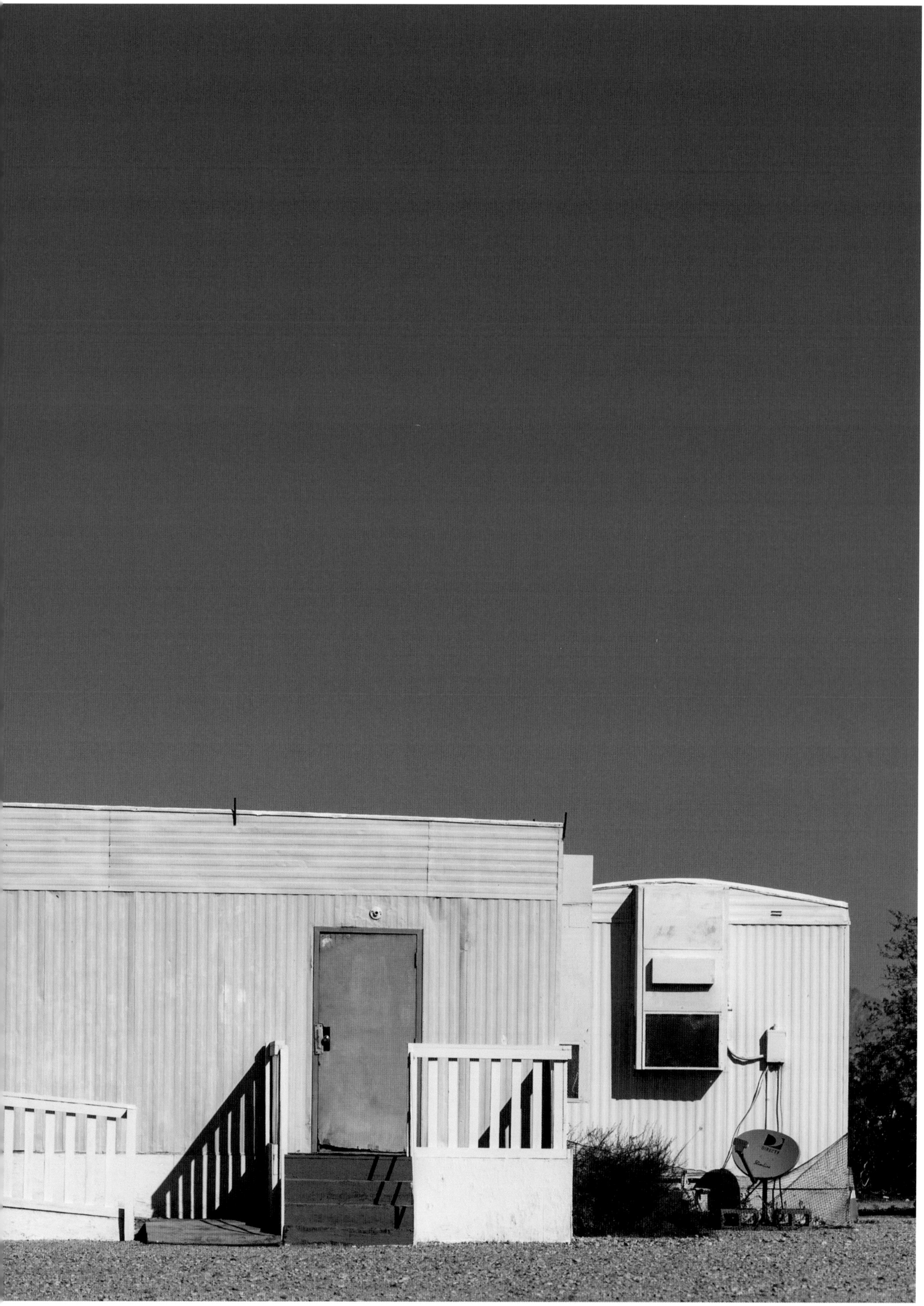

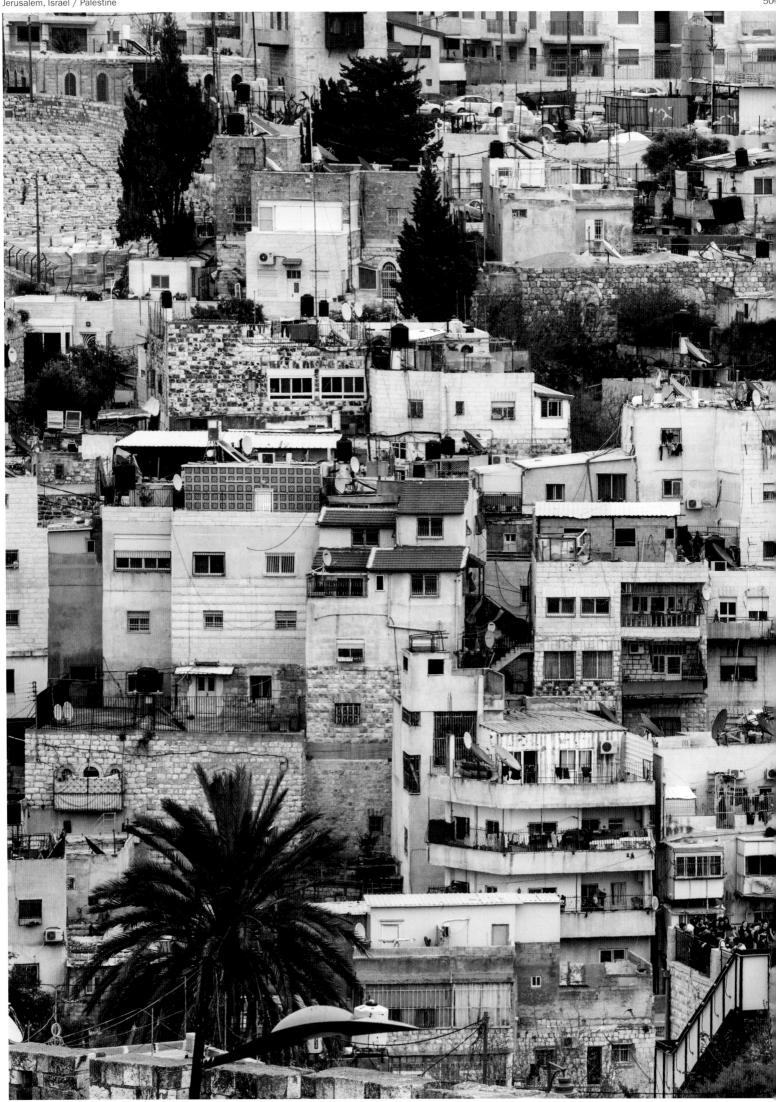

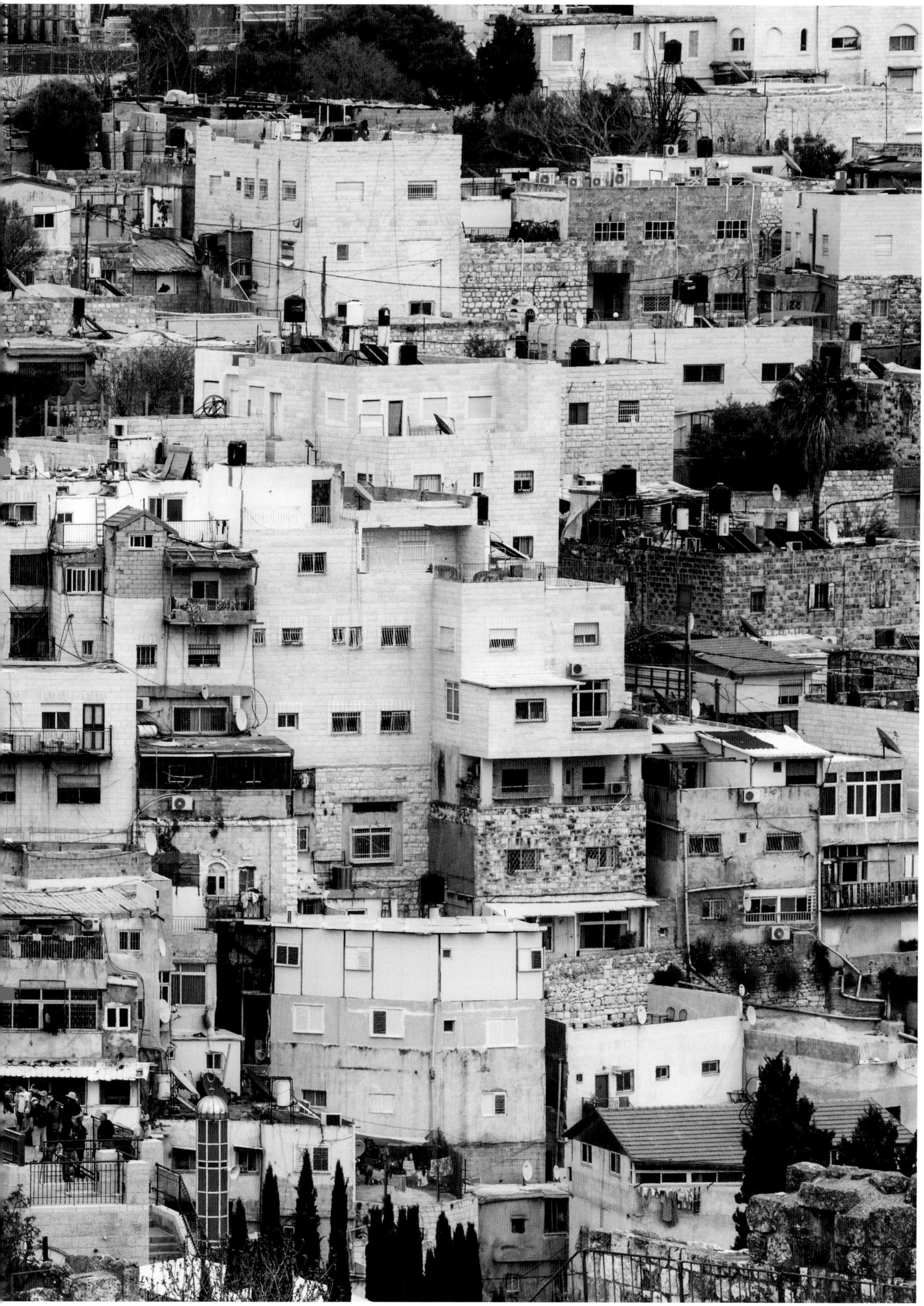

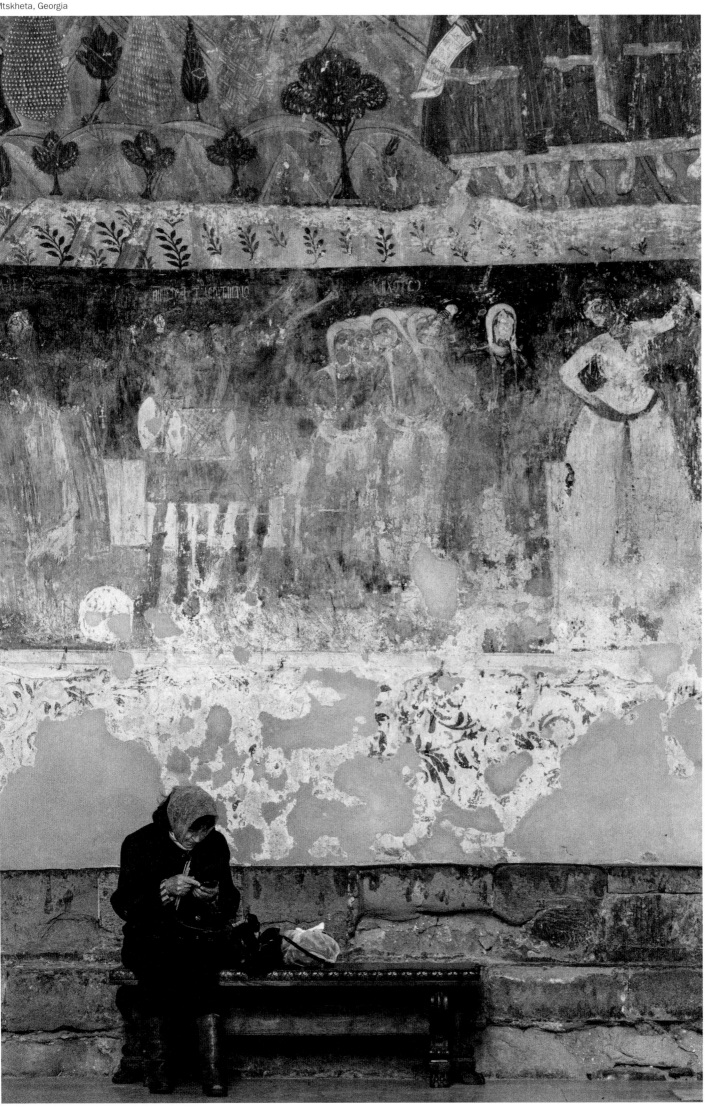

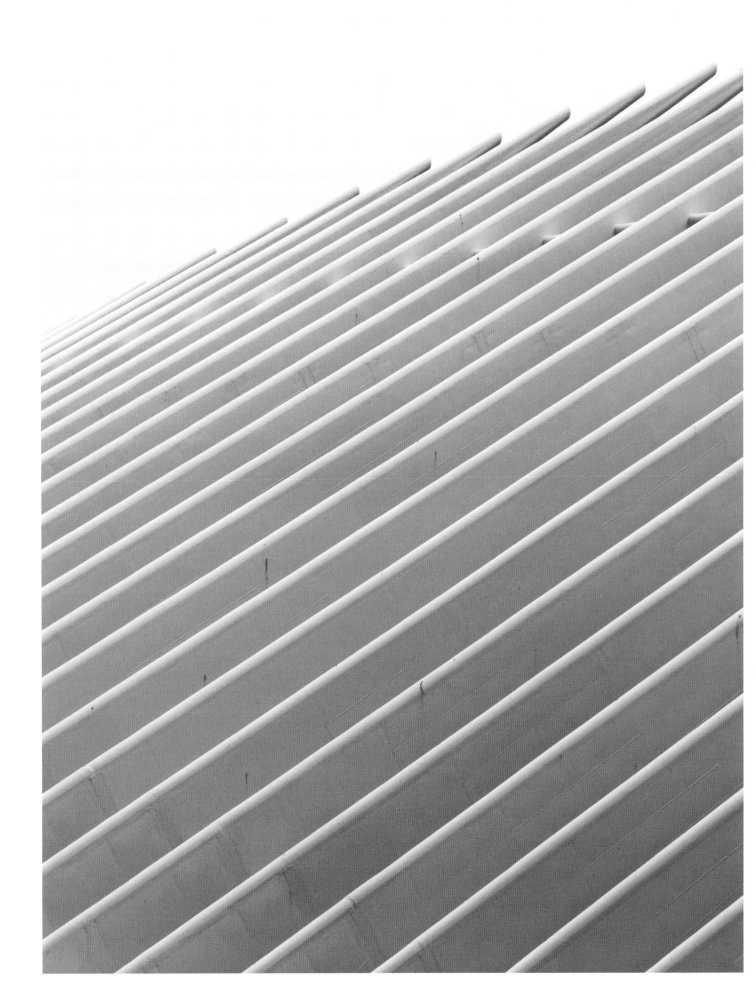

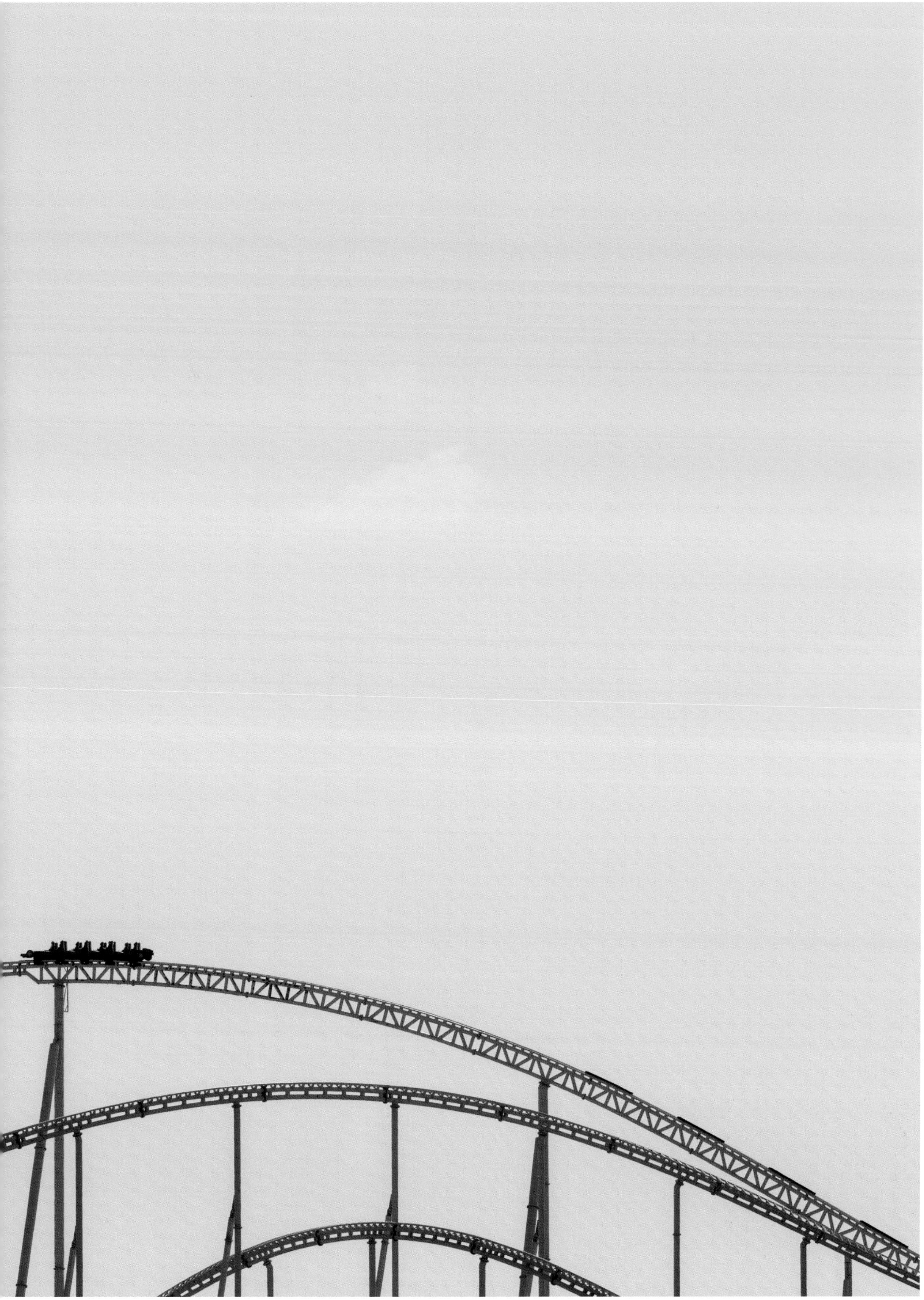

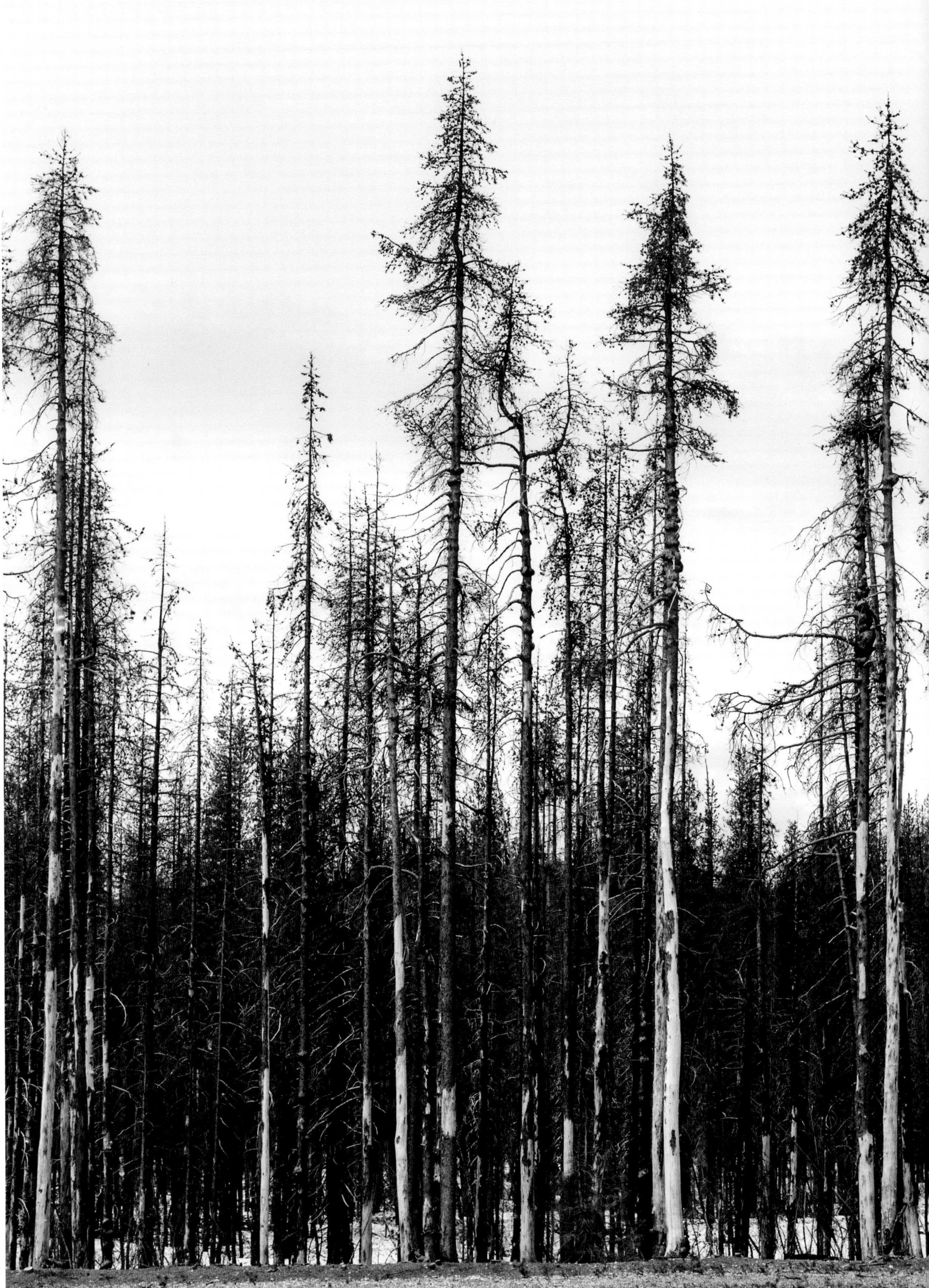

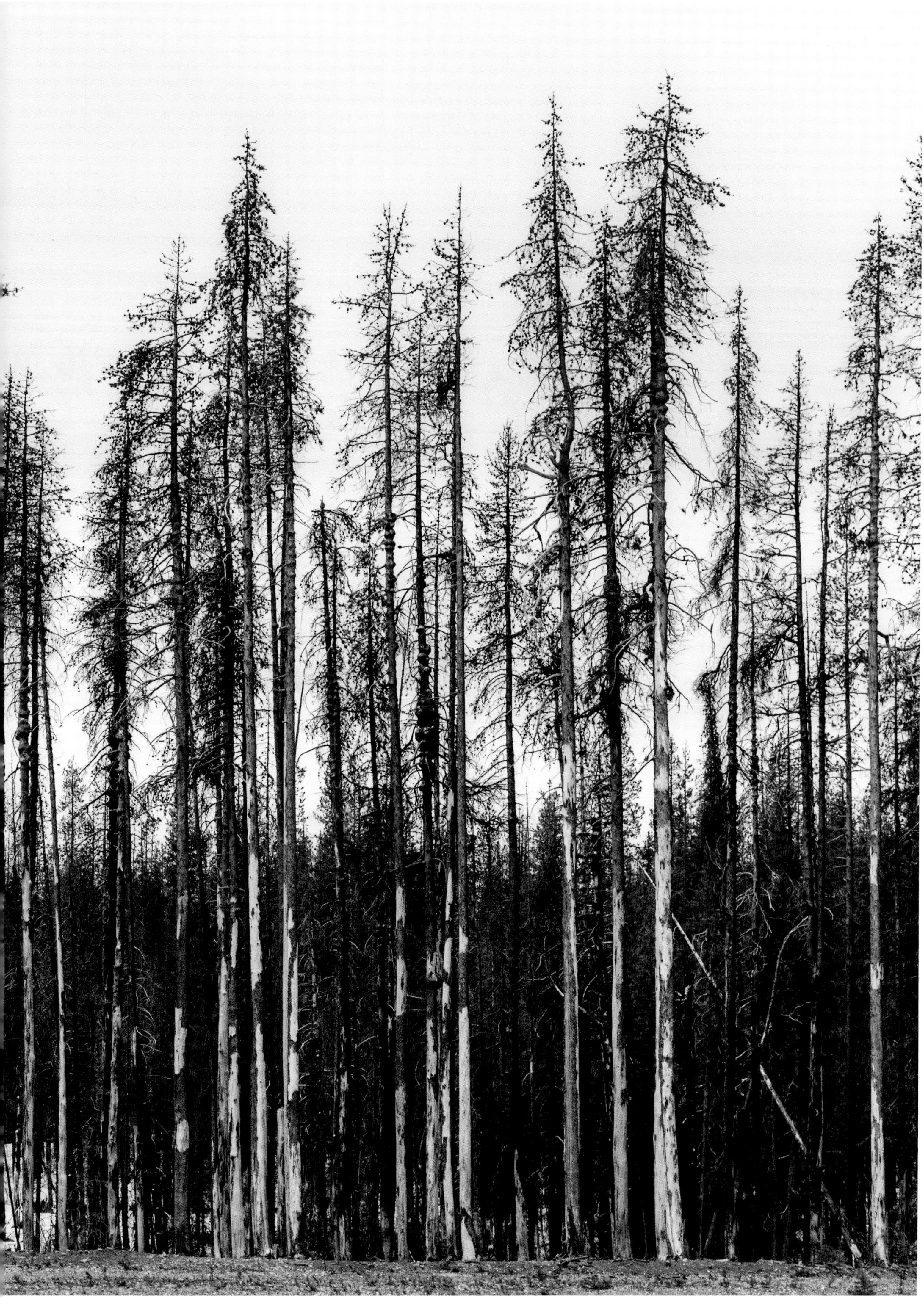

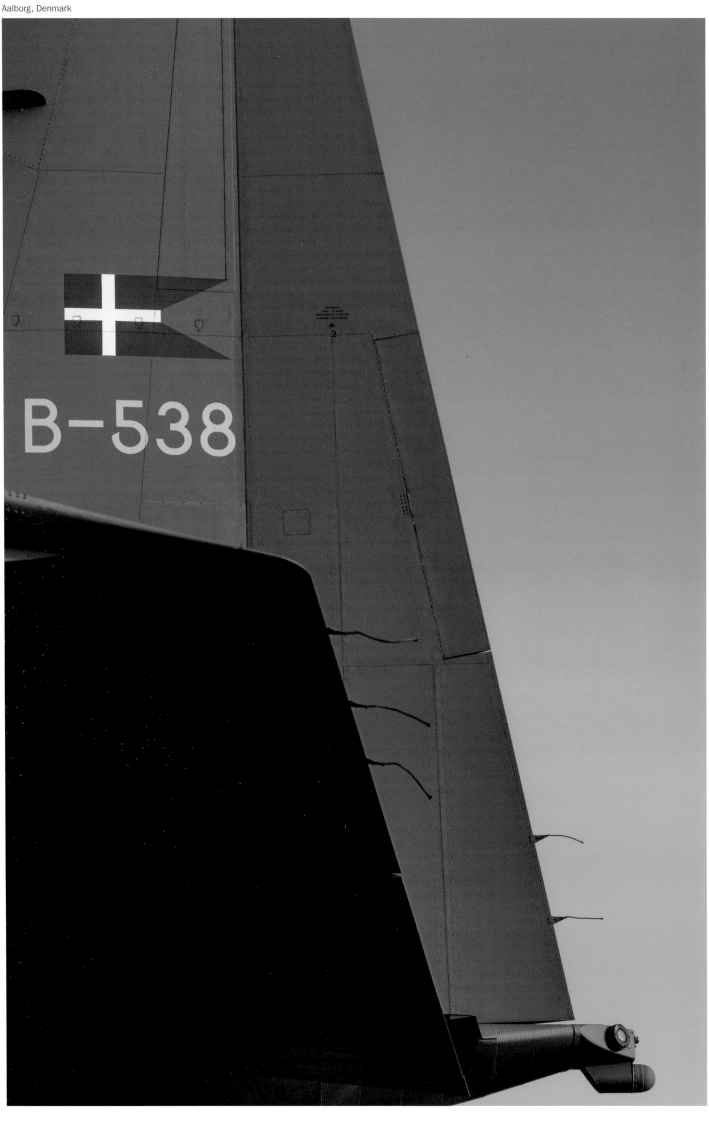

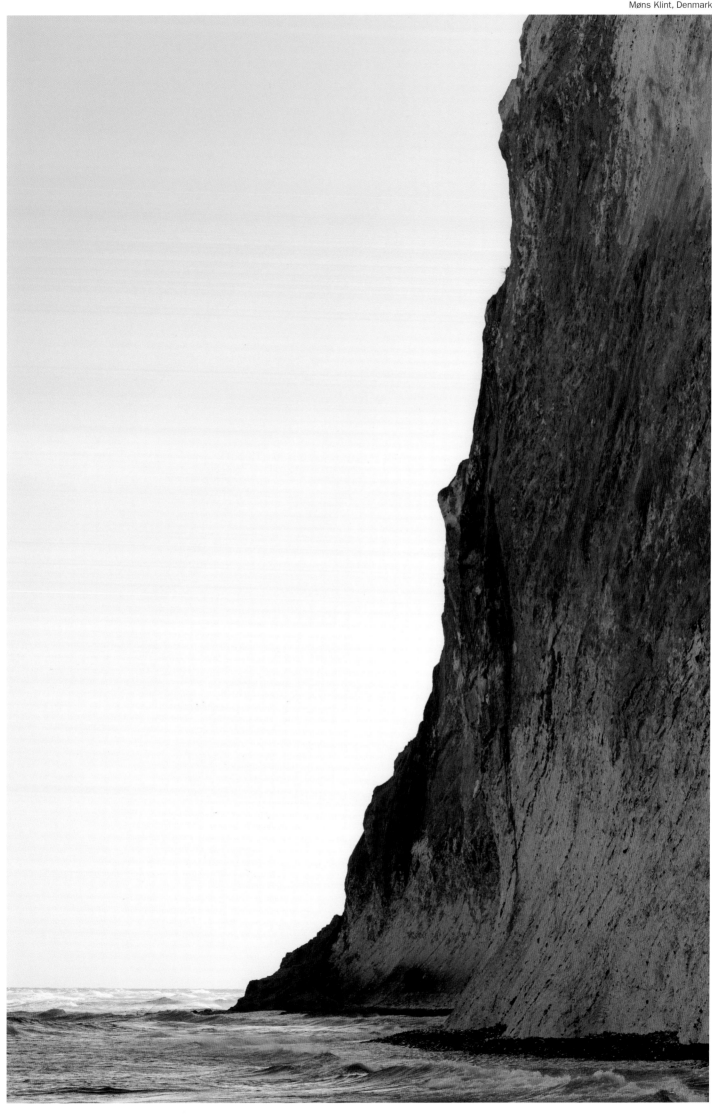

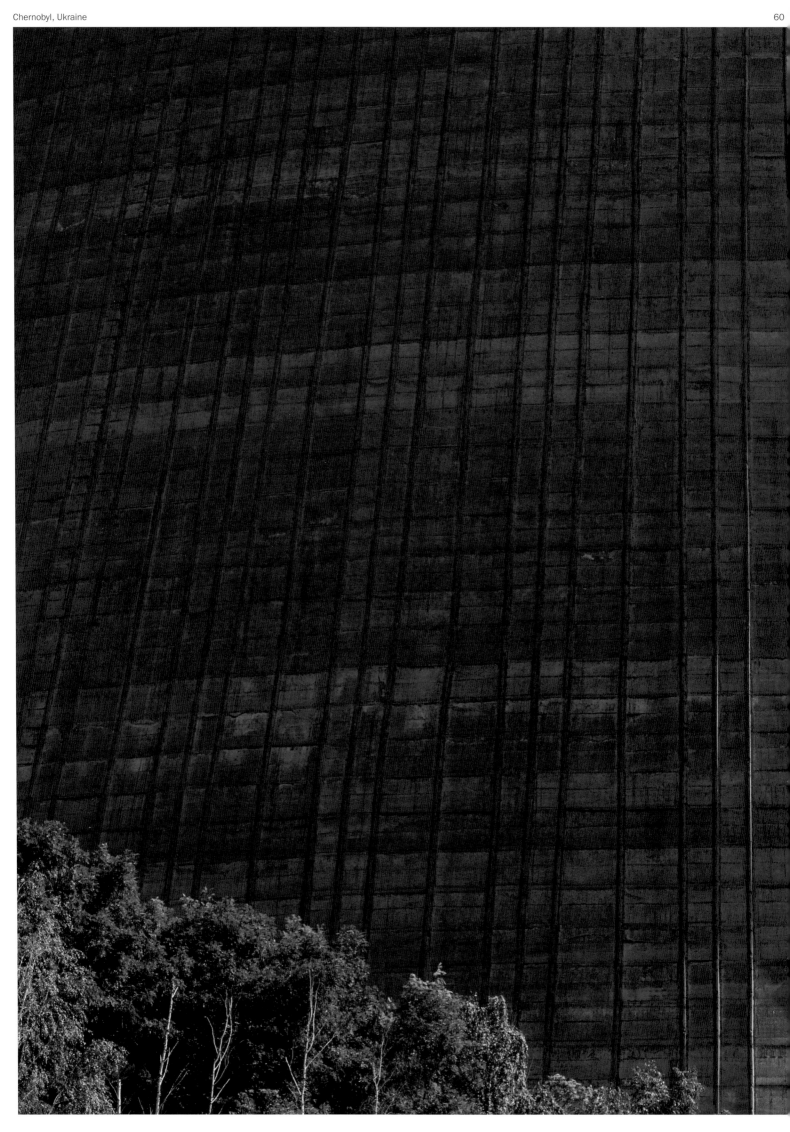

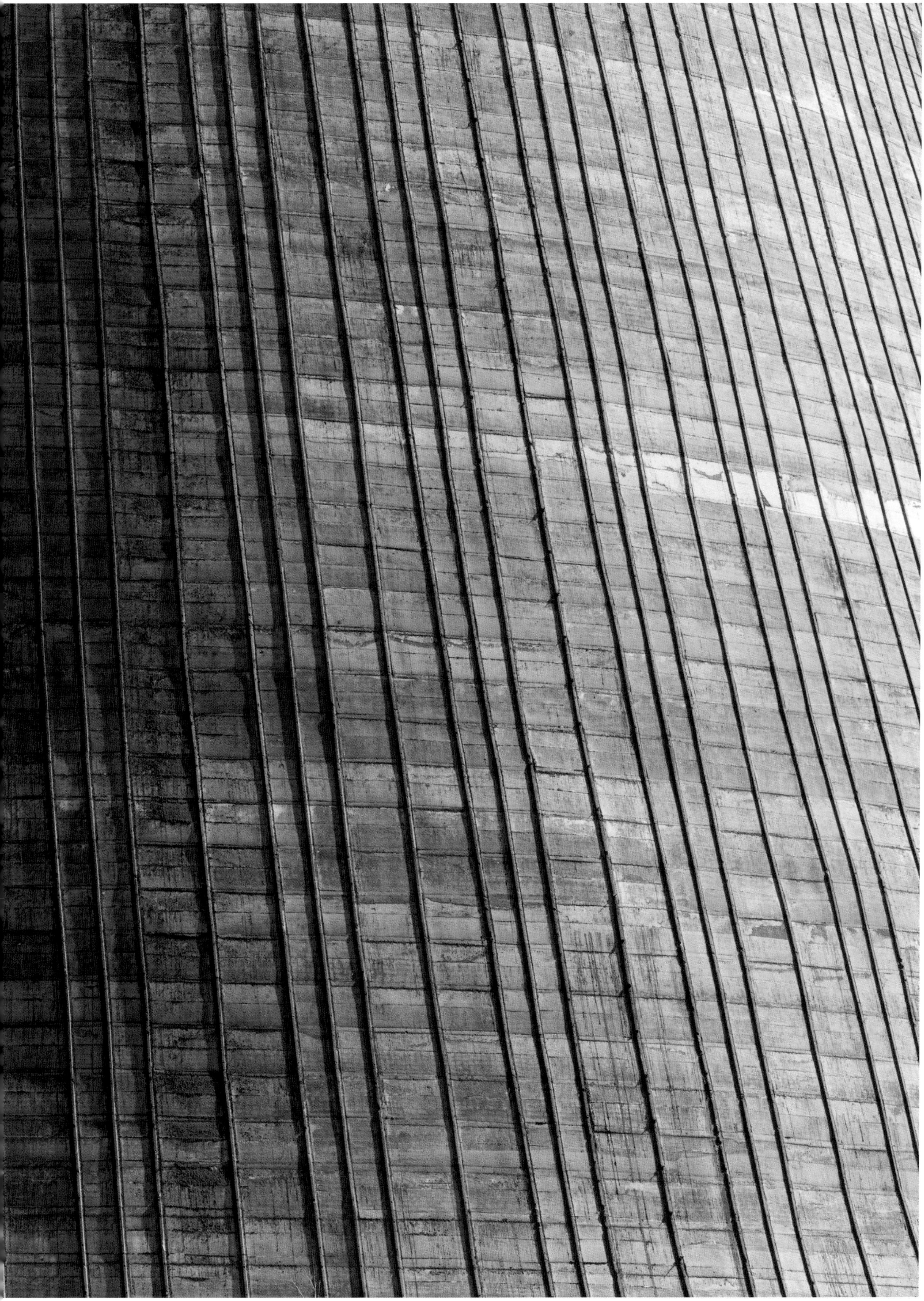

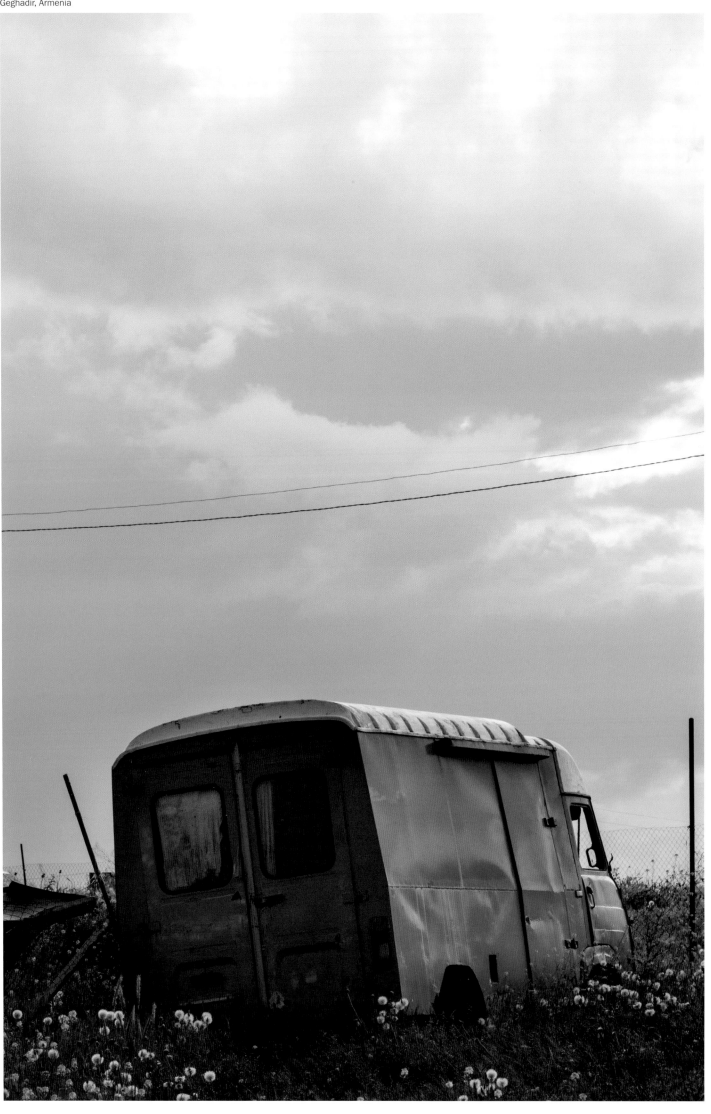

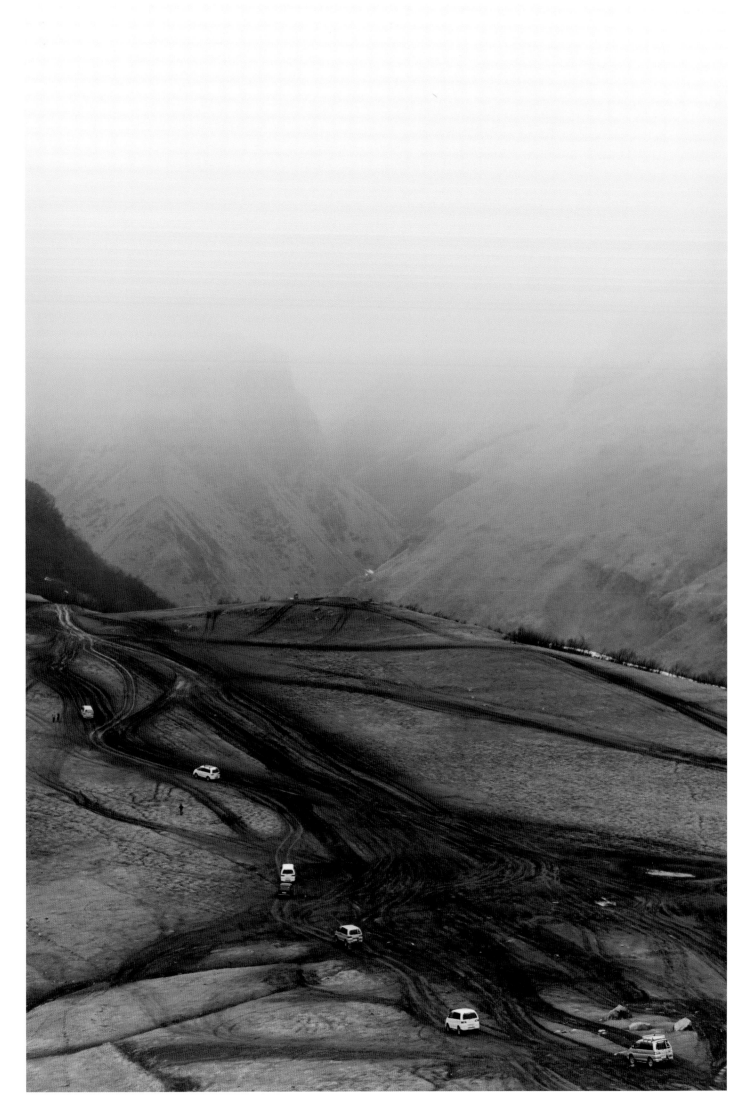

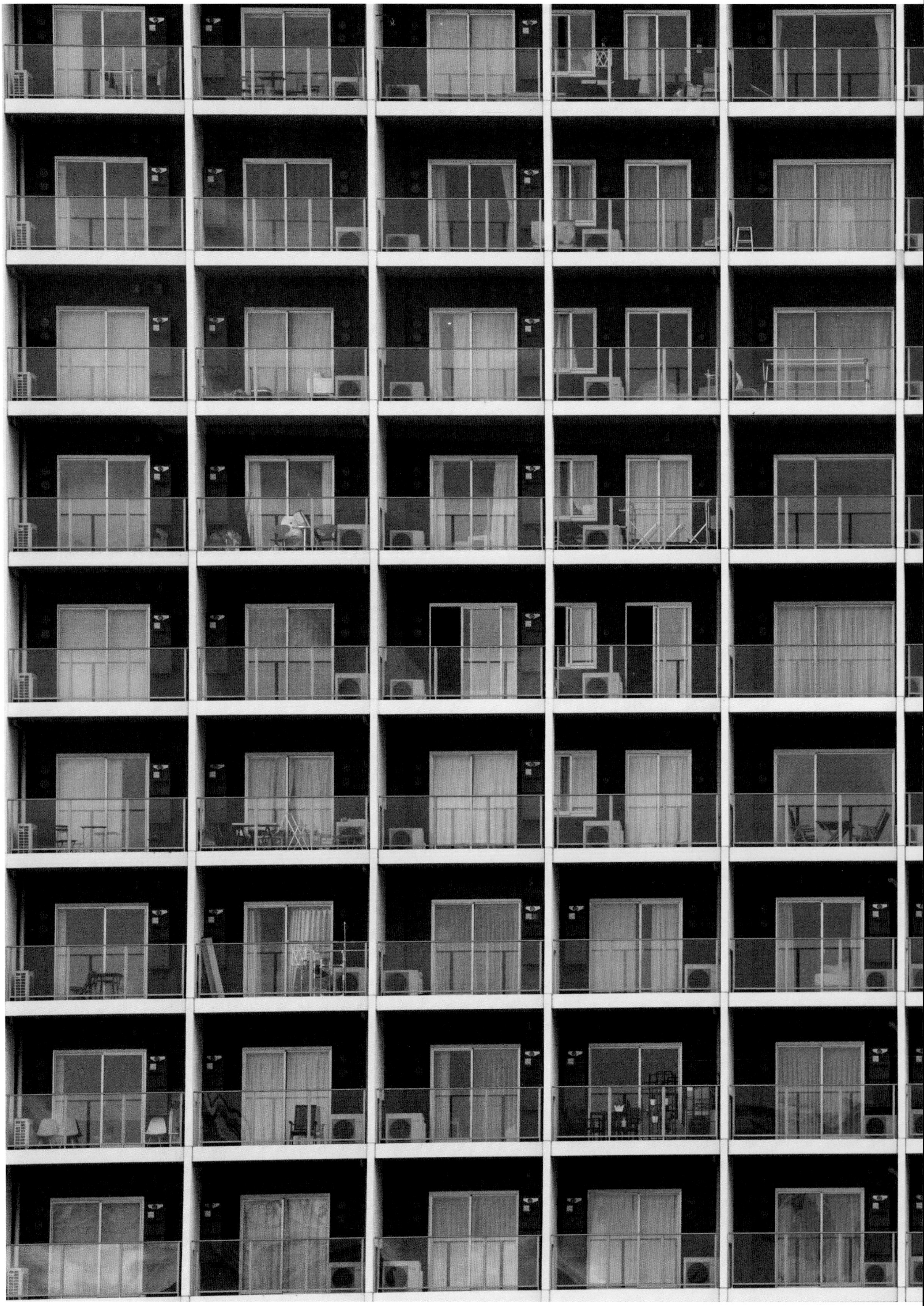

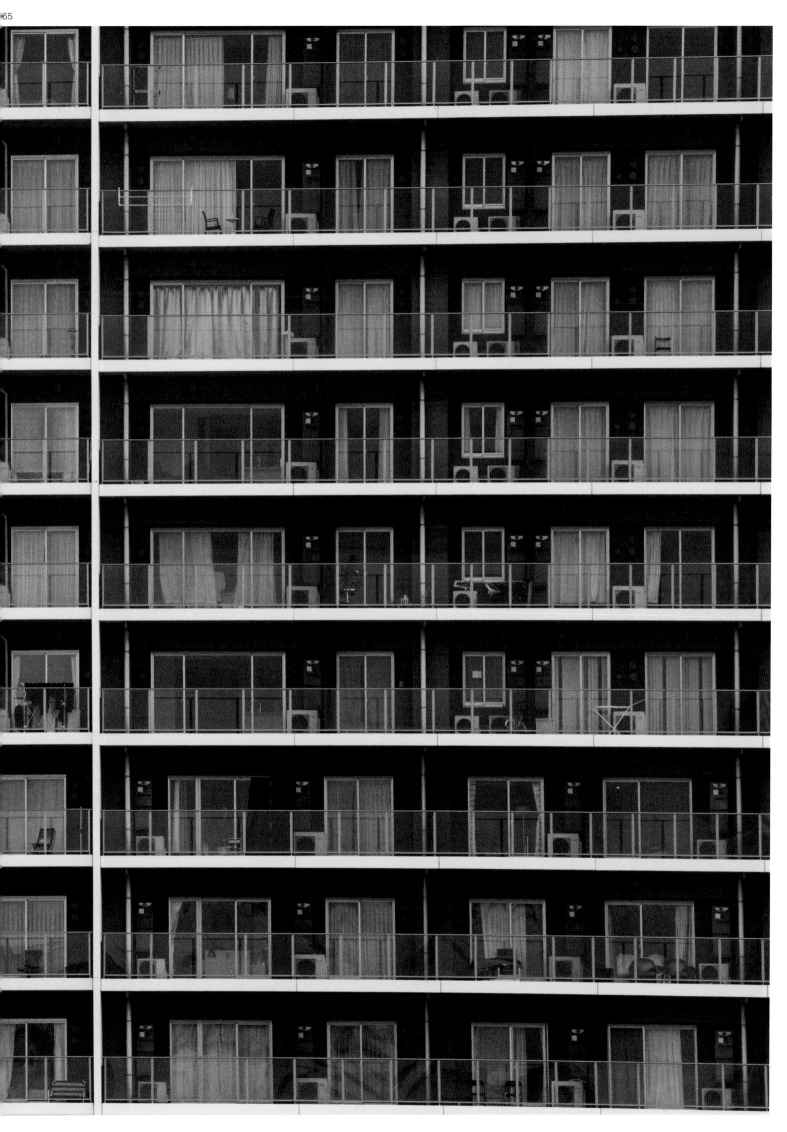

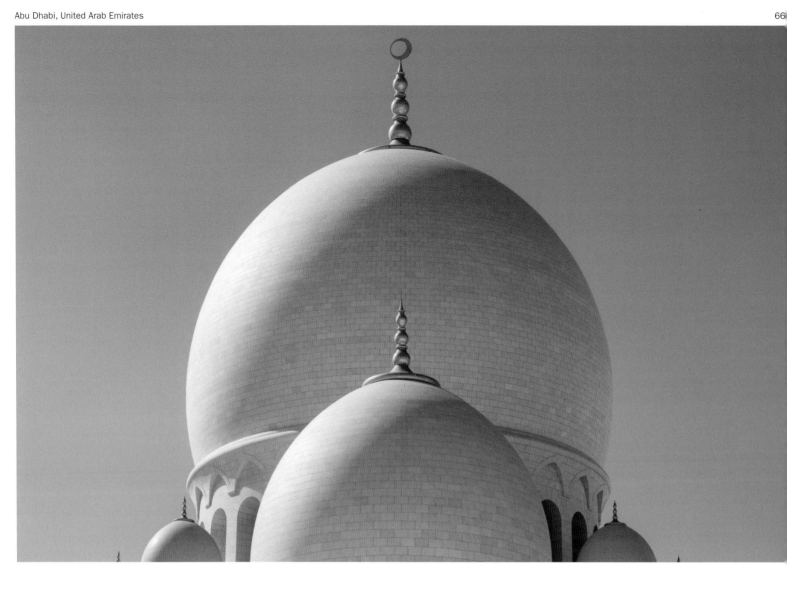

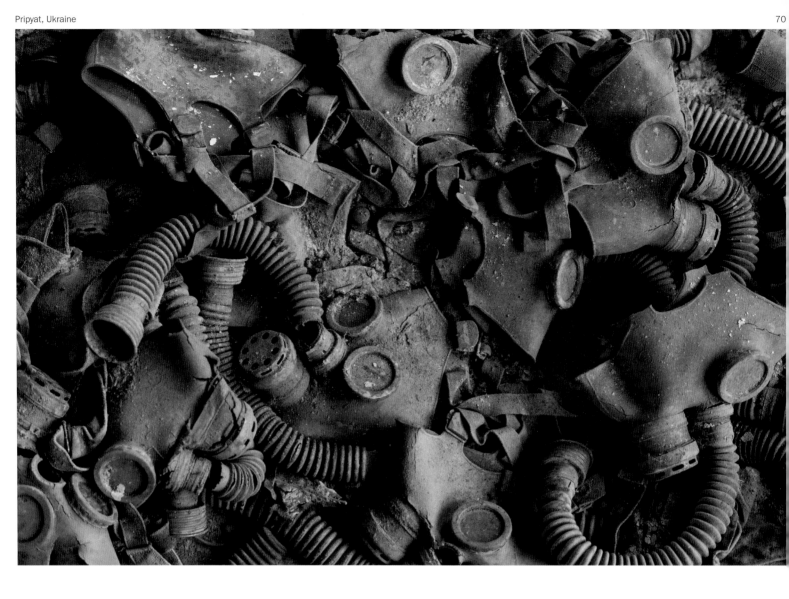

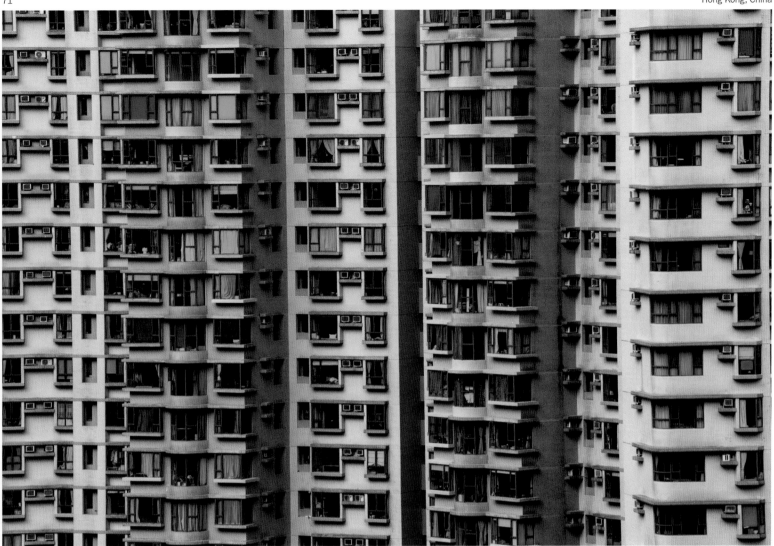

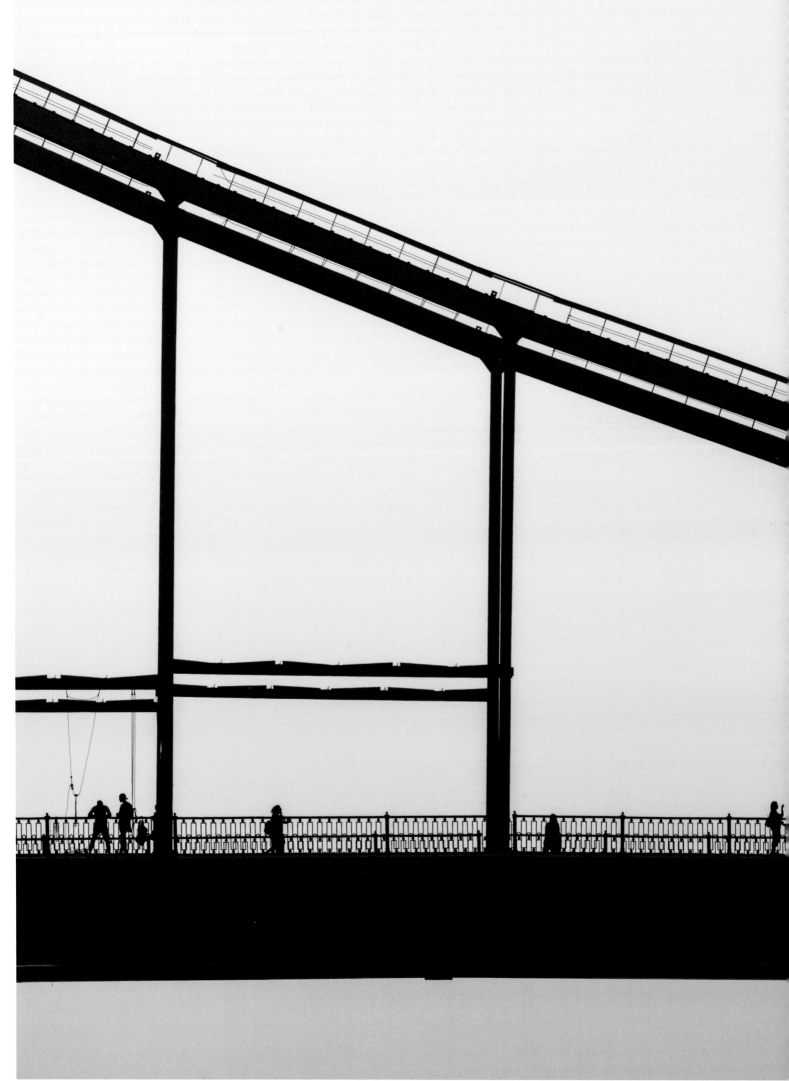

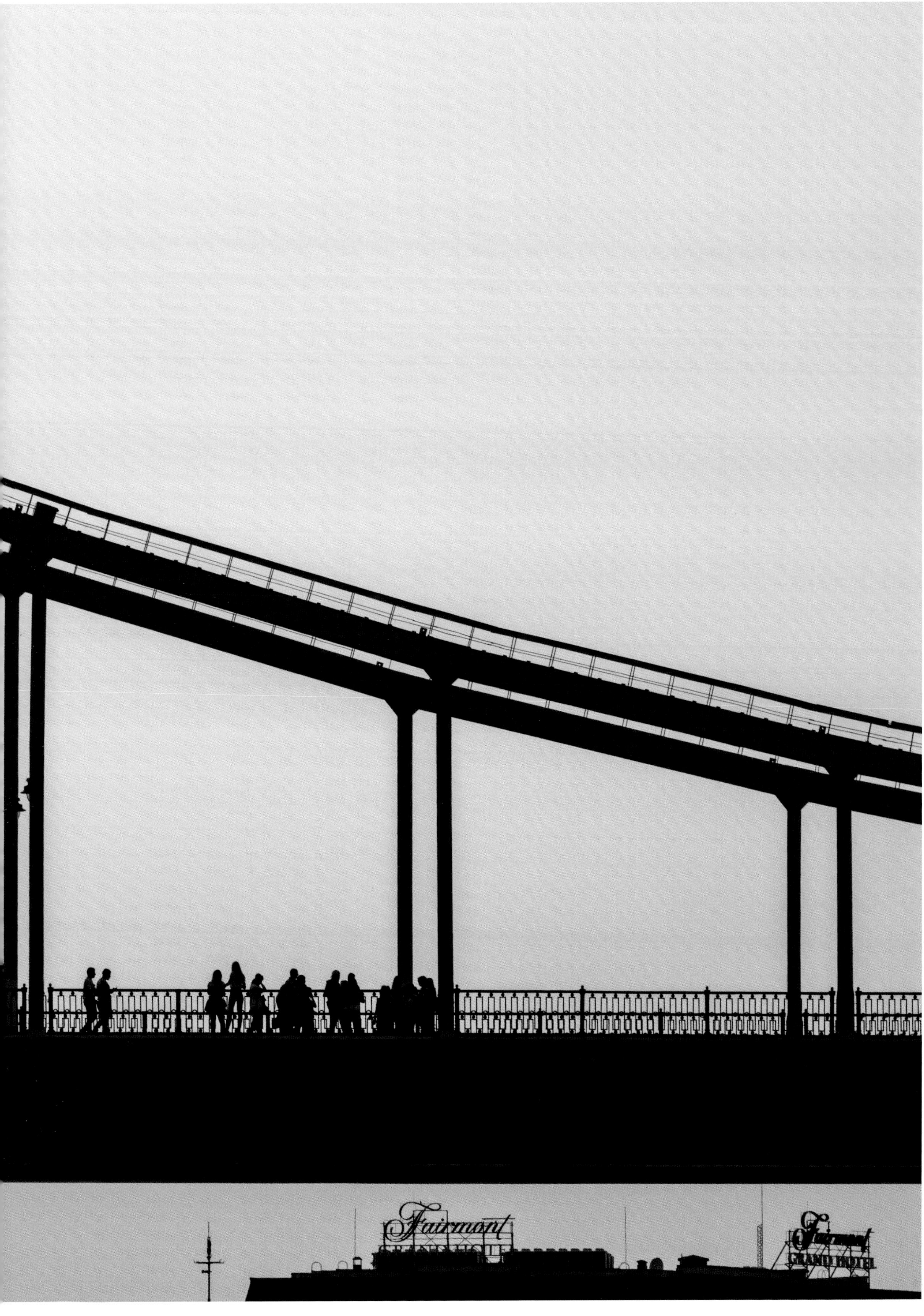
Fairmont
GRAND HOTEL

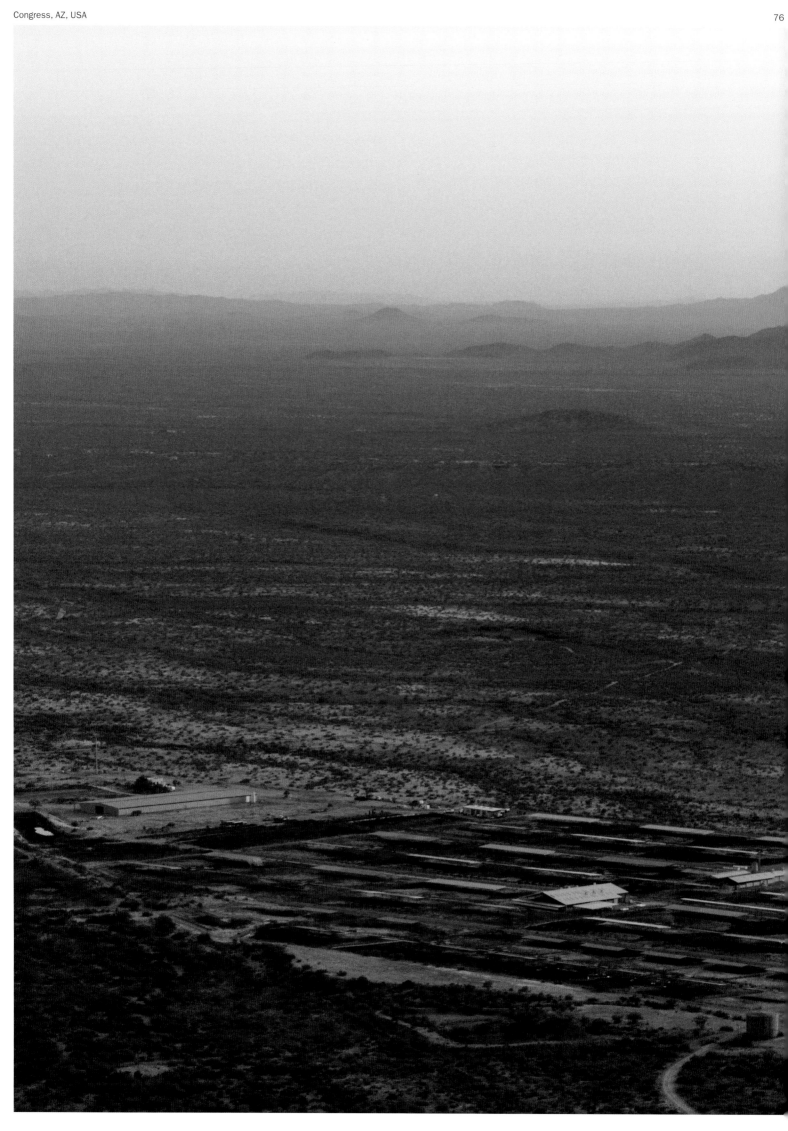

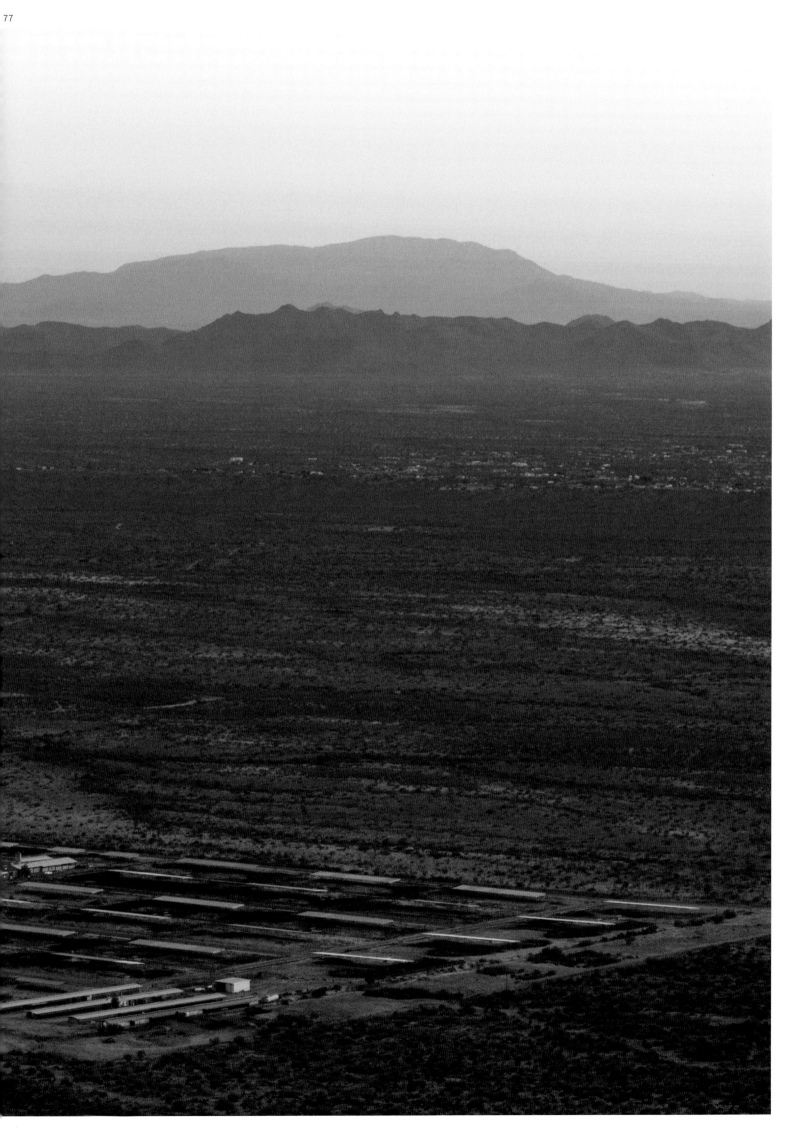

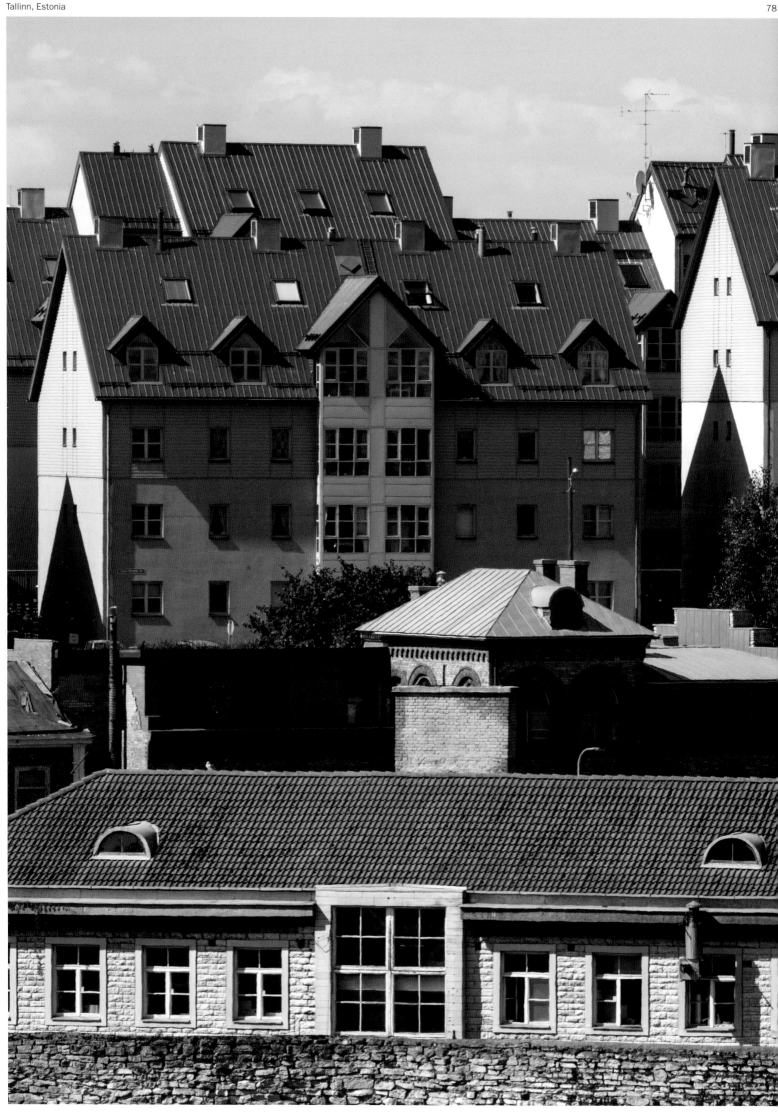

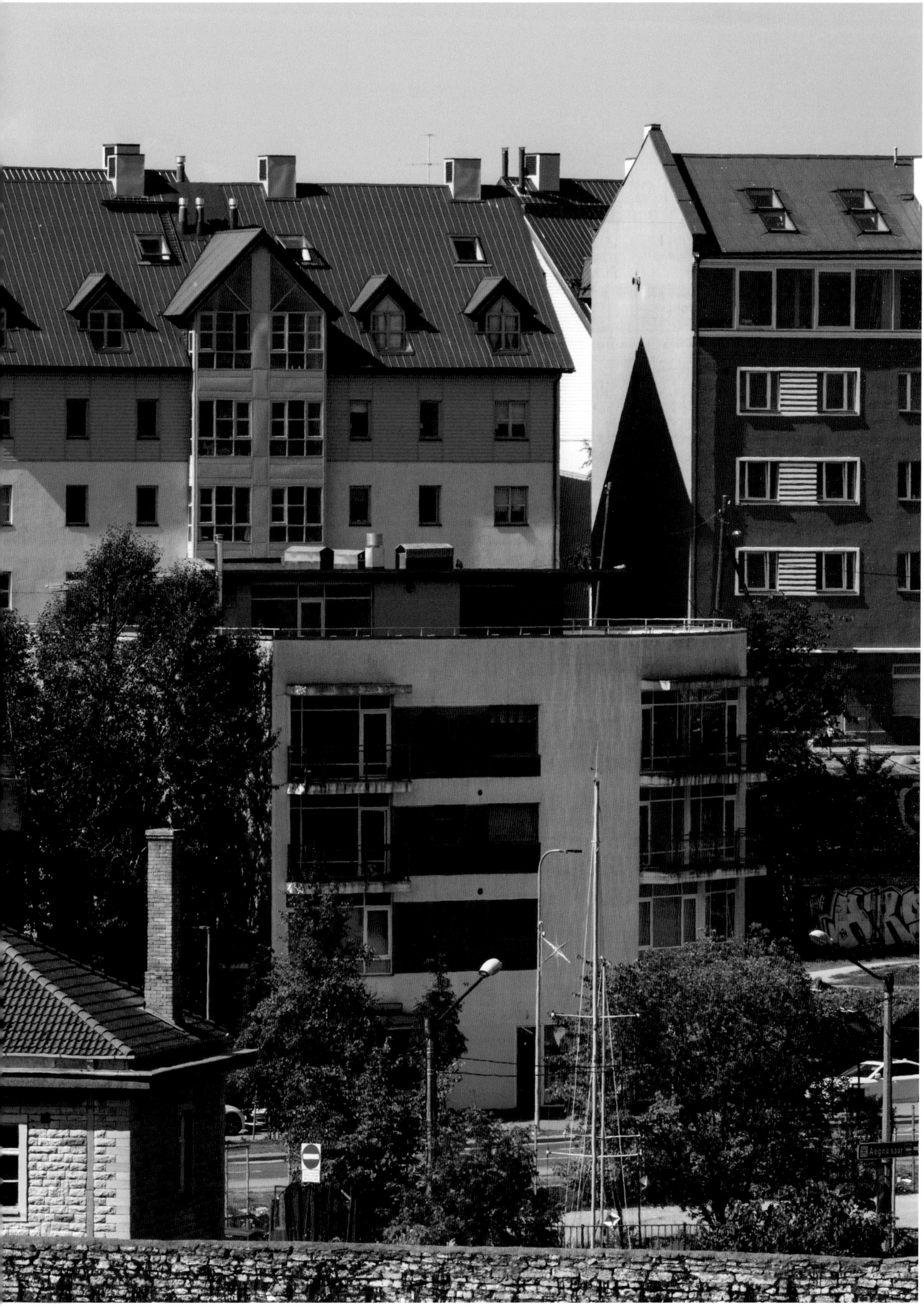

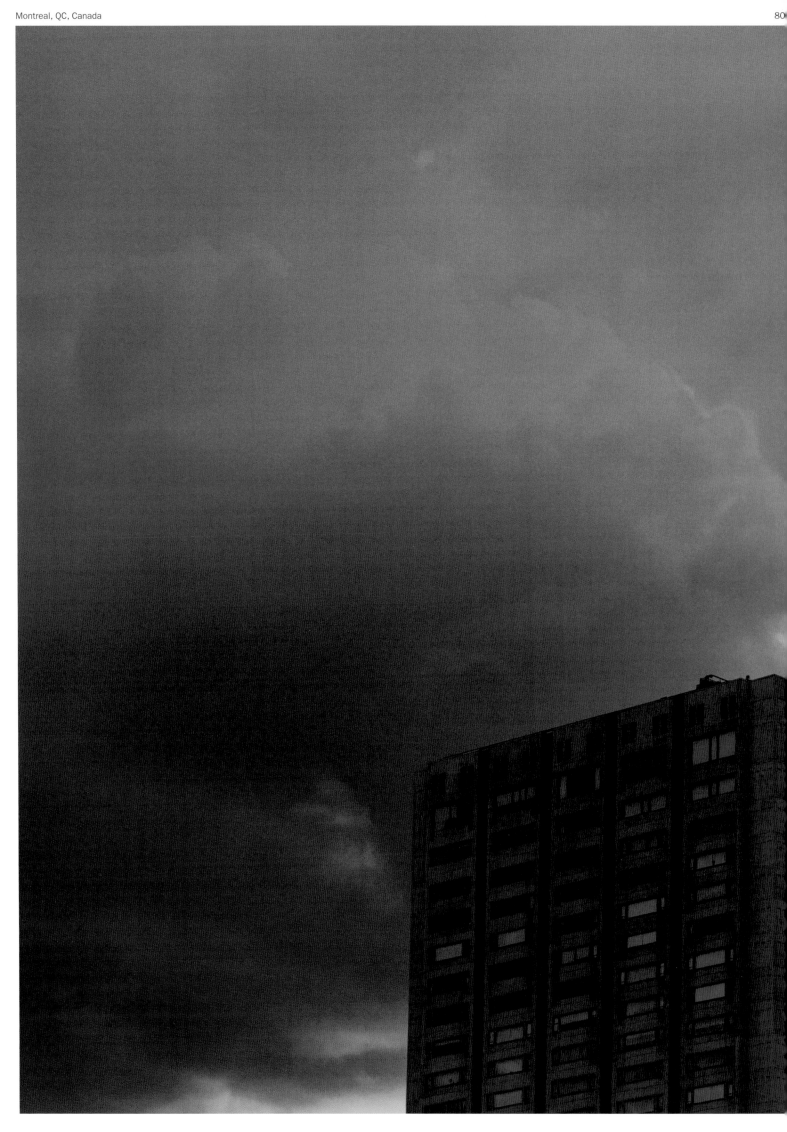

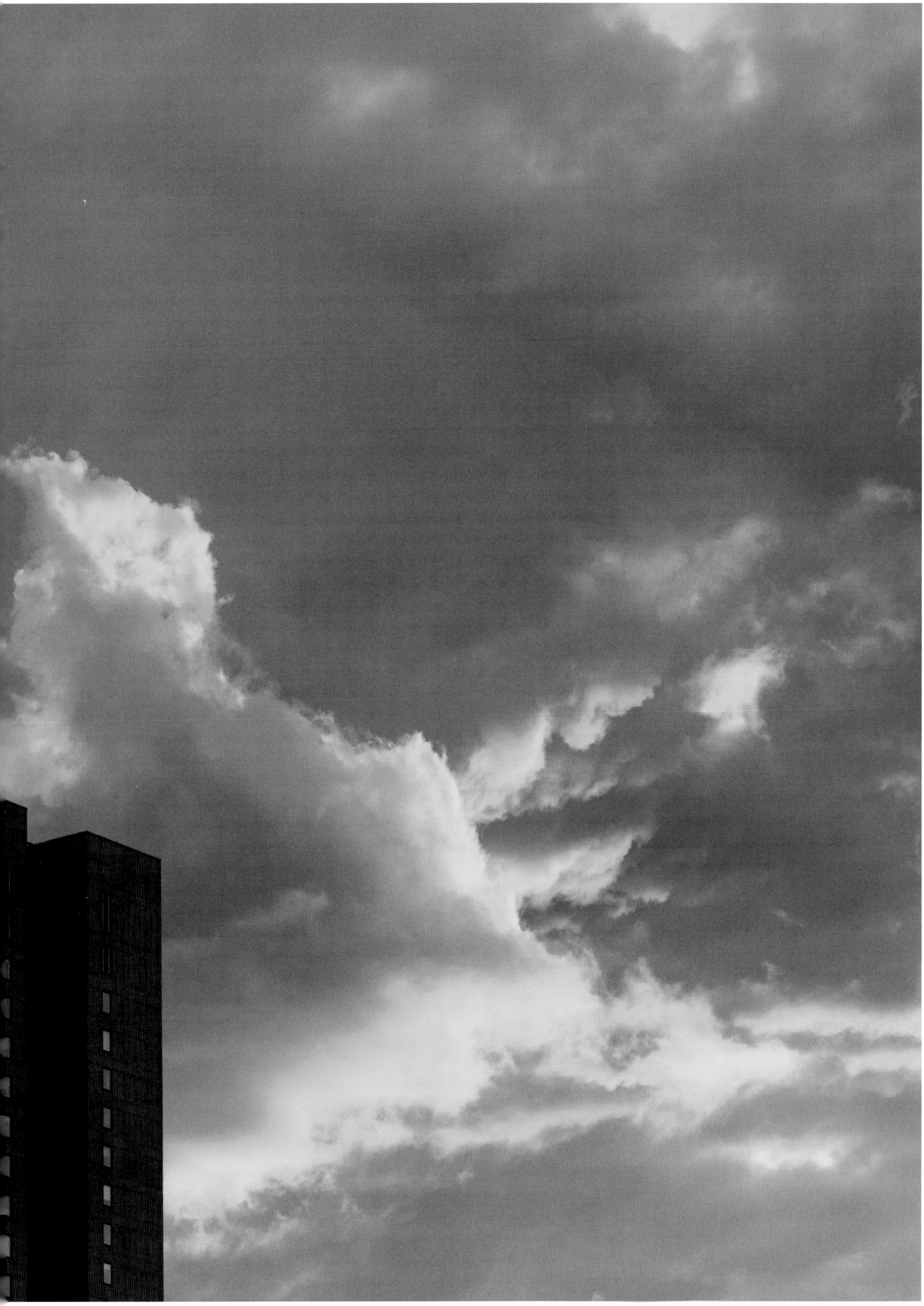

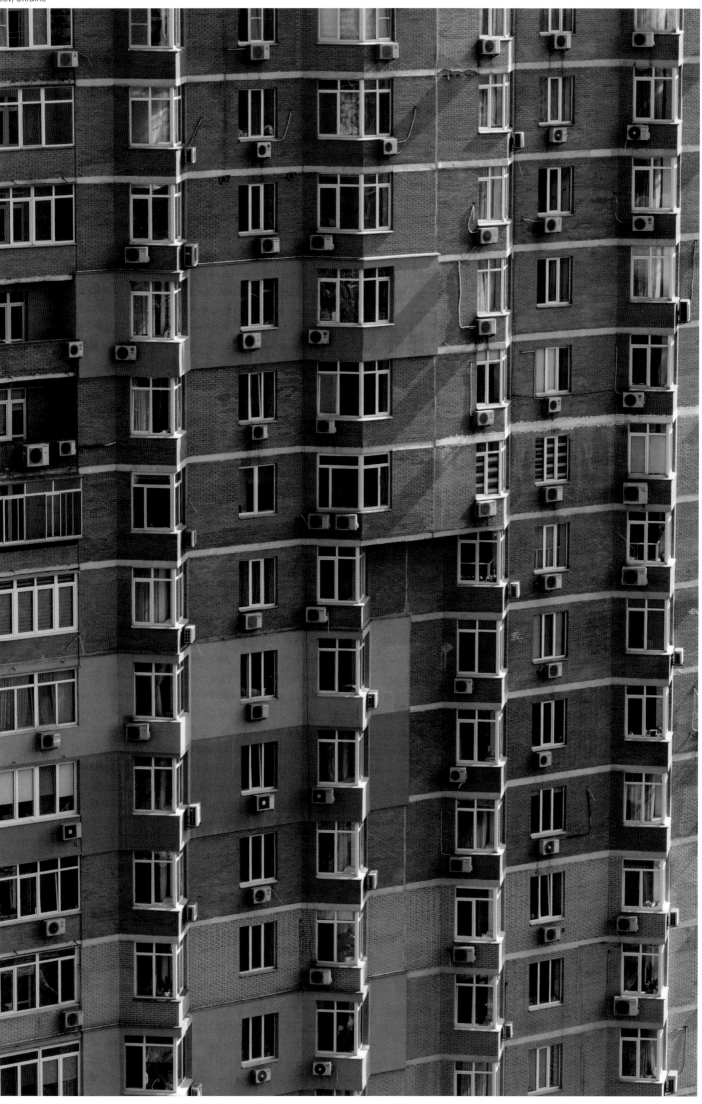

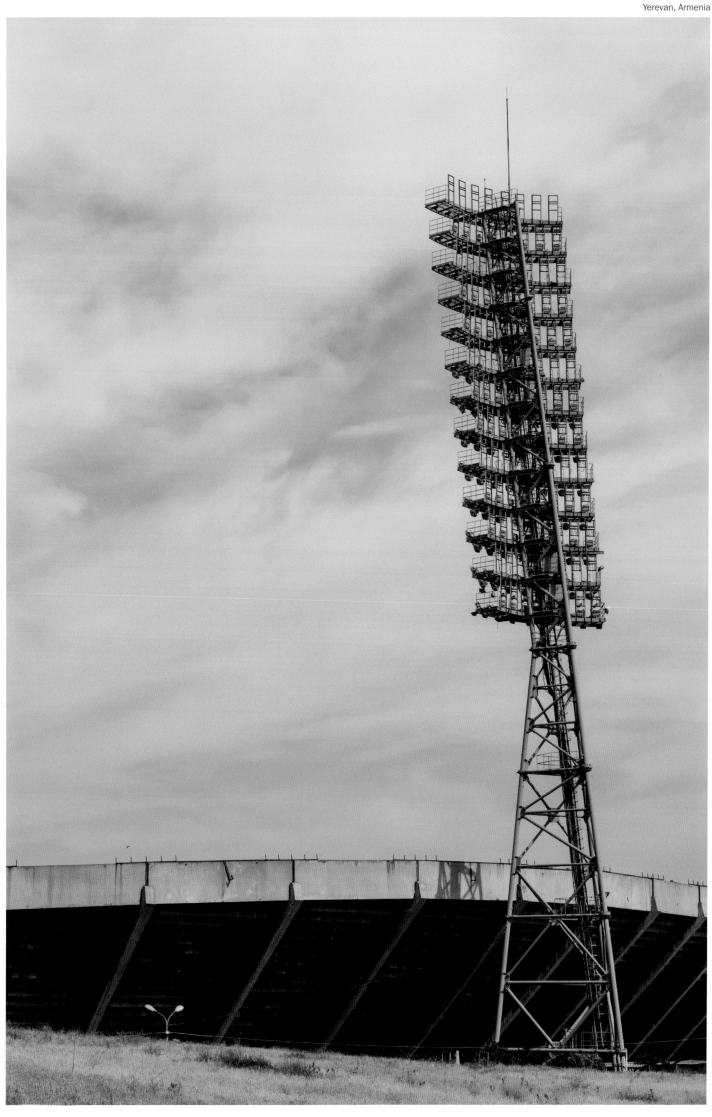

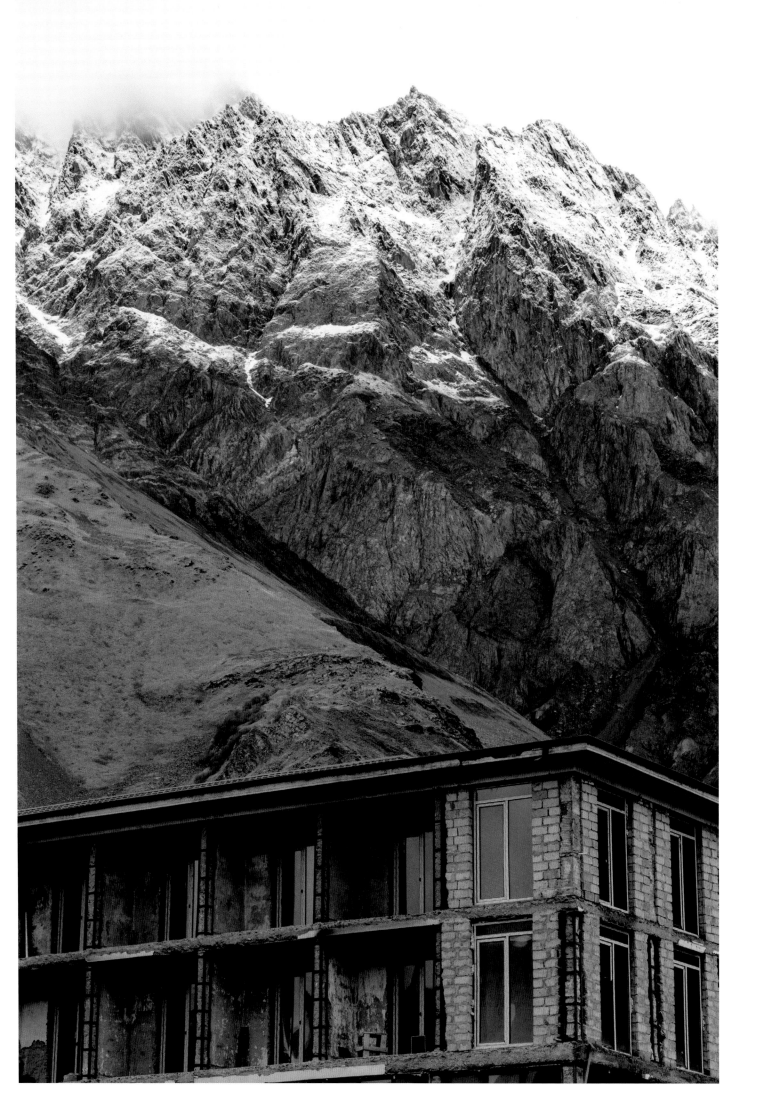

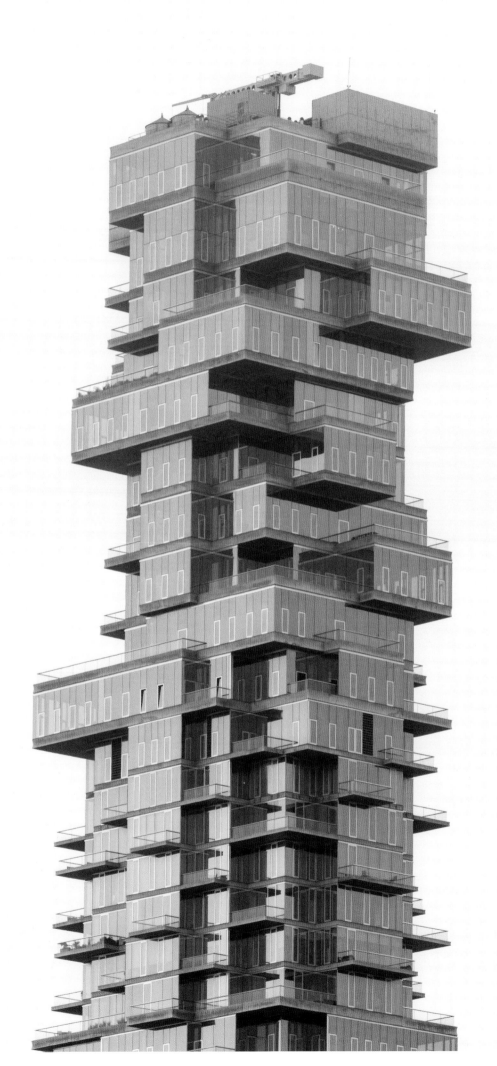

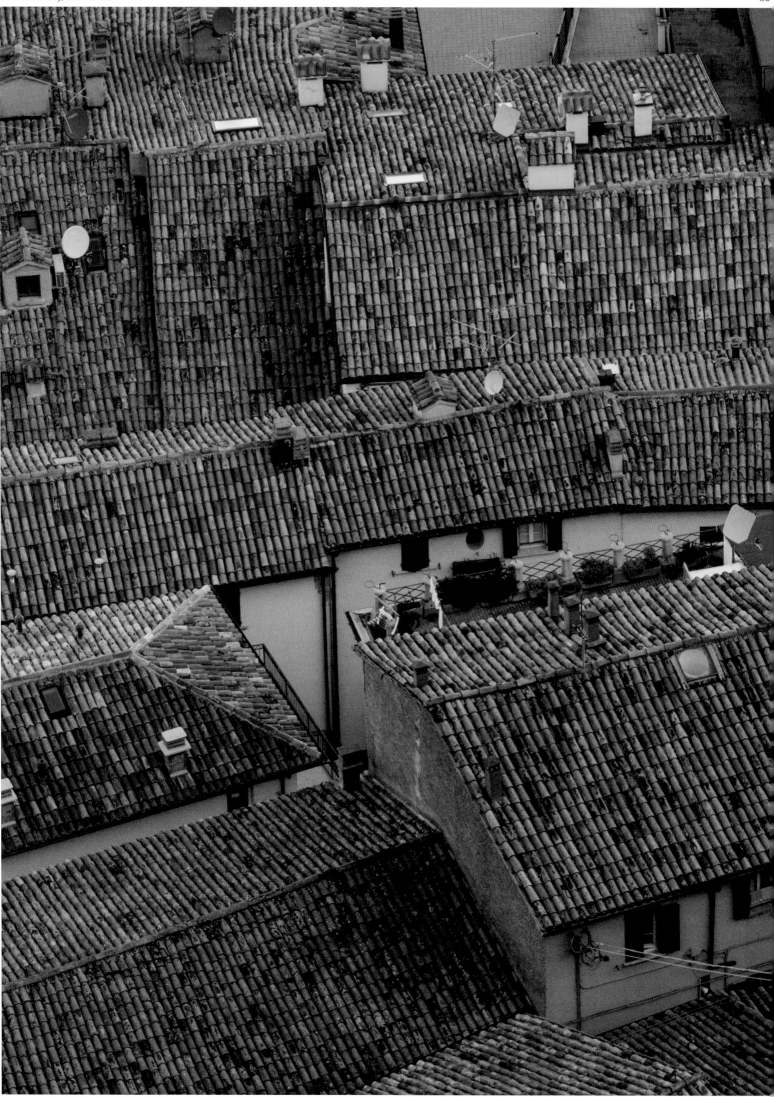

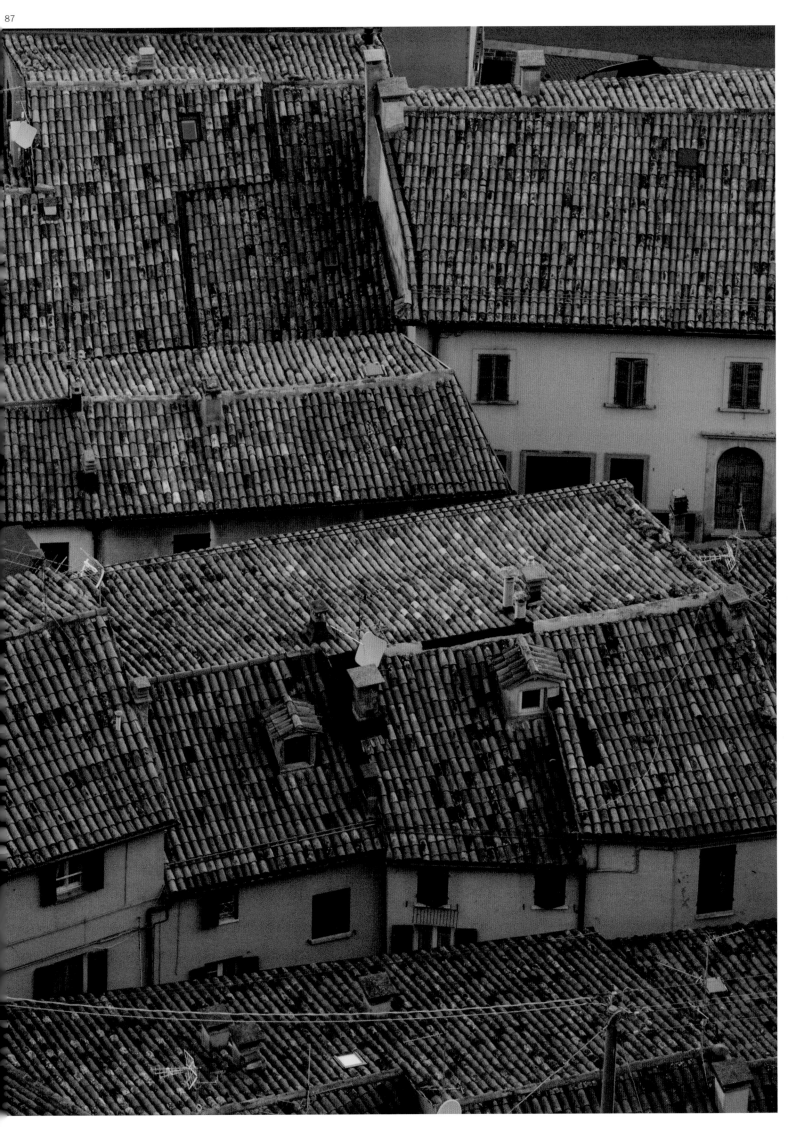

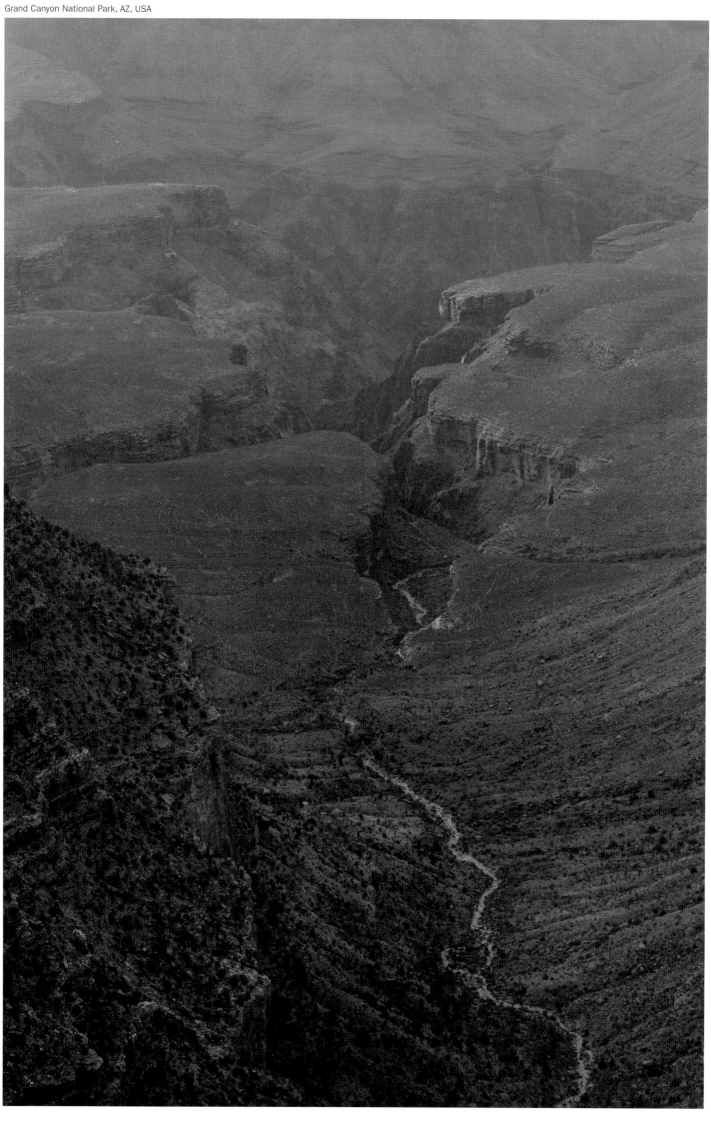

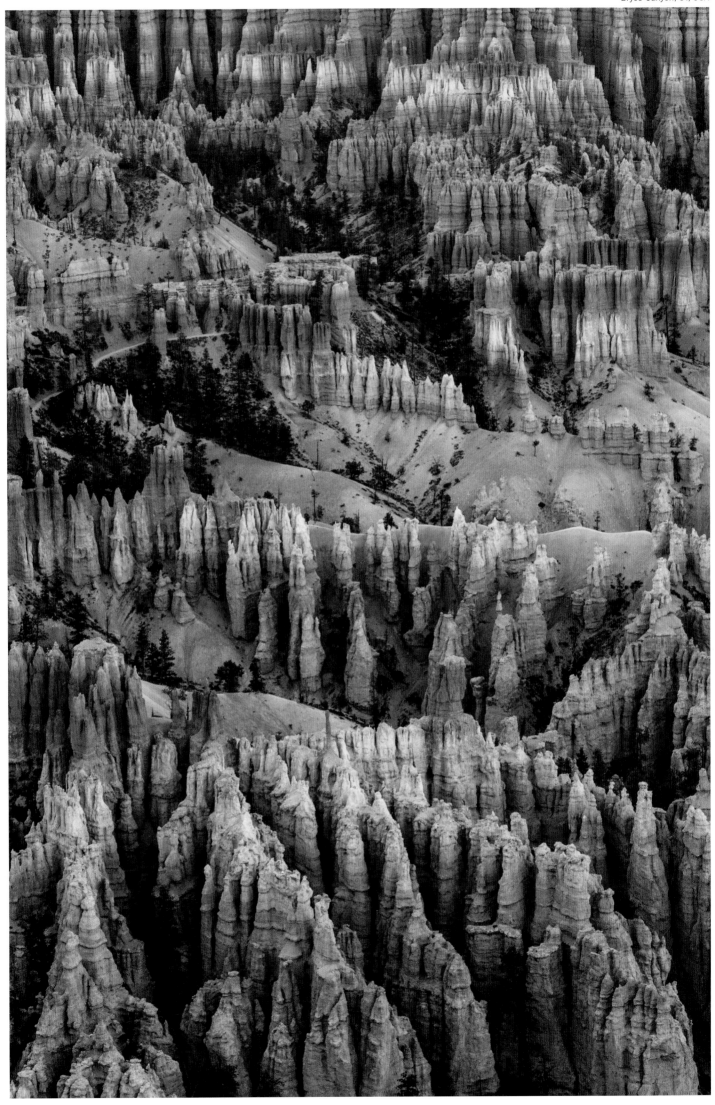

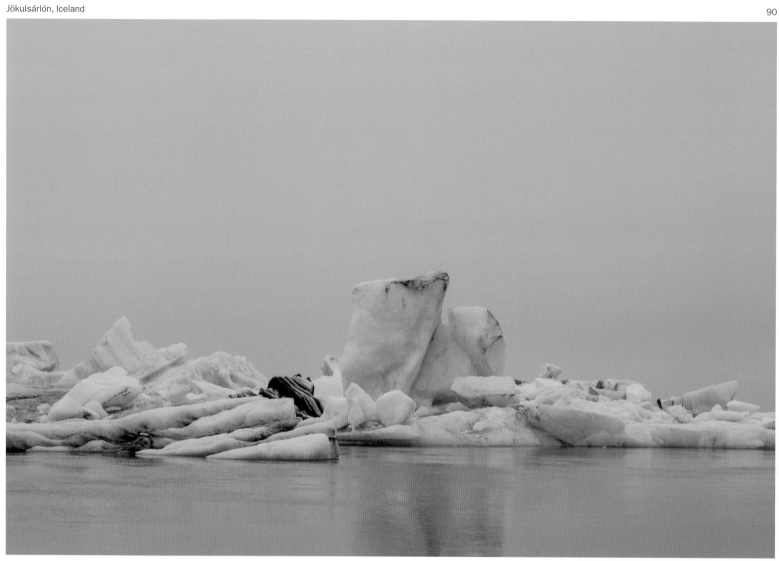

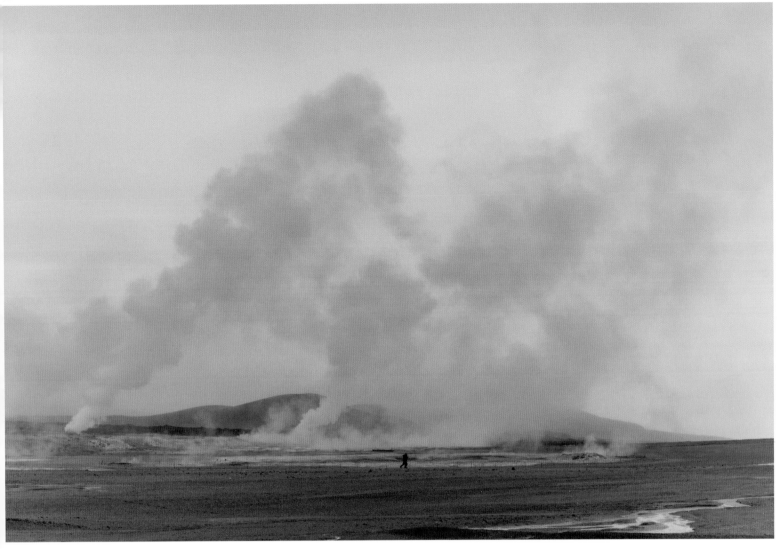

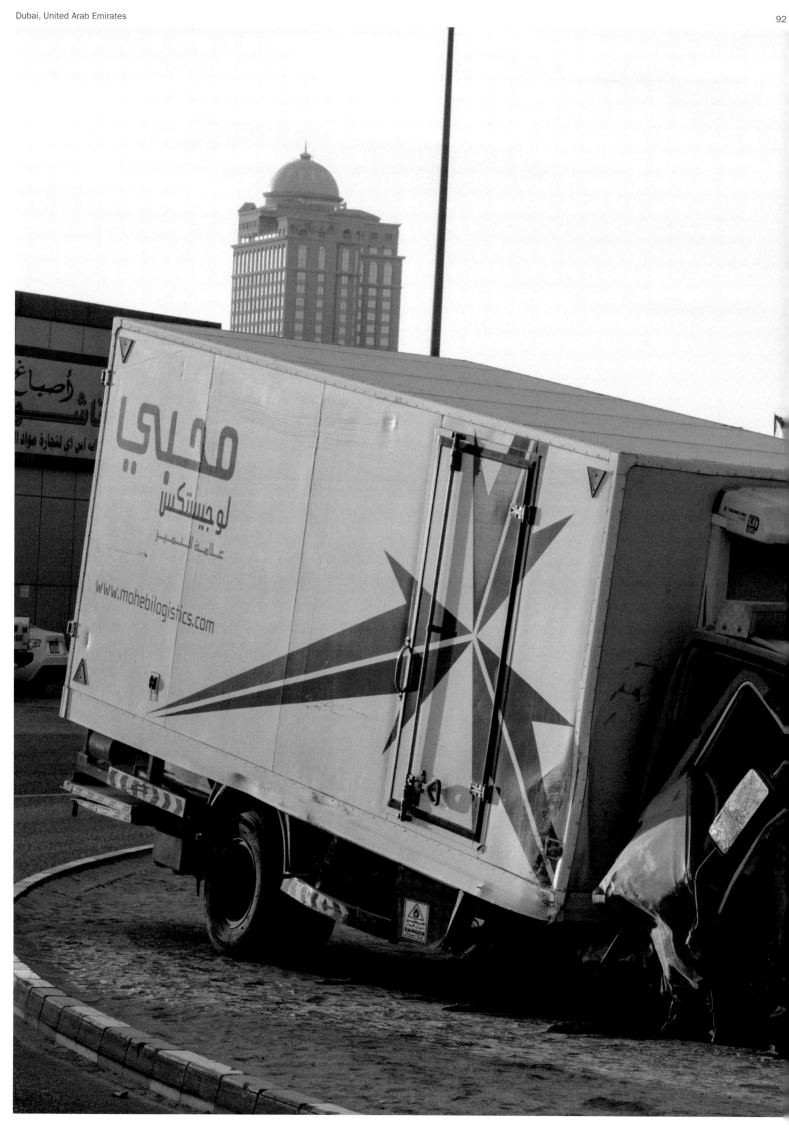

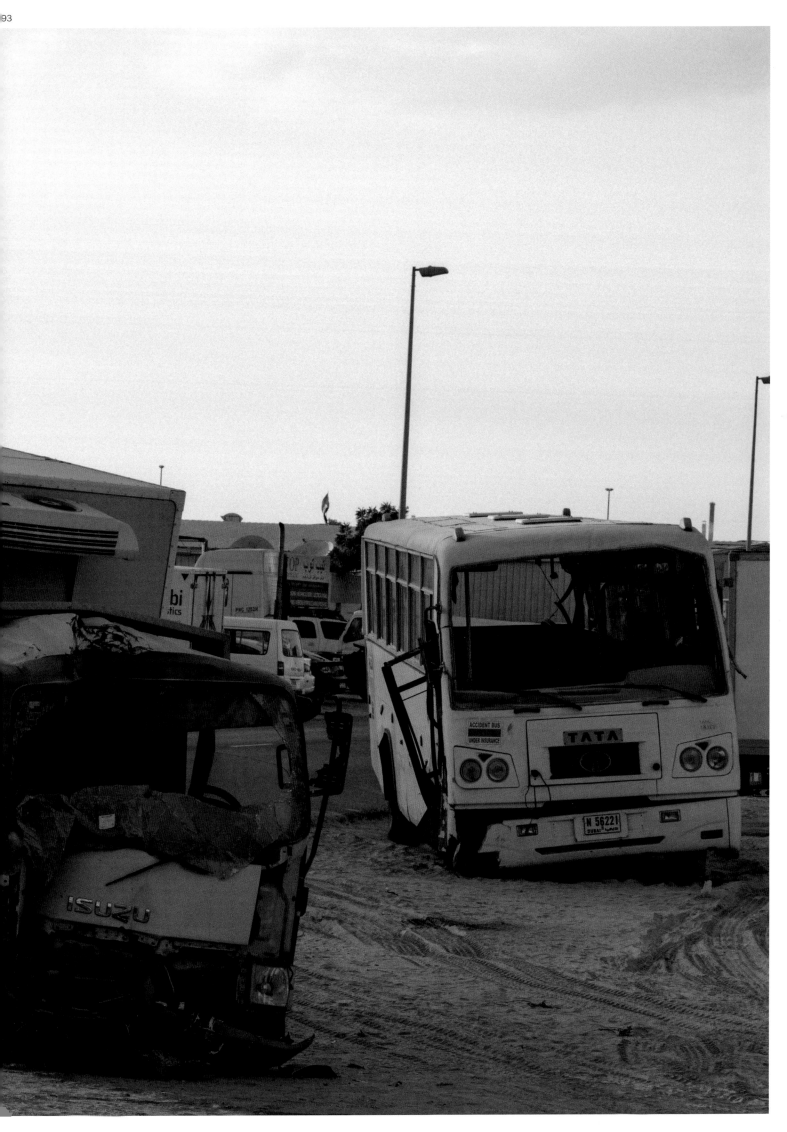

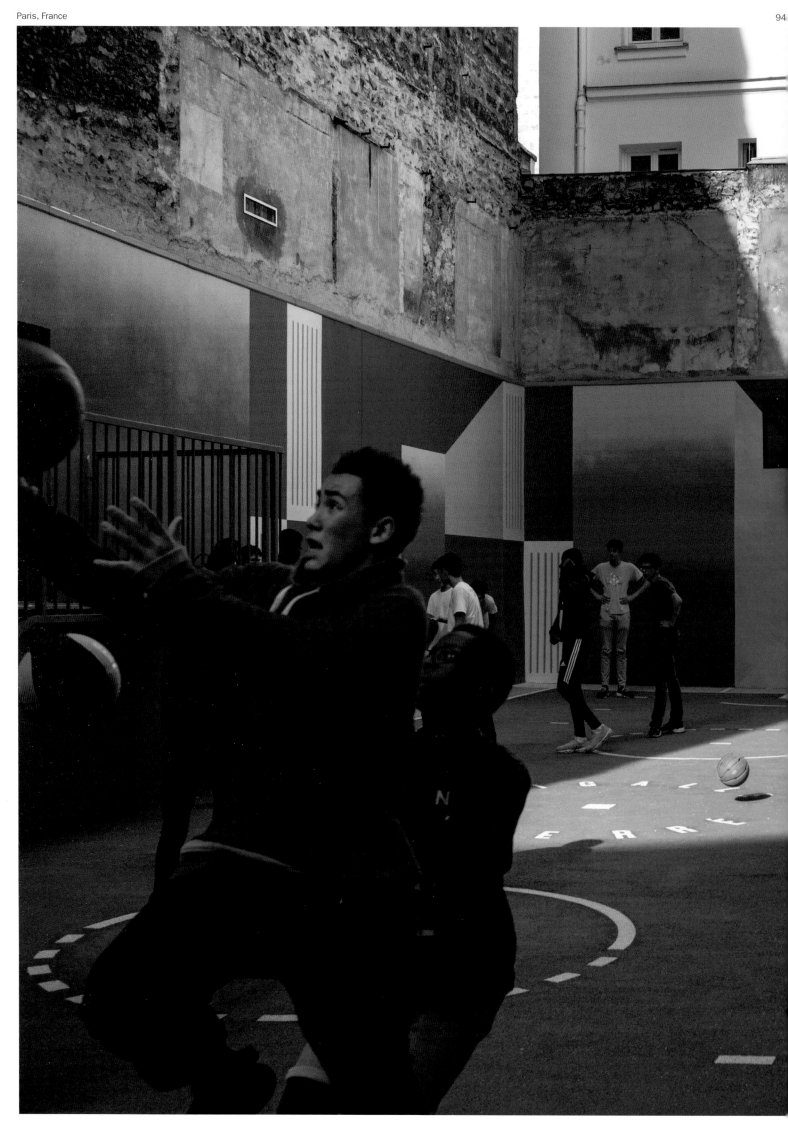

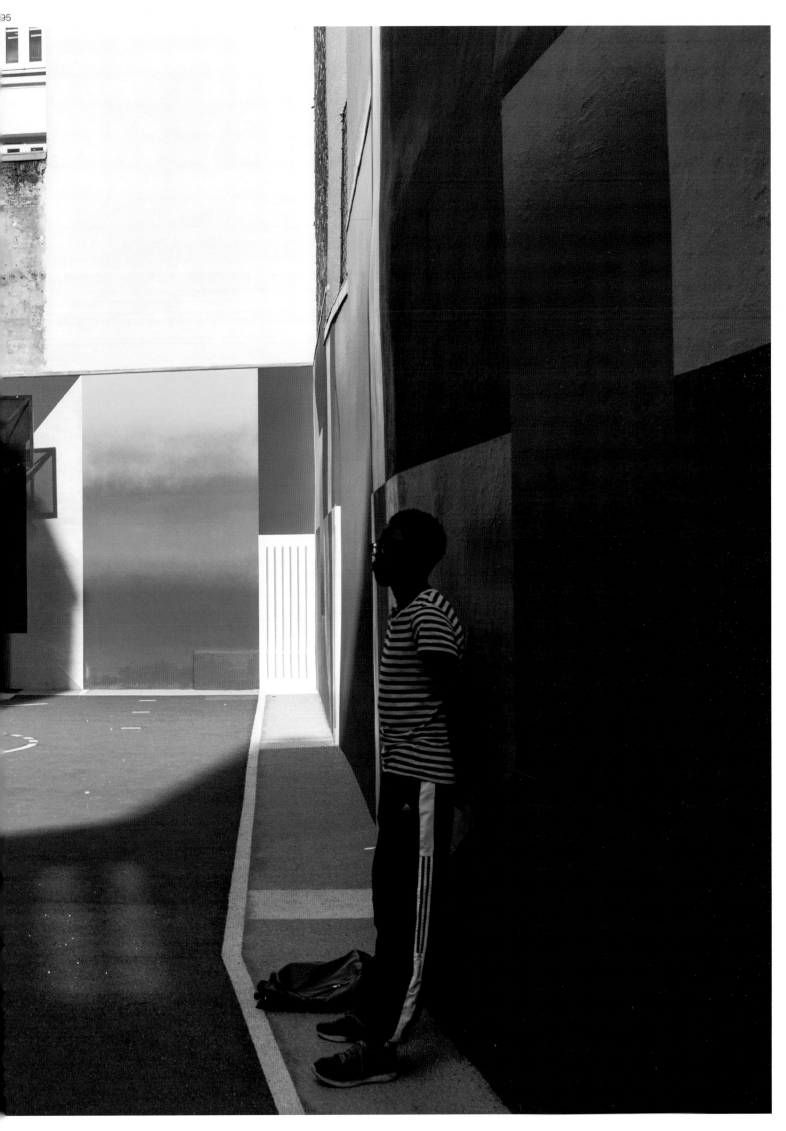

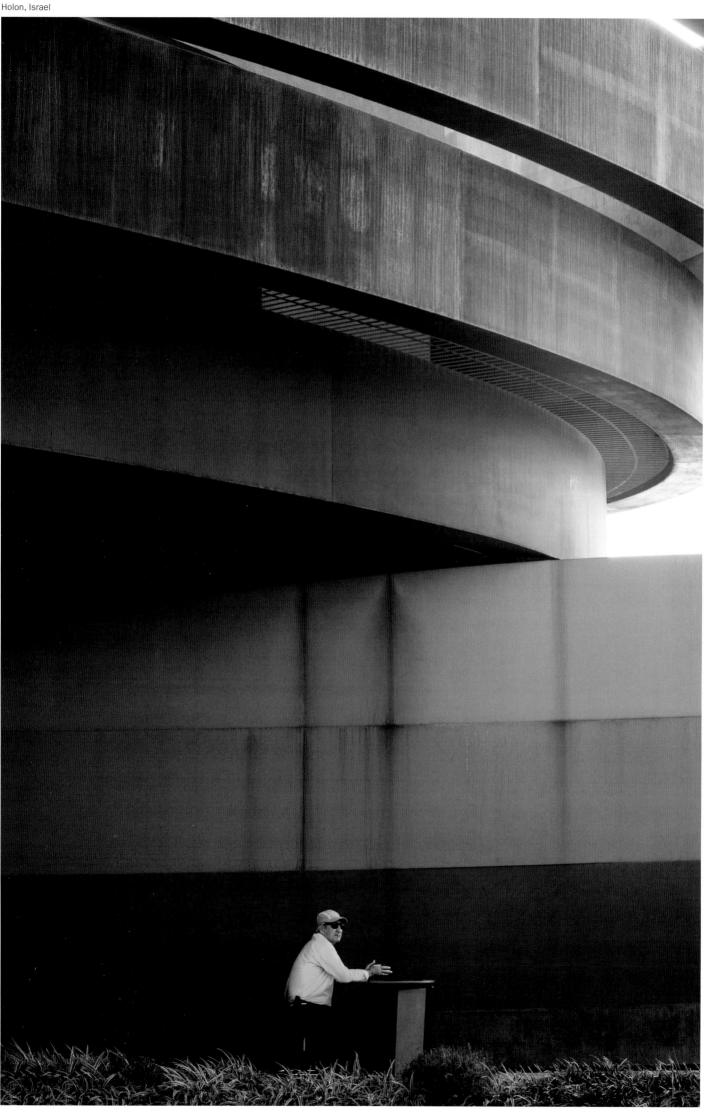

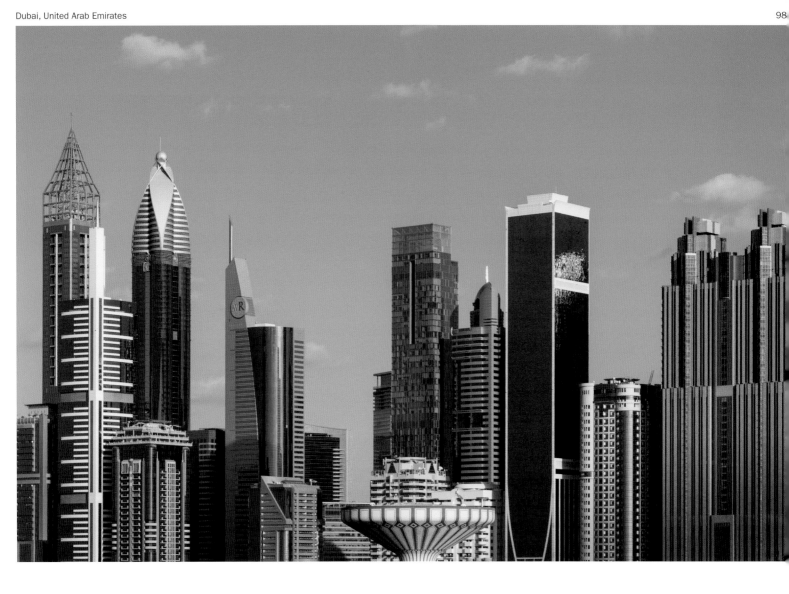

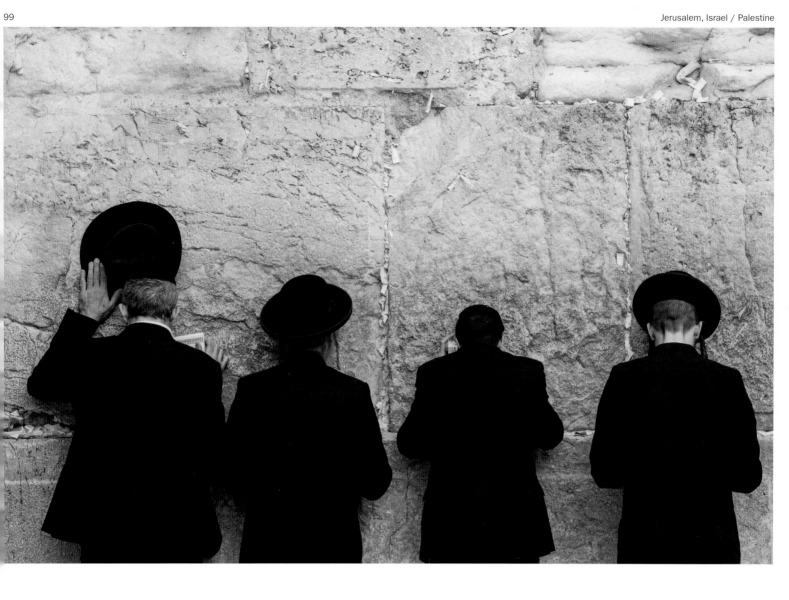

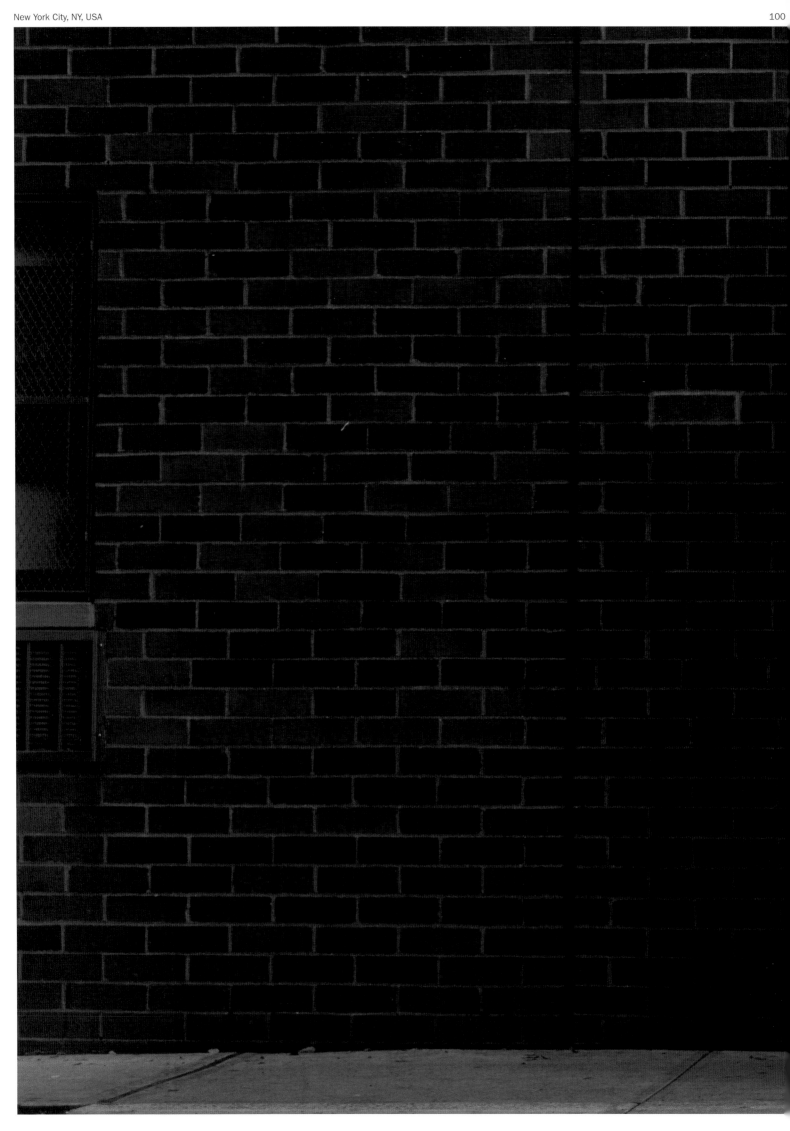

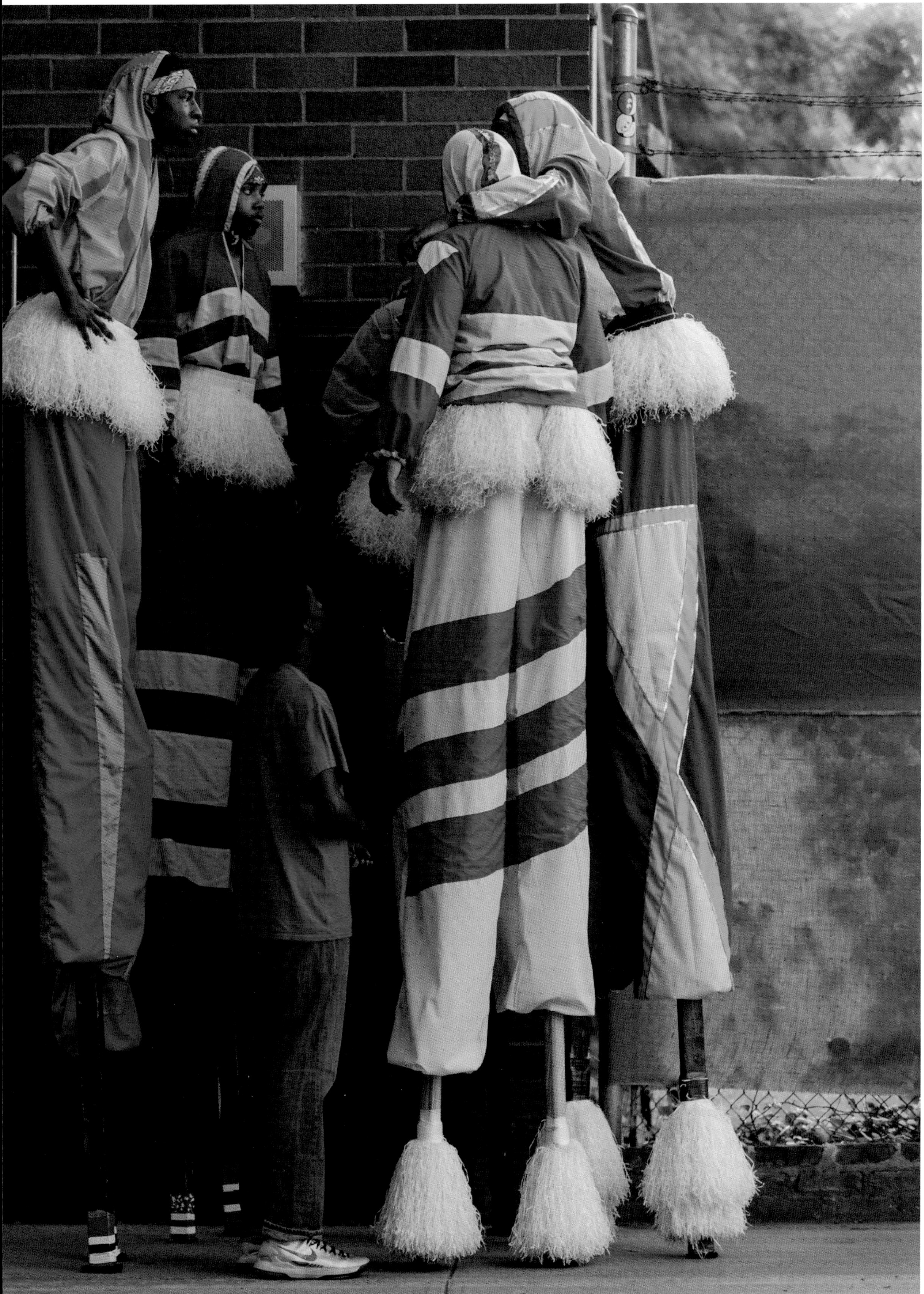

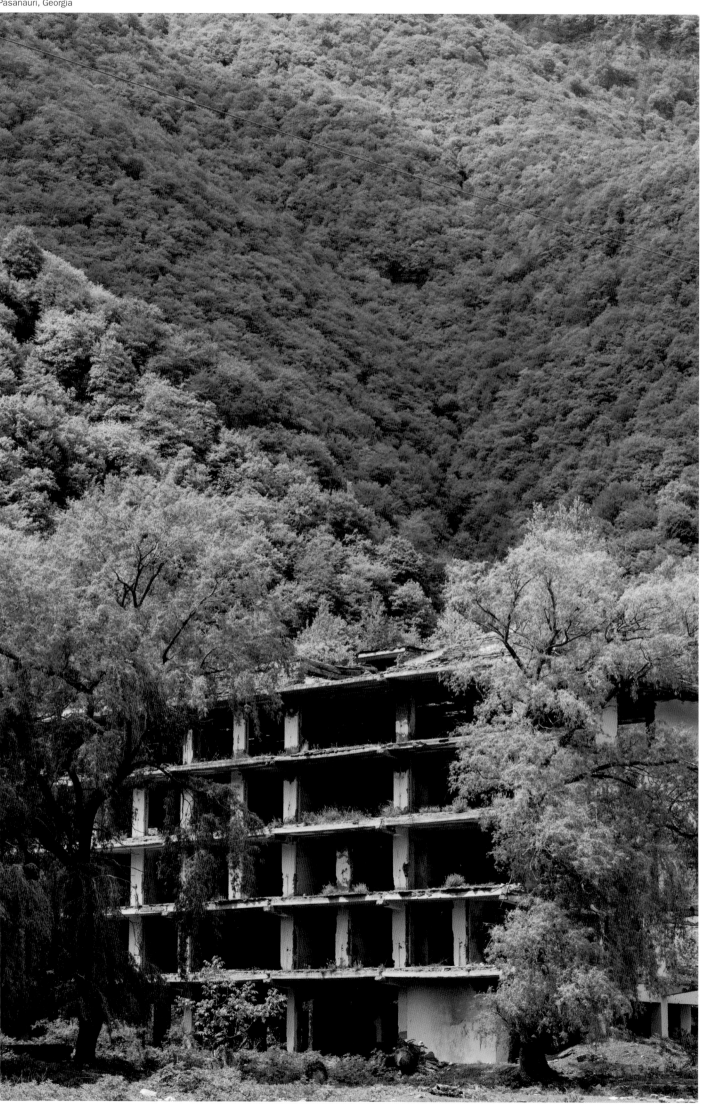

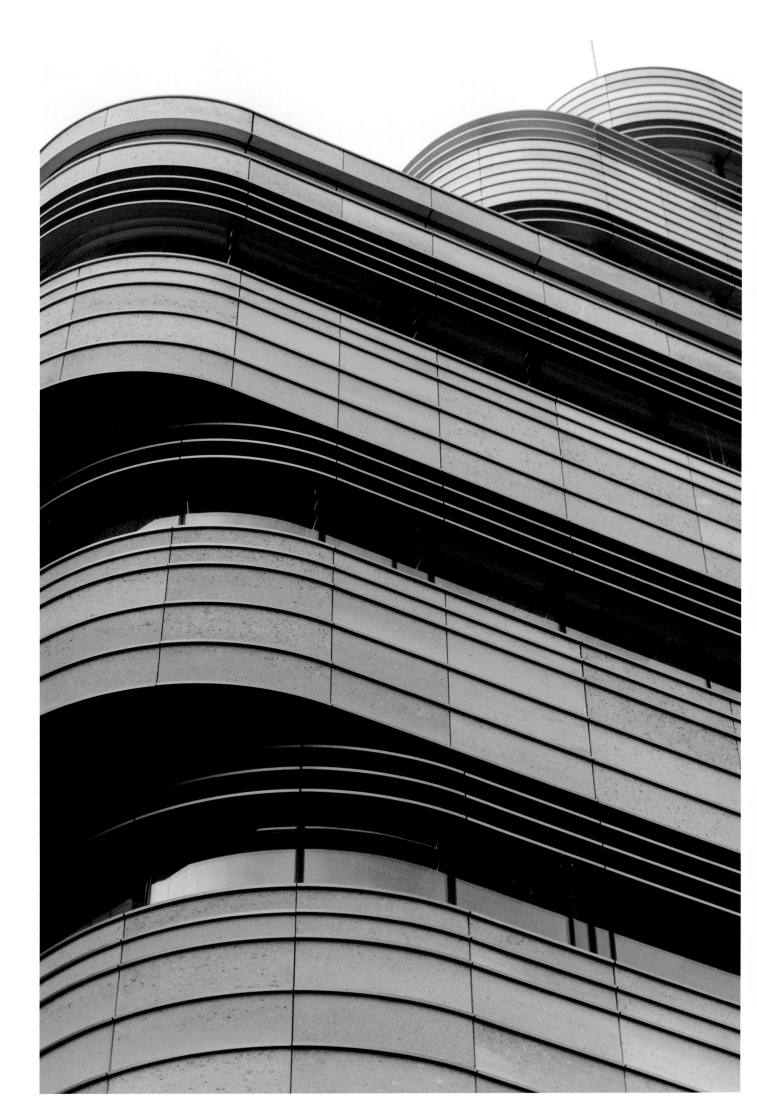

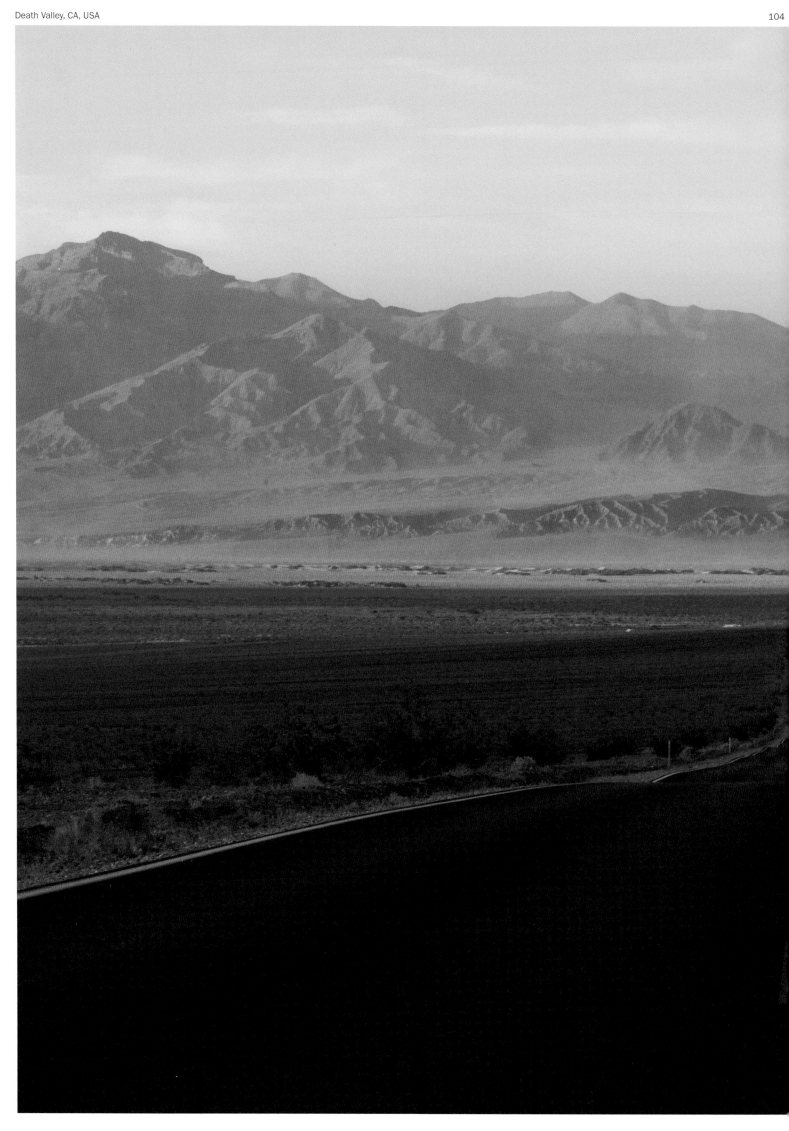

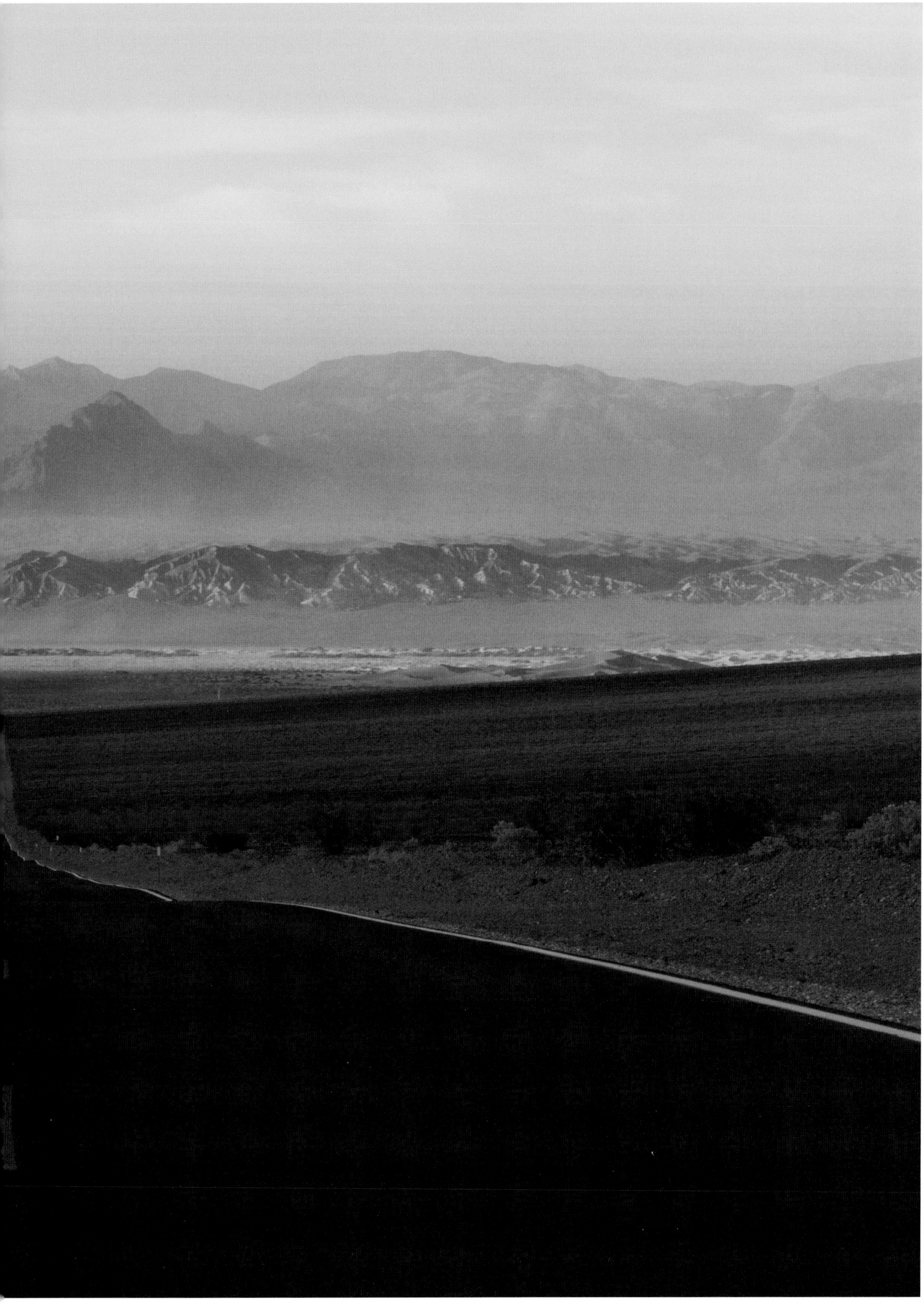

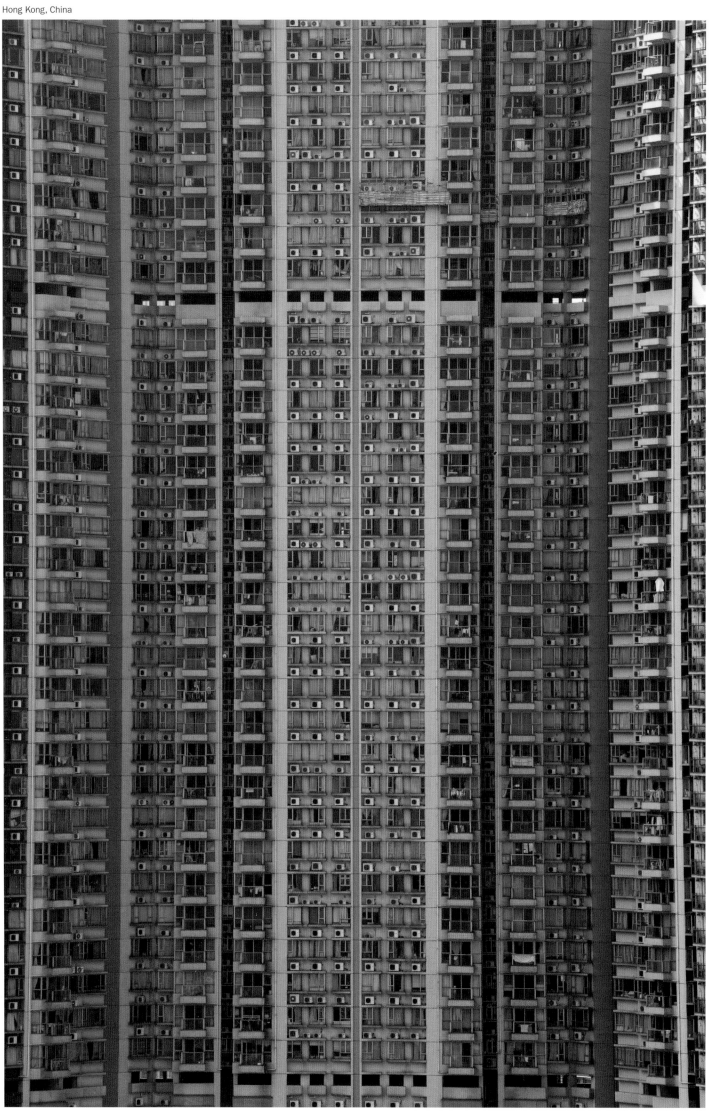

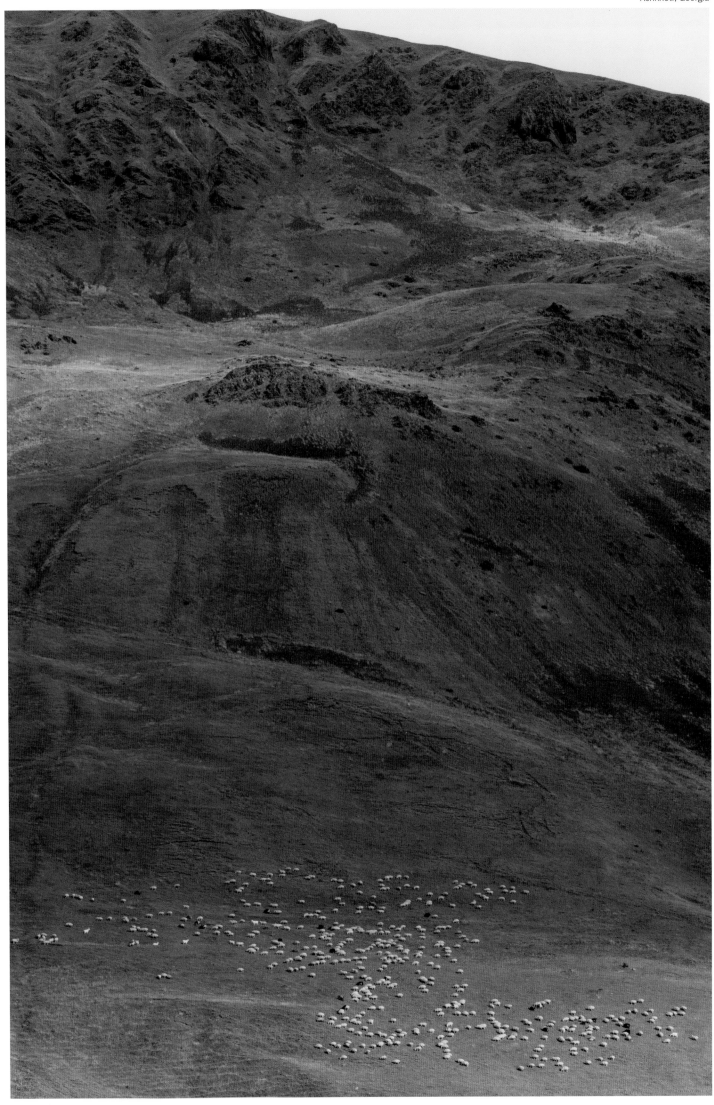

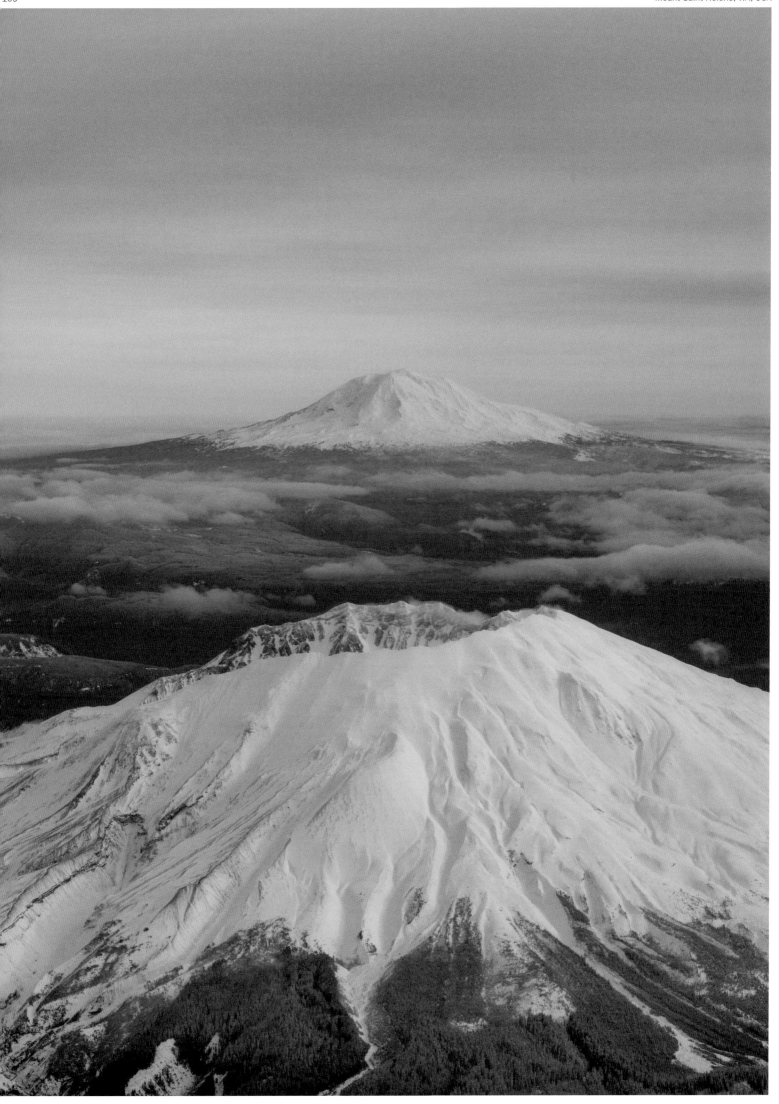

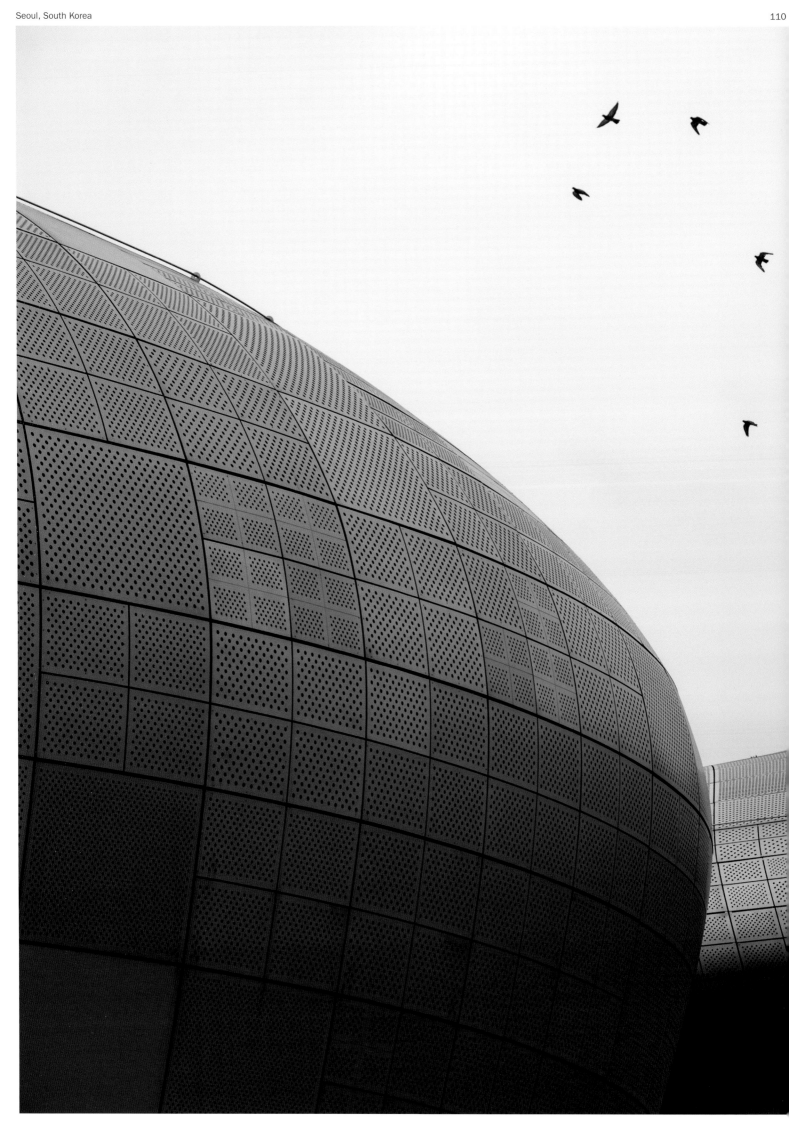

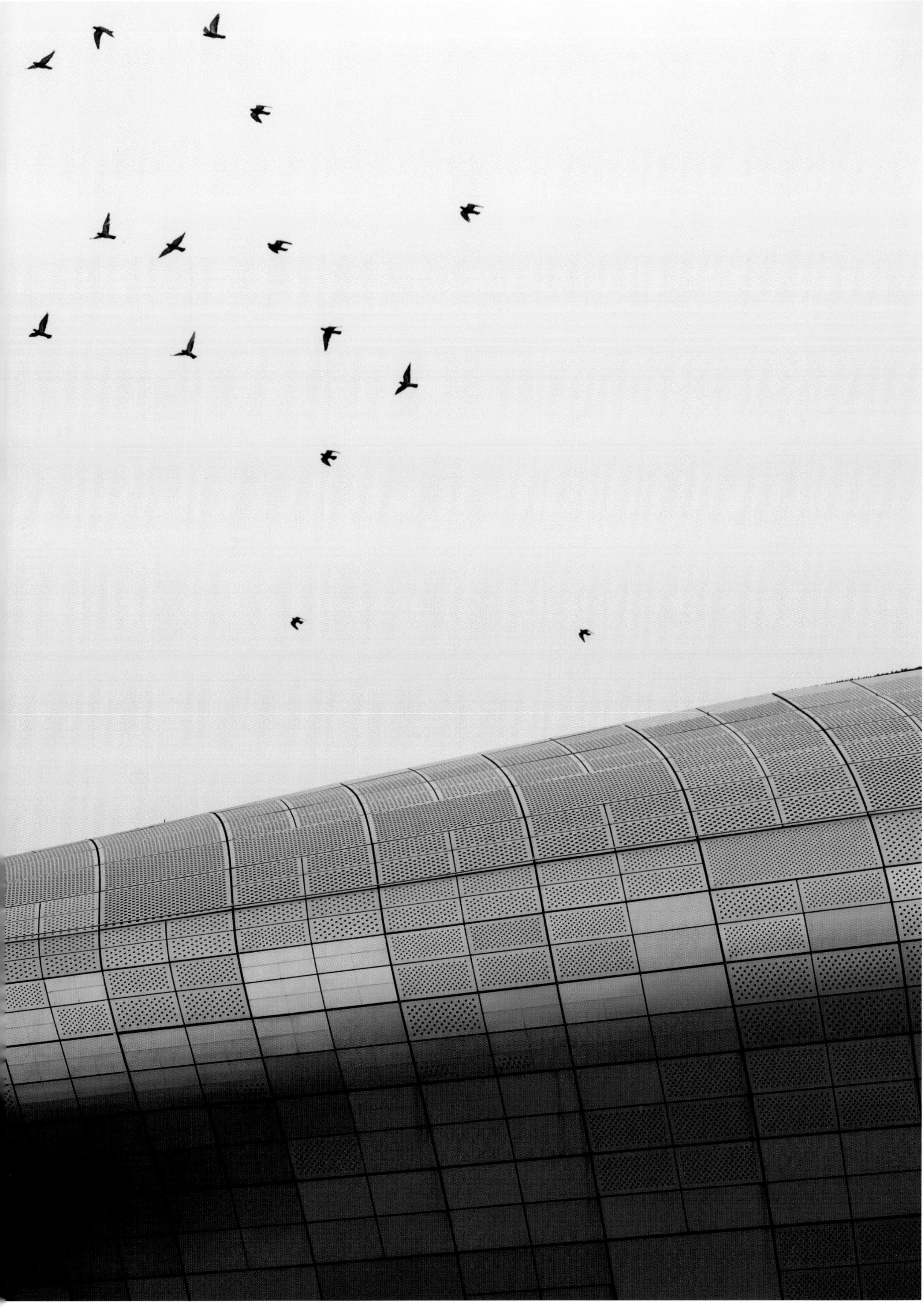

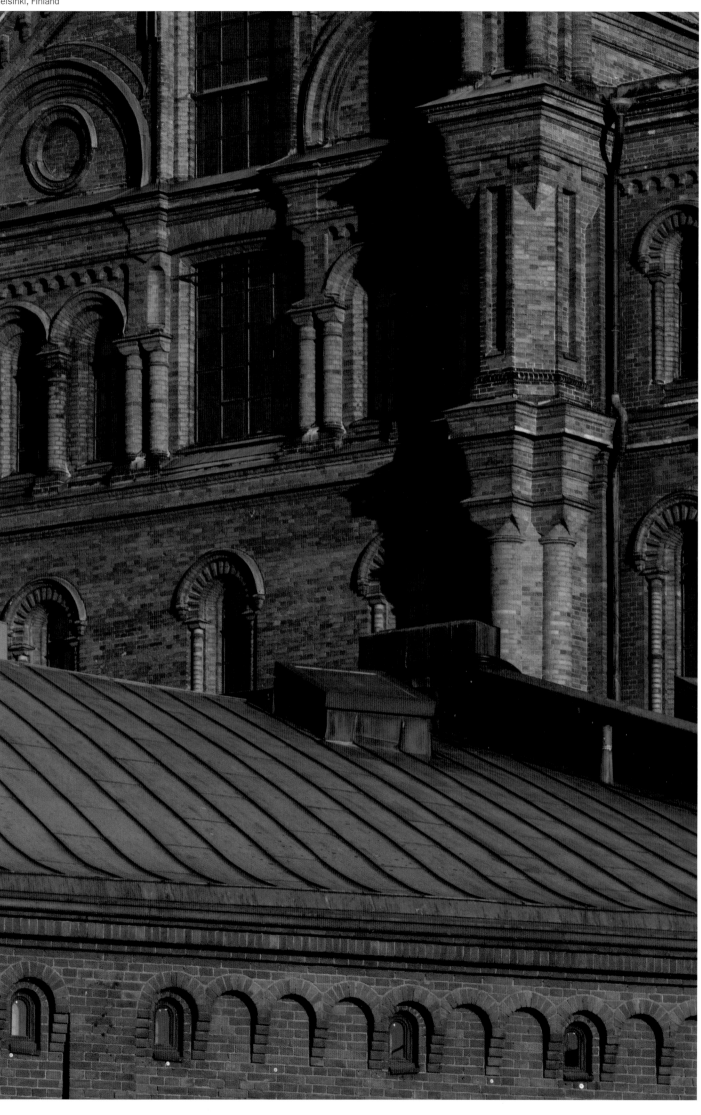

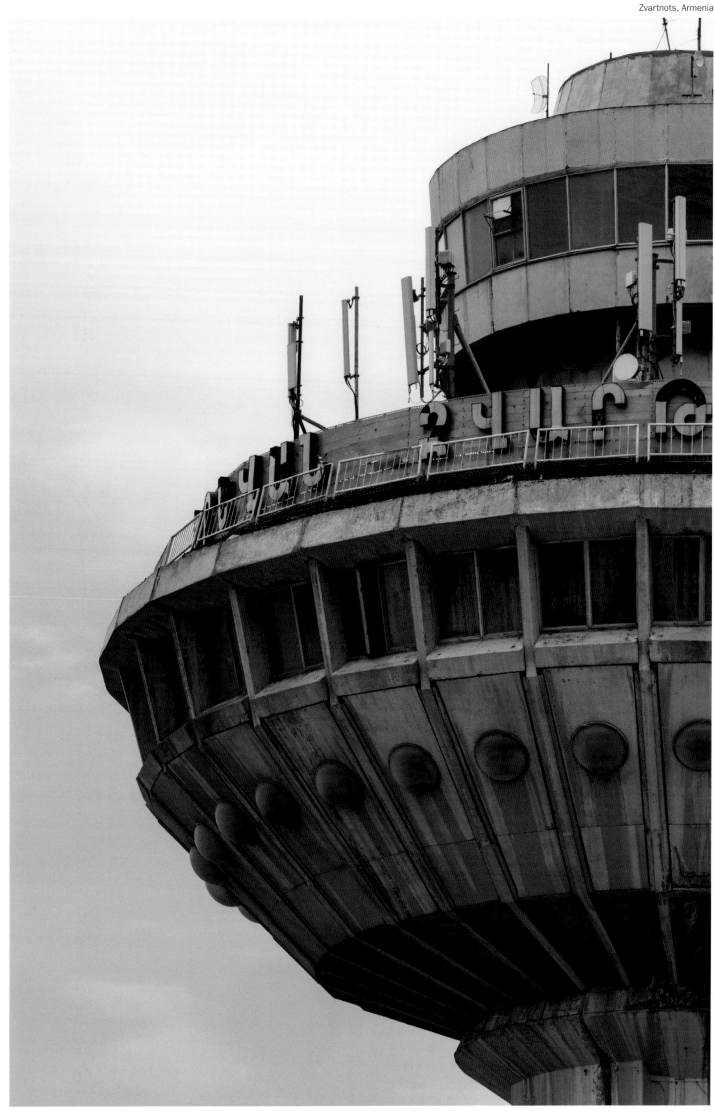

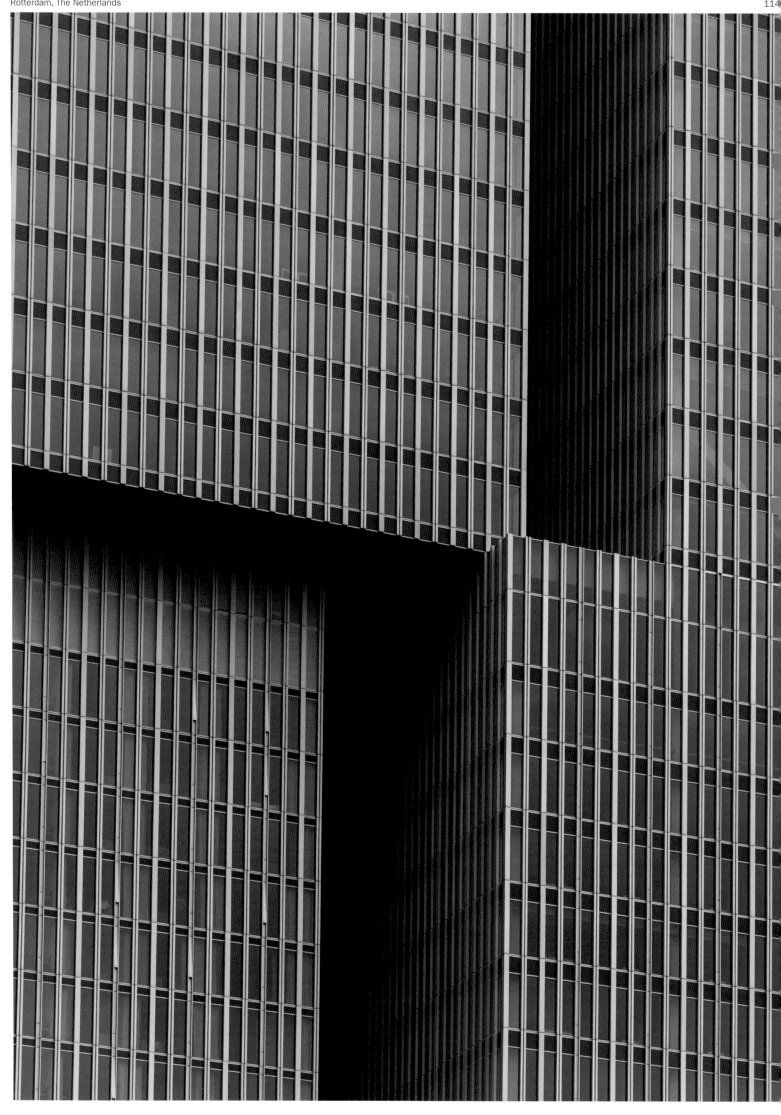

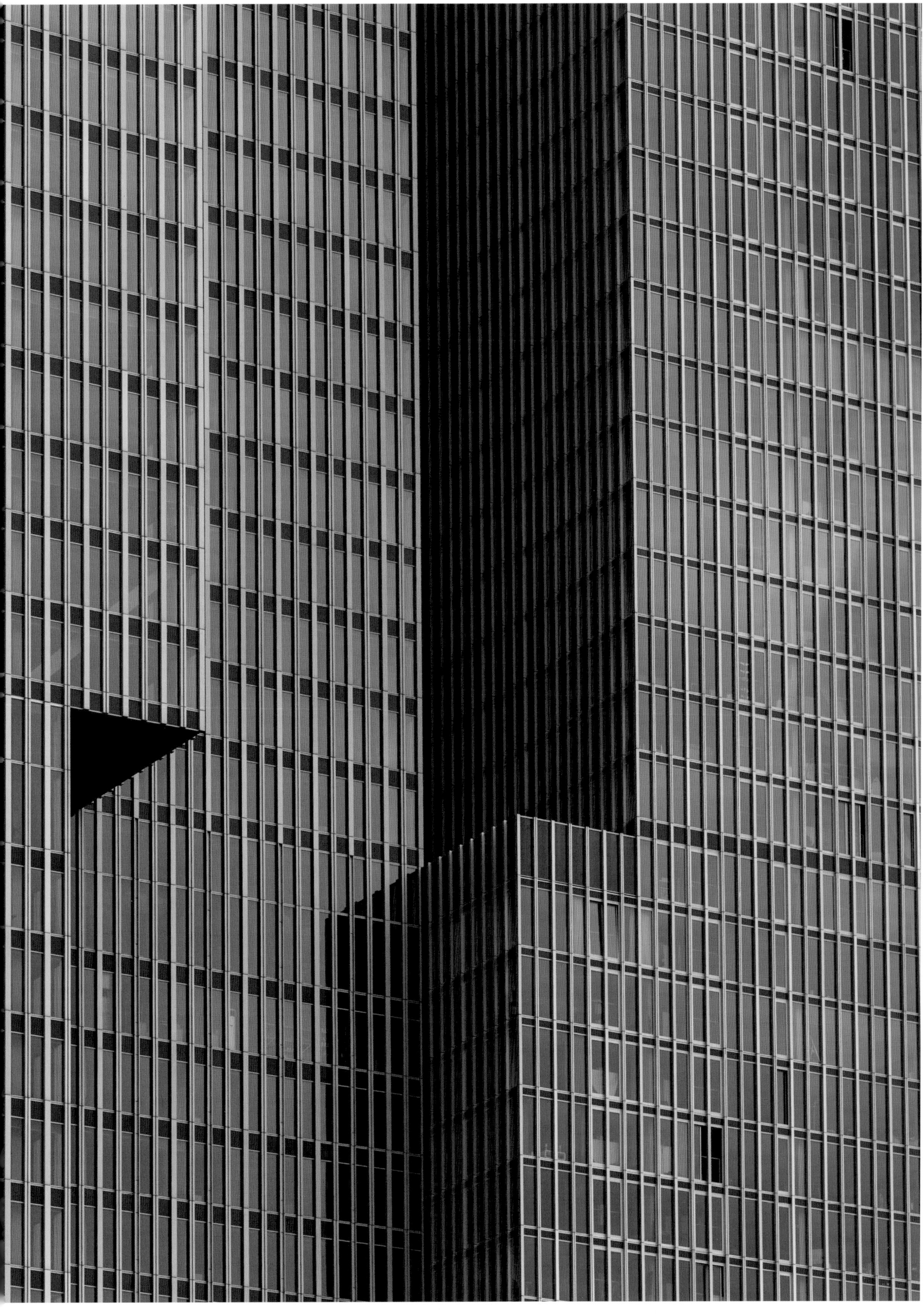

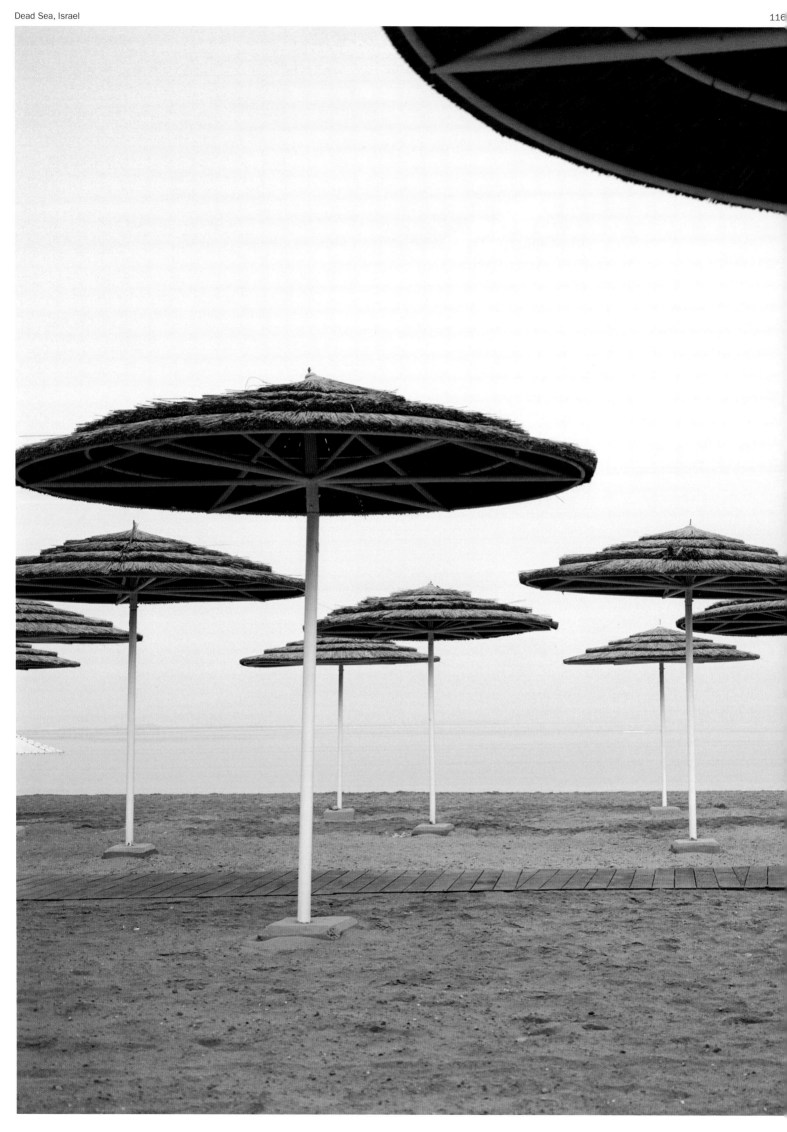

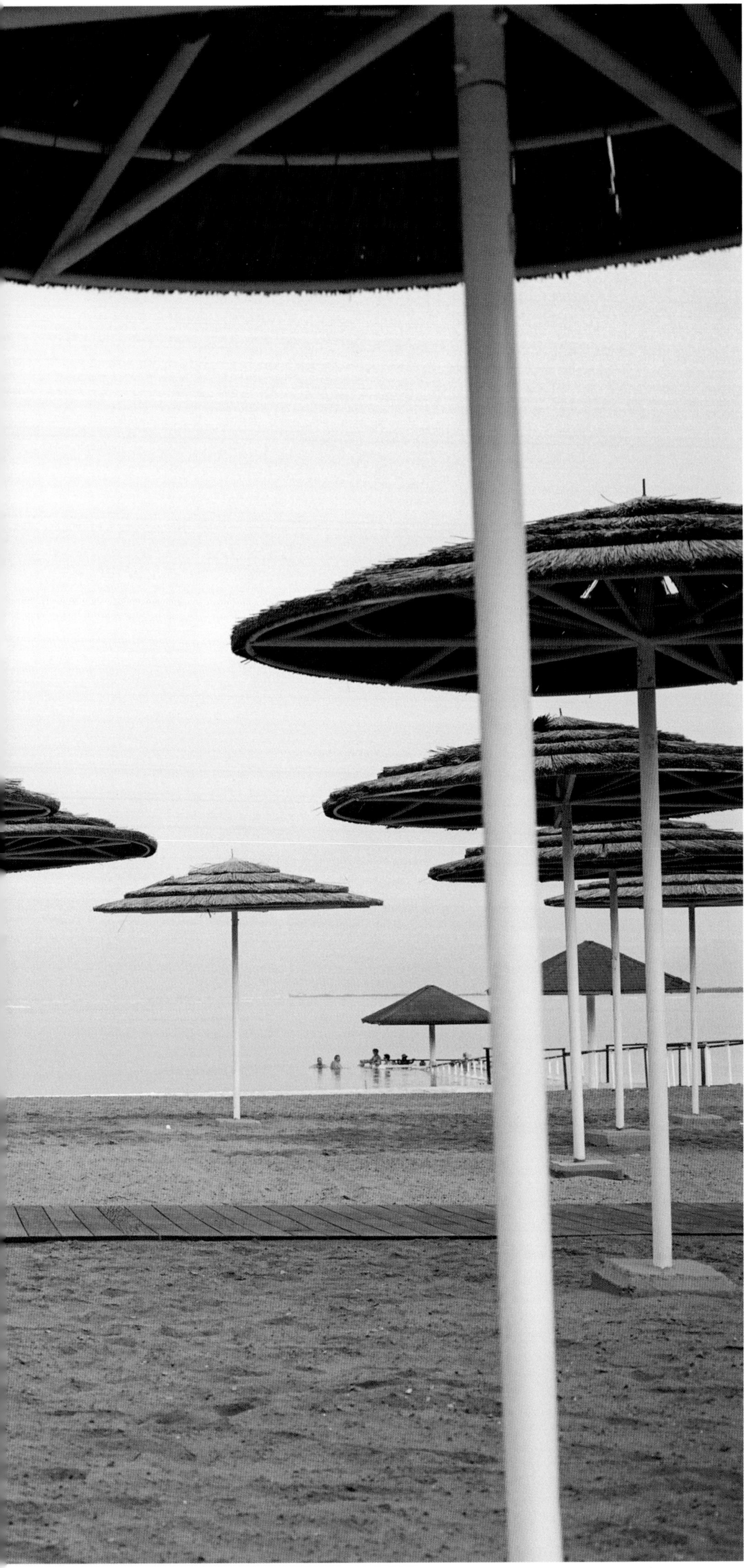

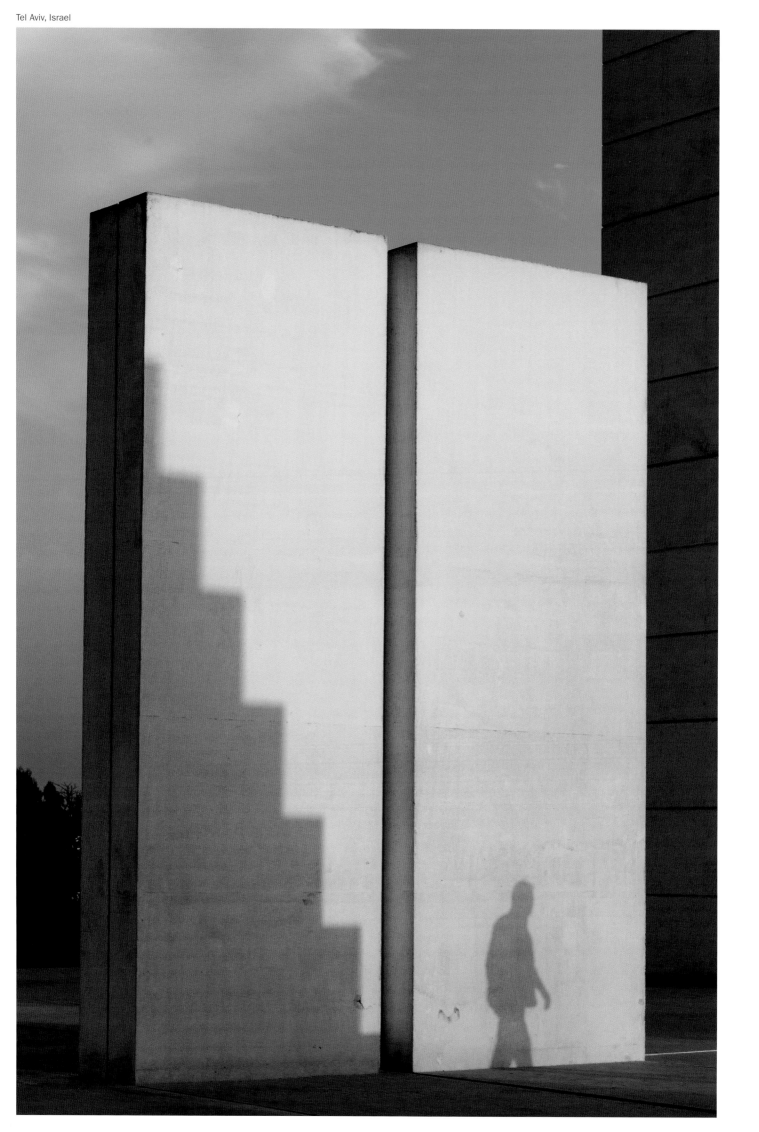

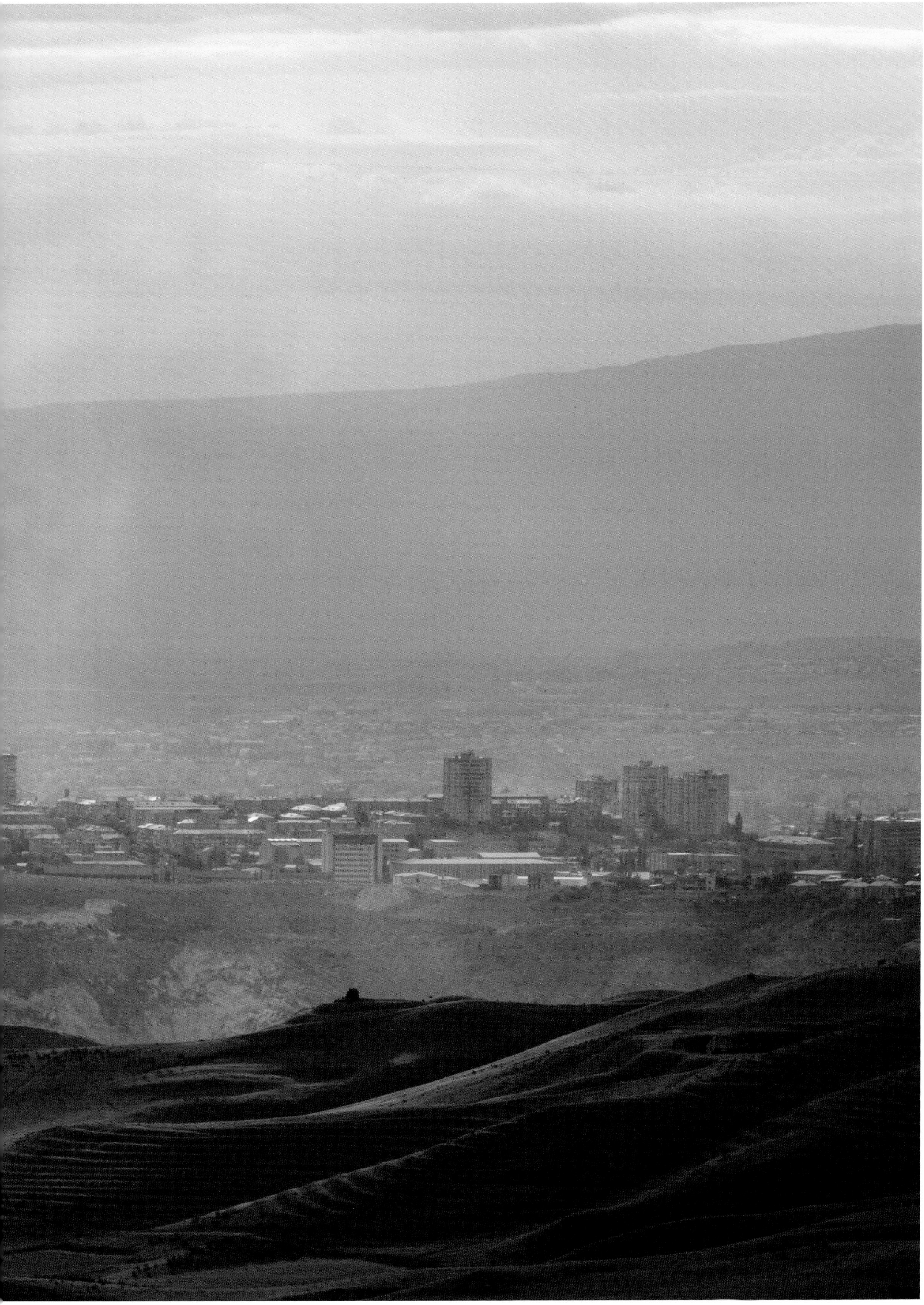

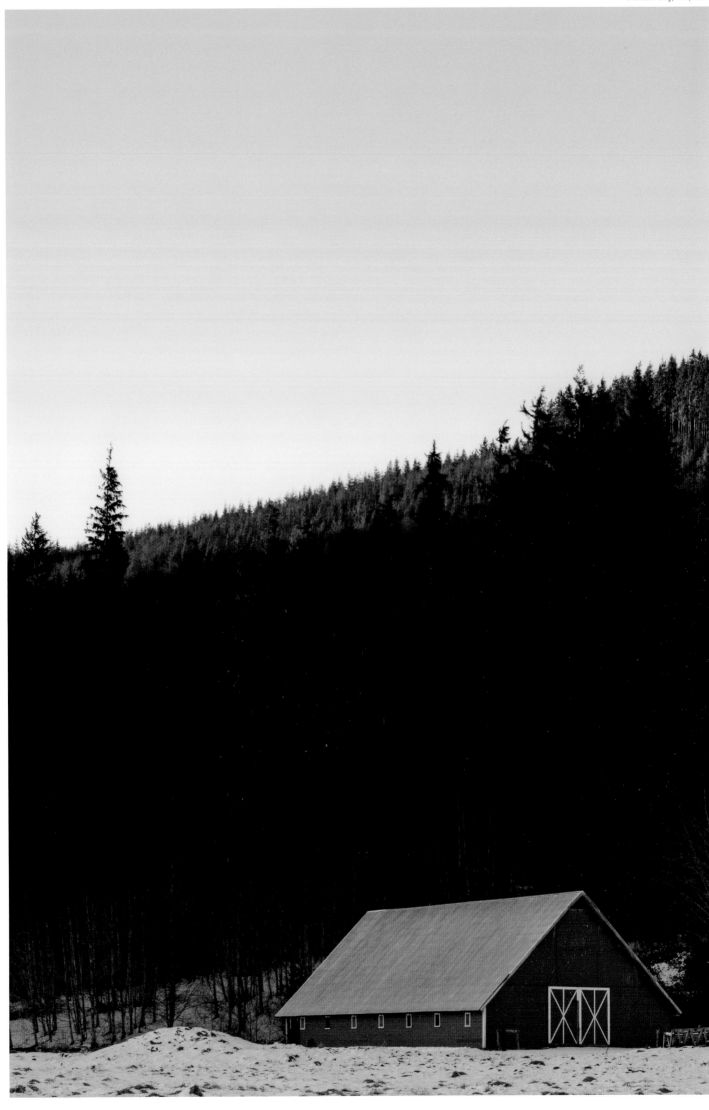

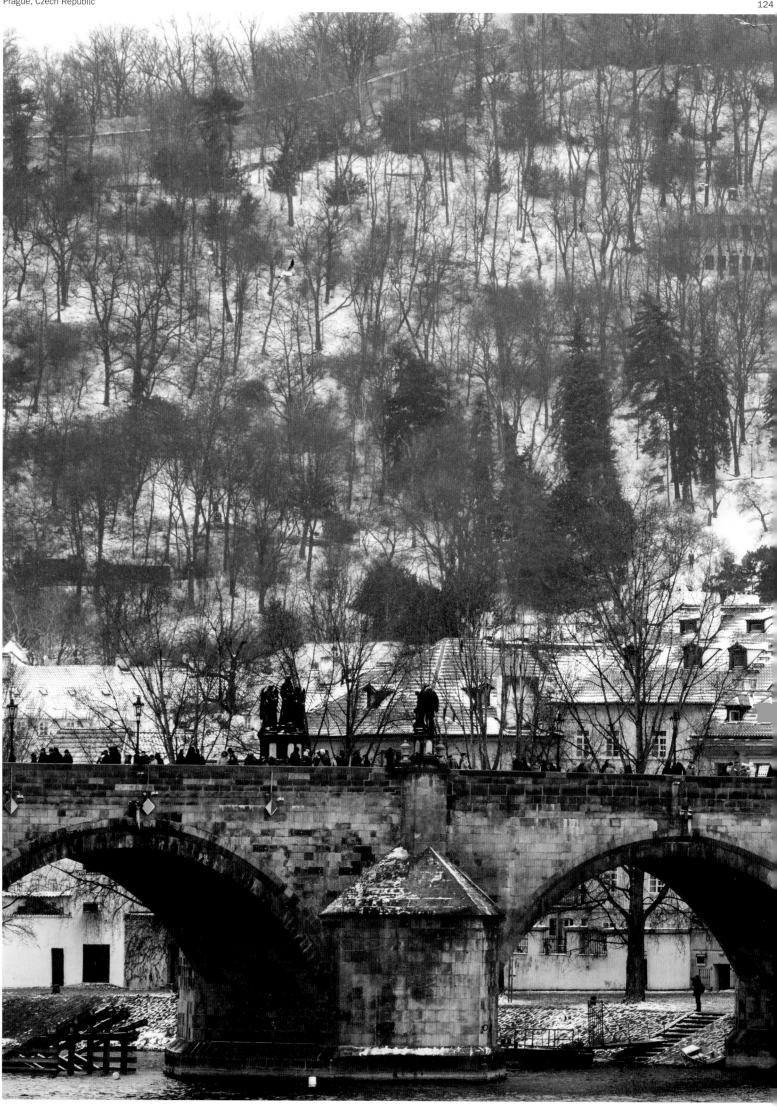

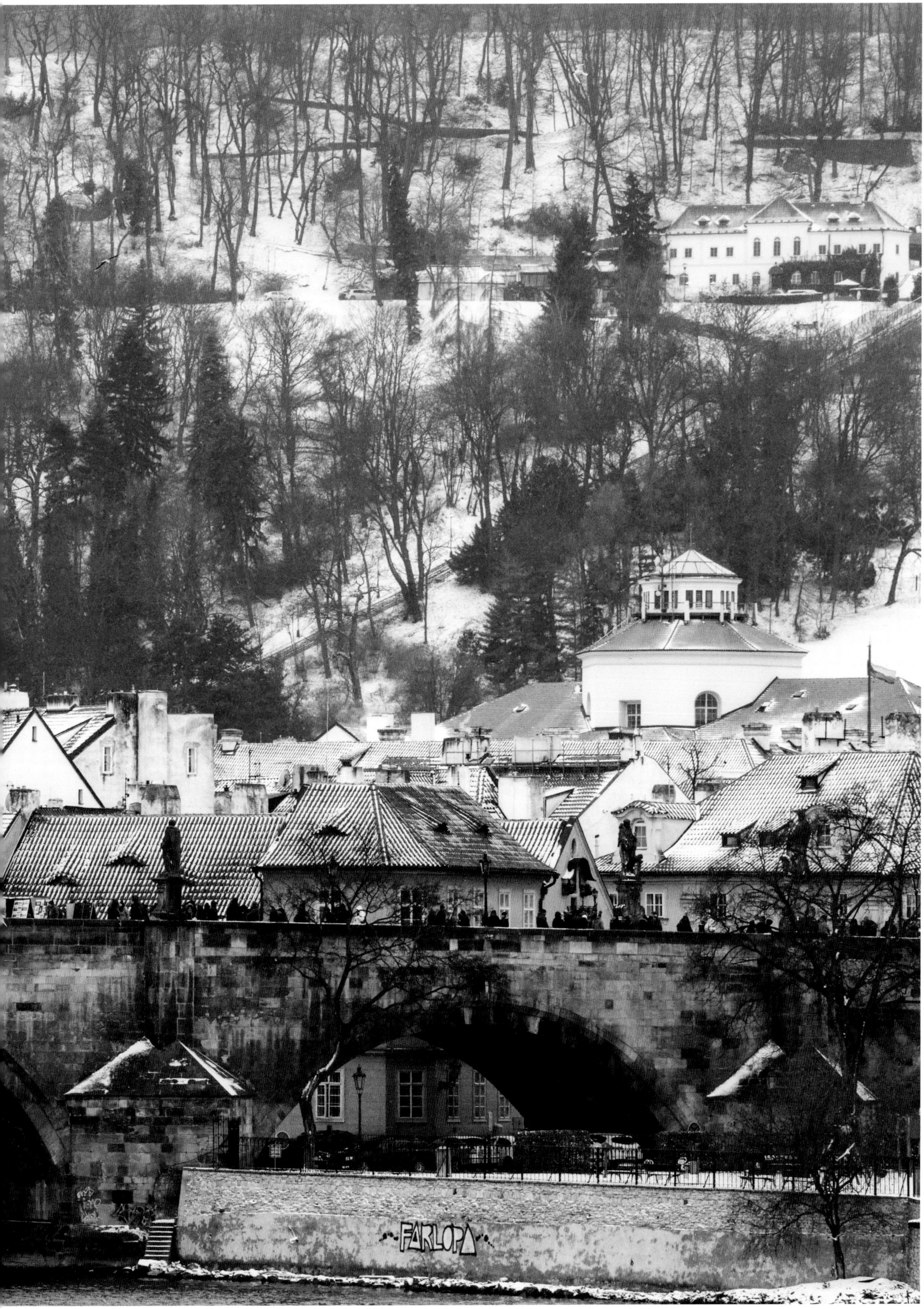
FARLOPA

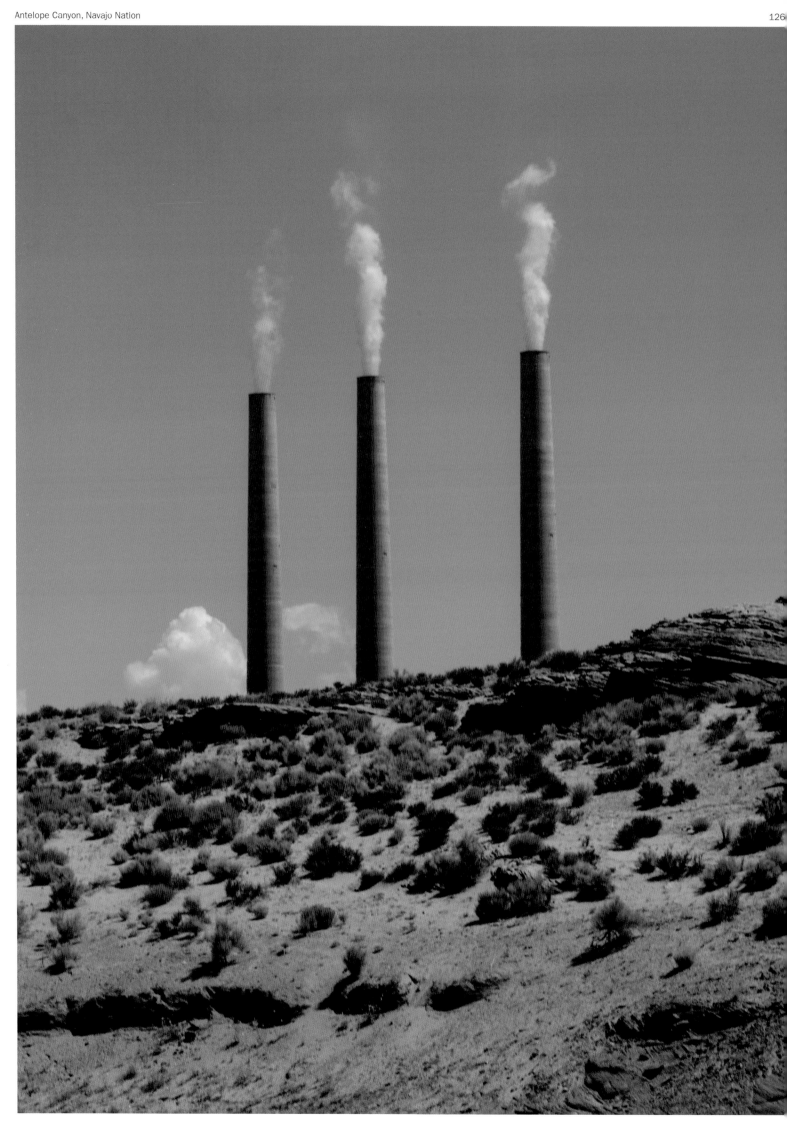

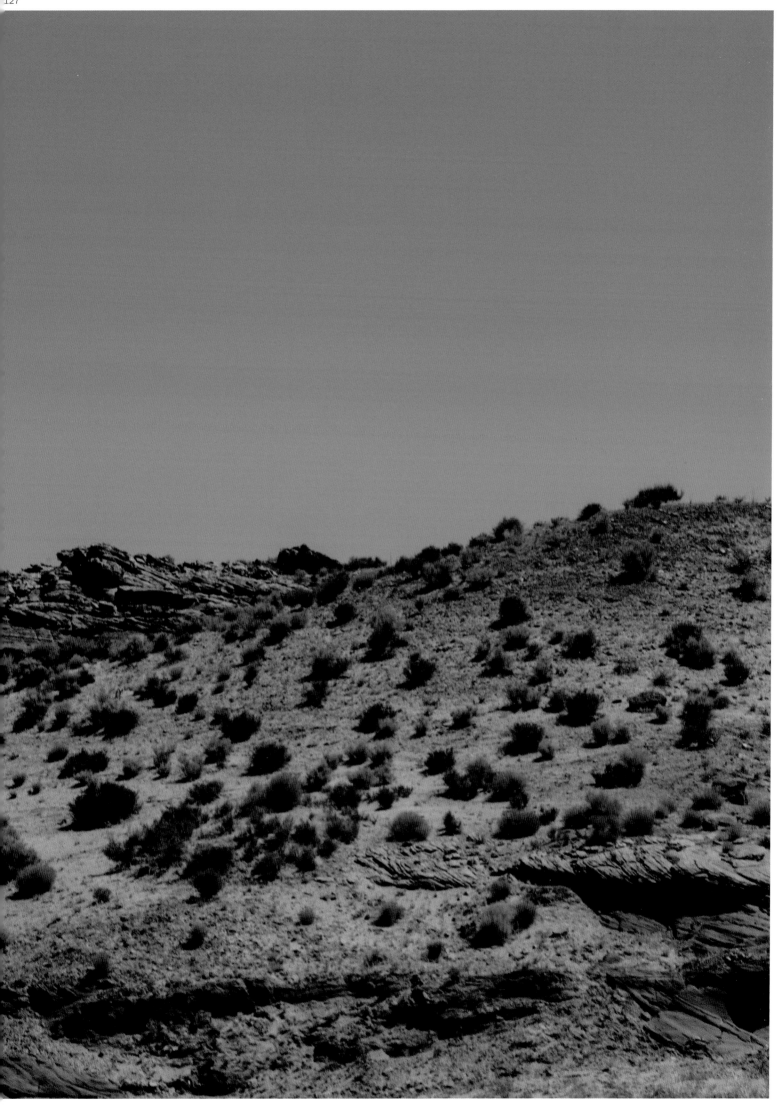

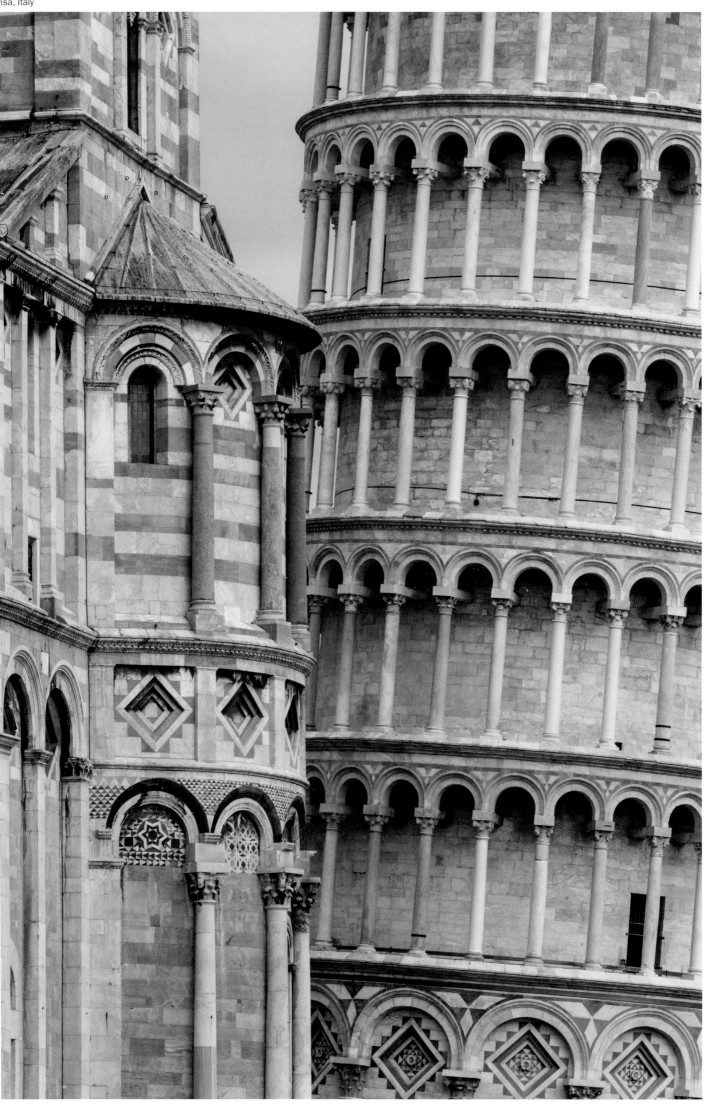

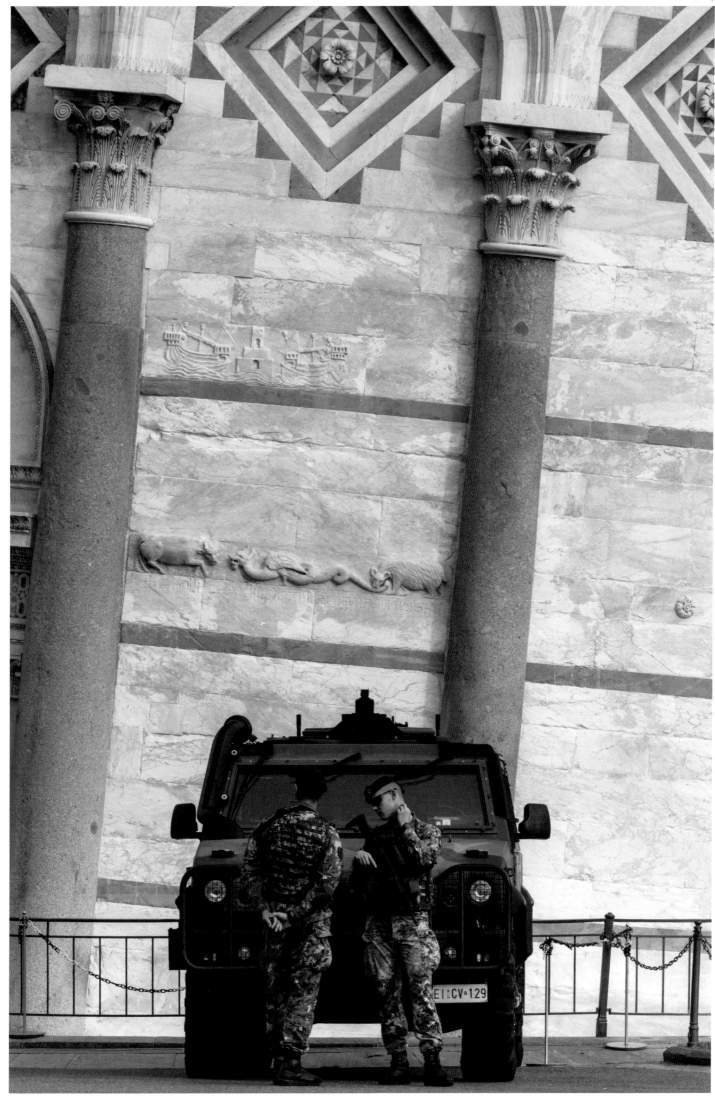

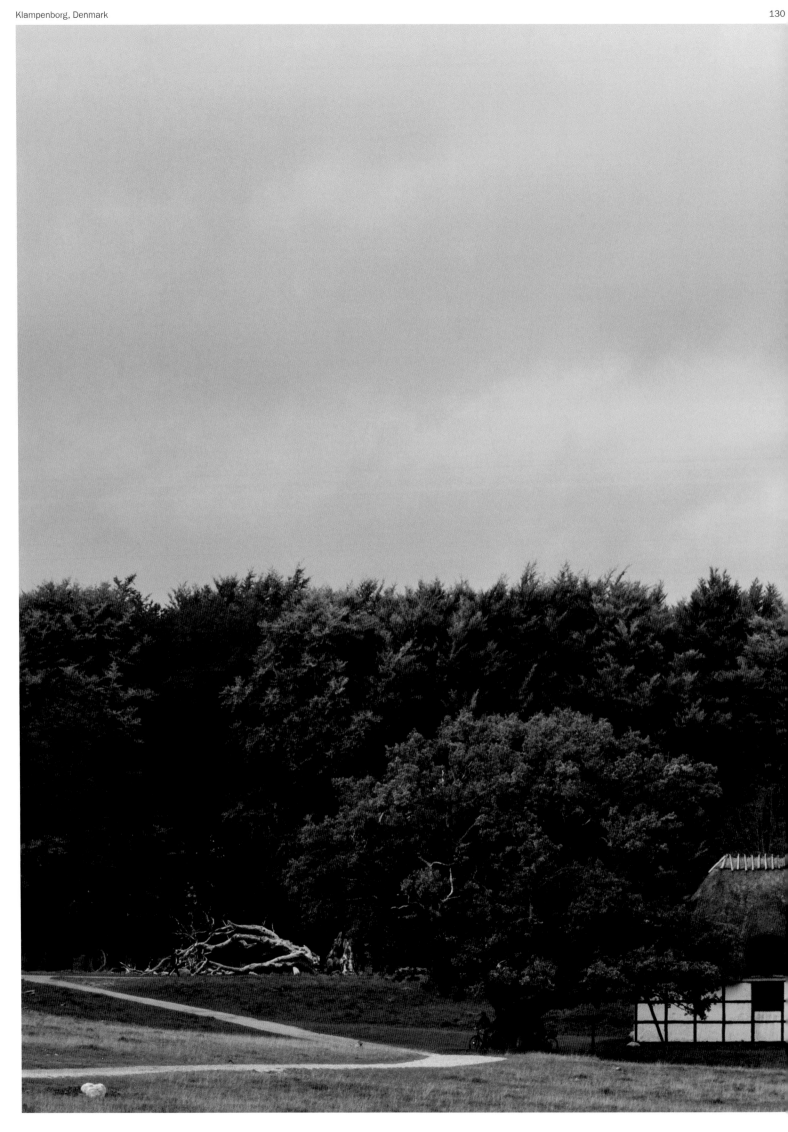

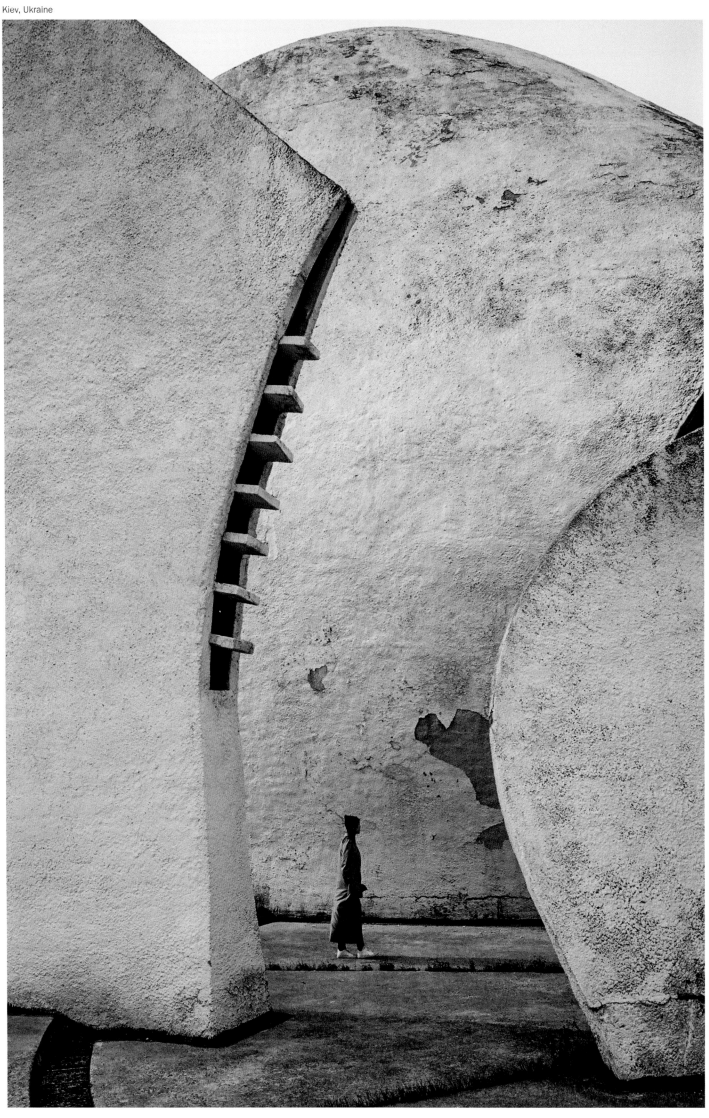

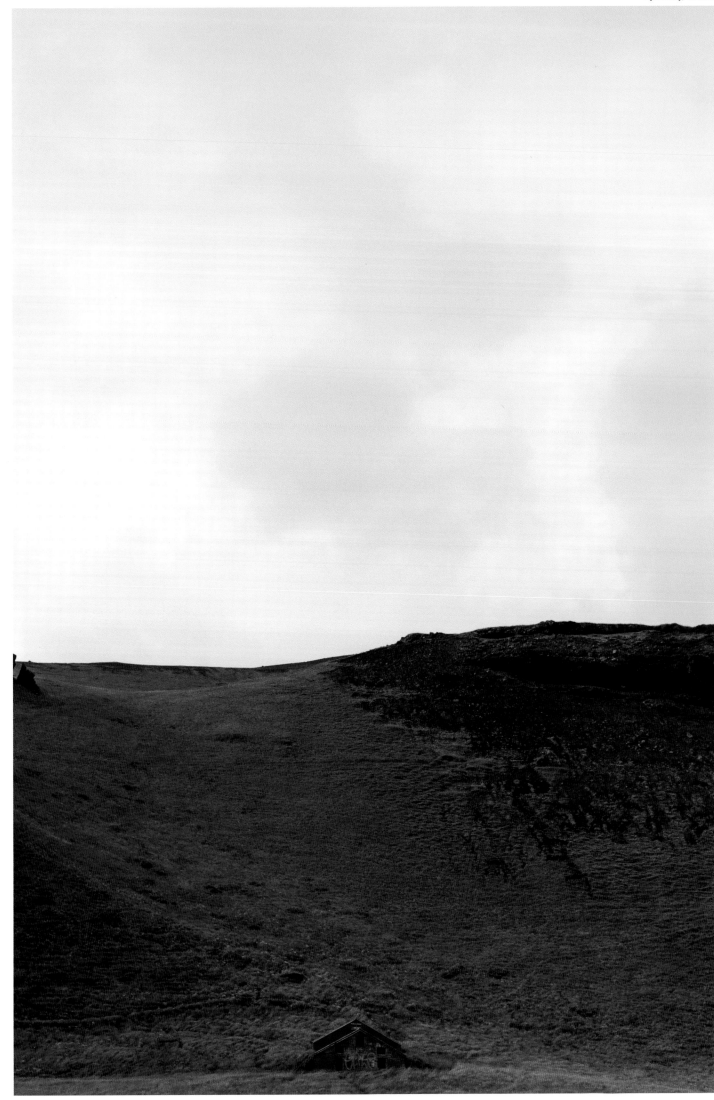

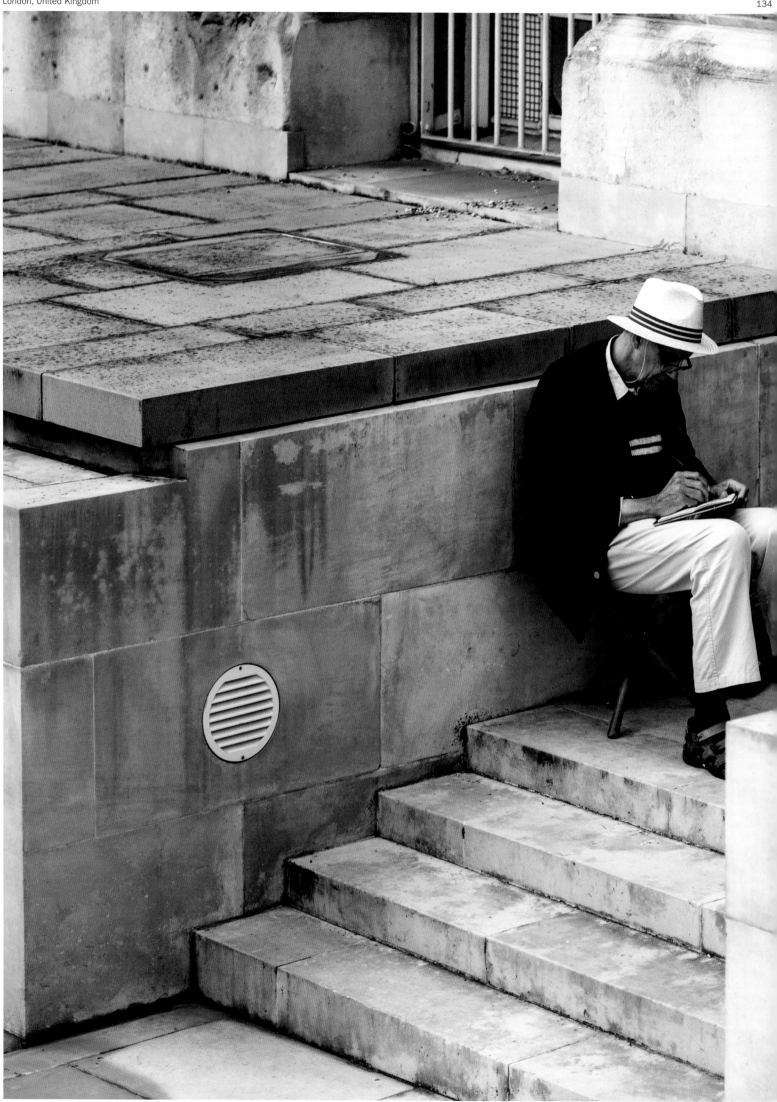

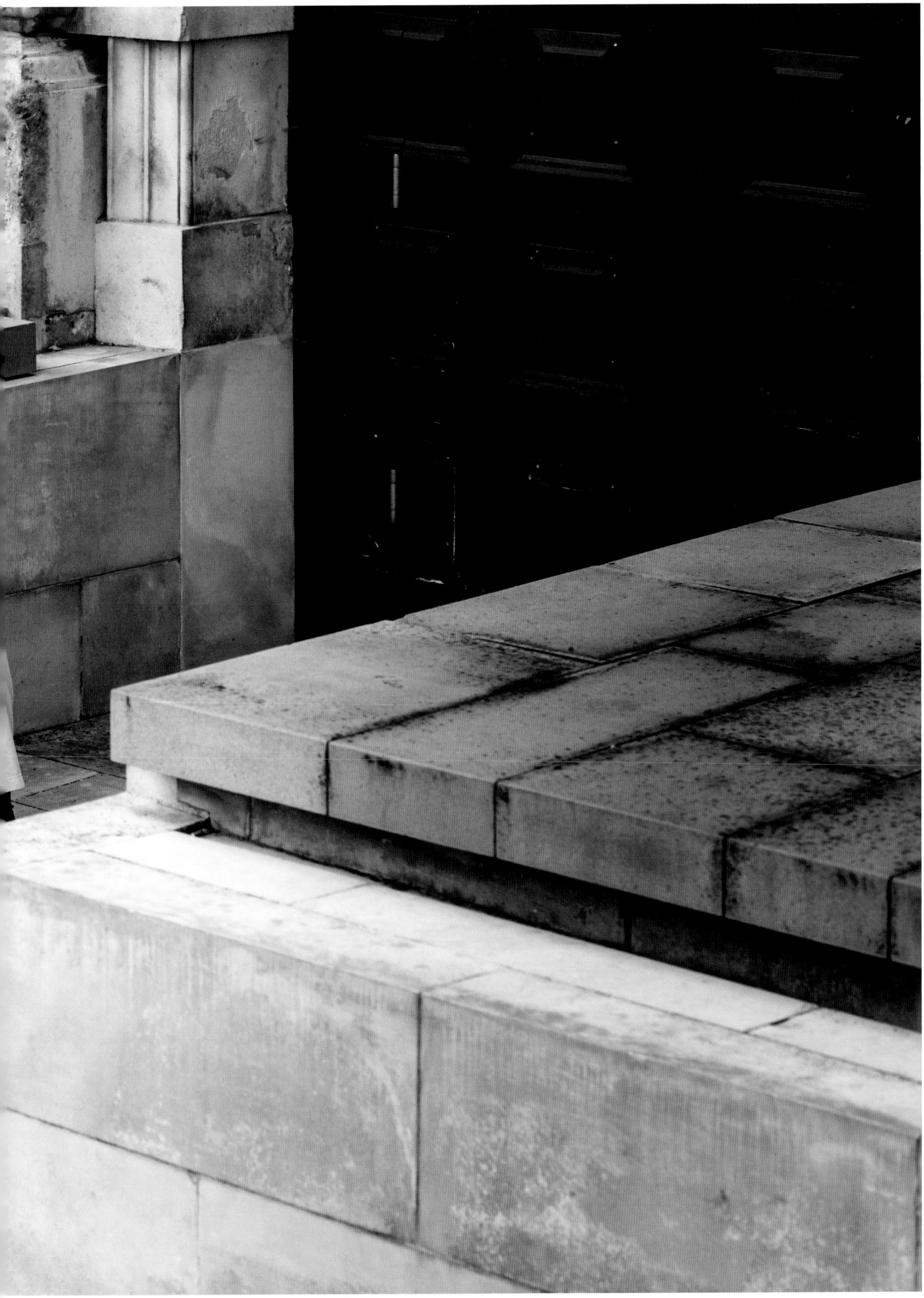

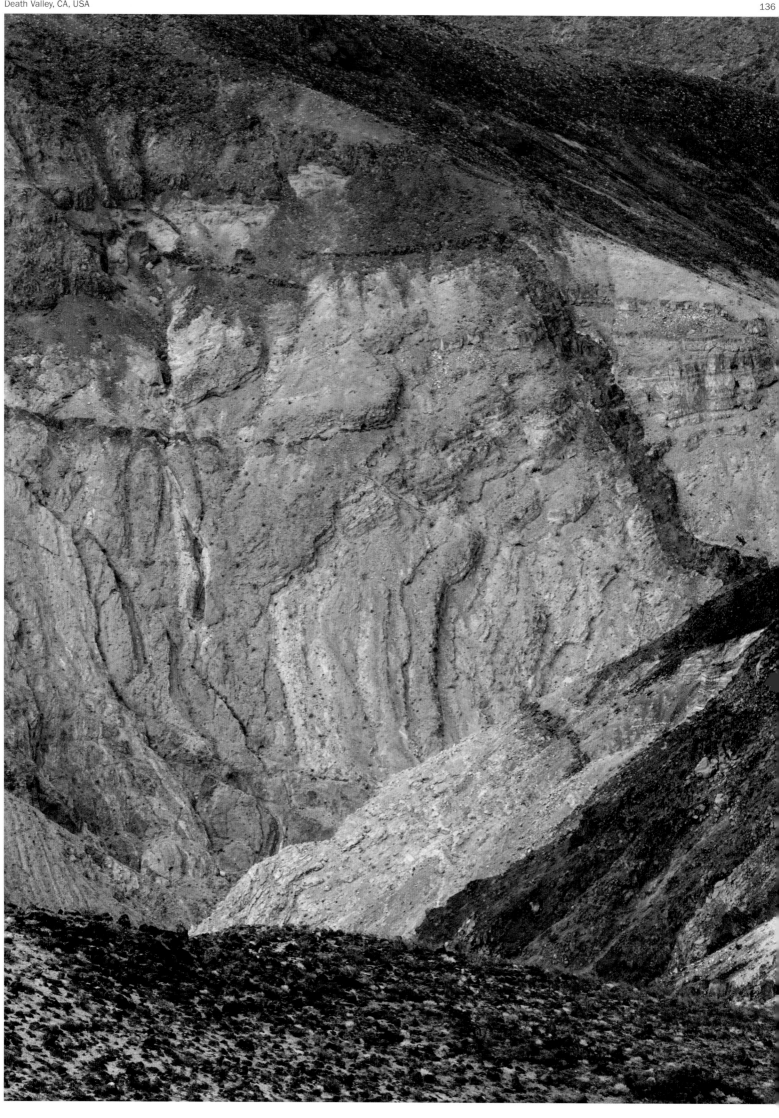

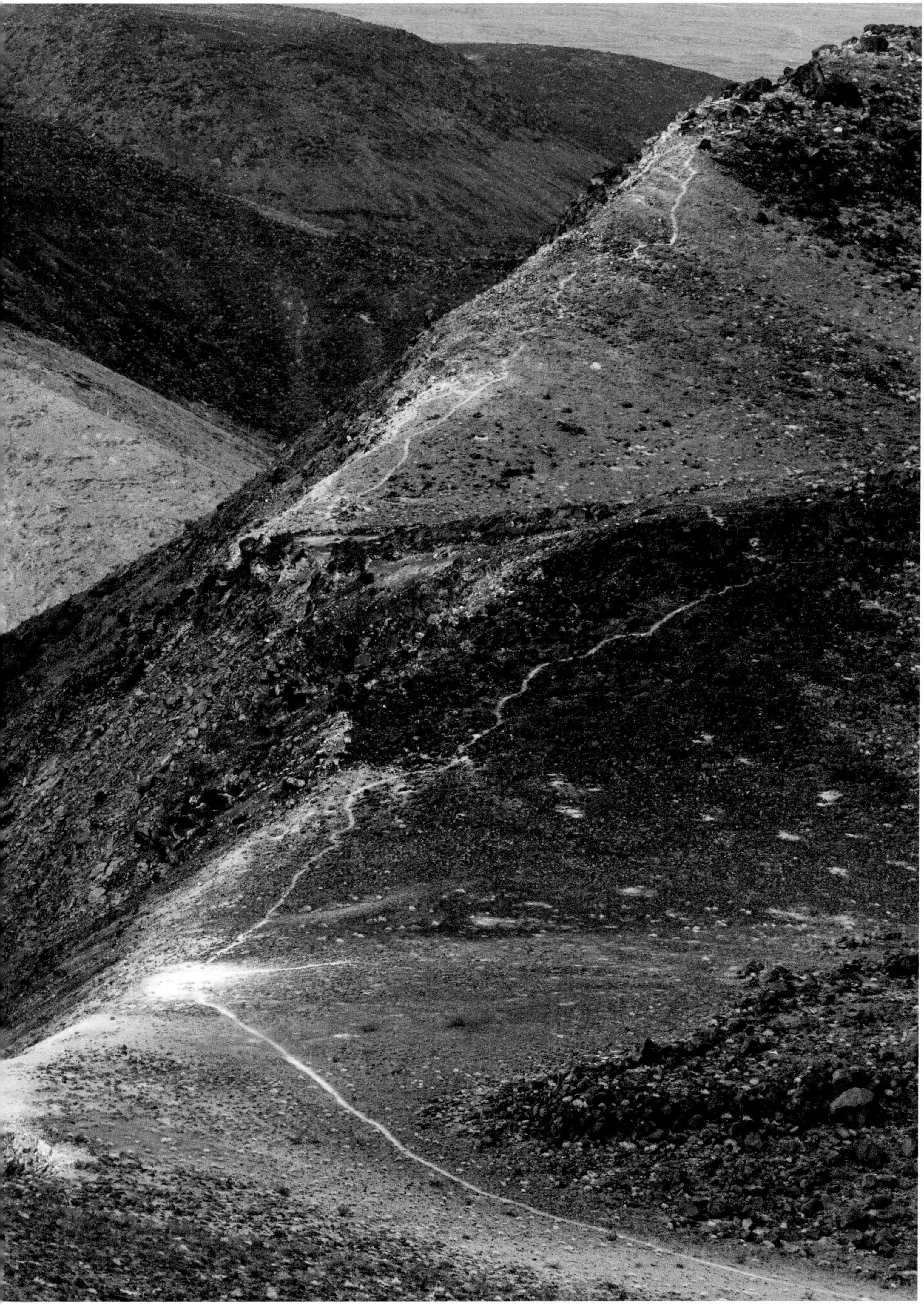

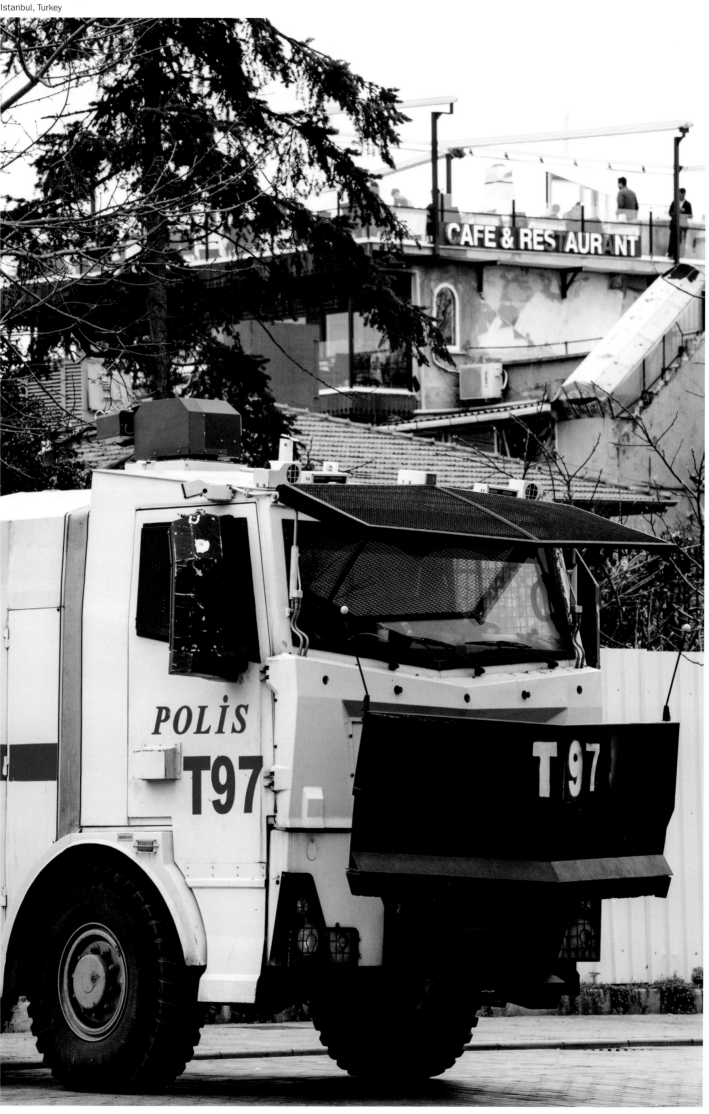

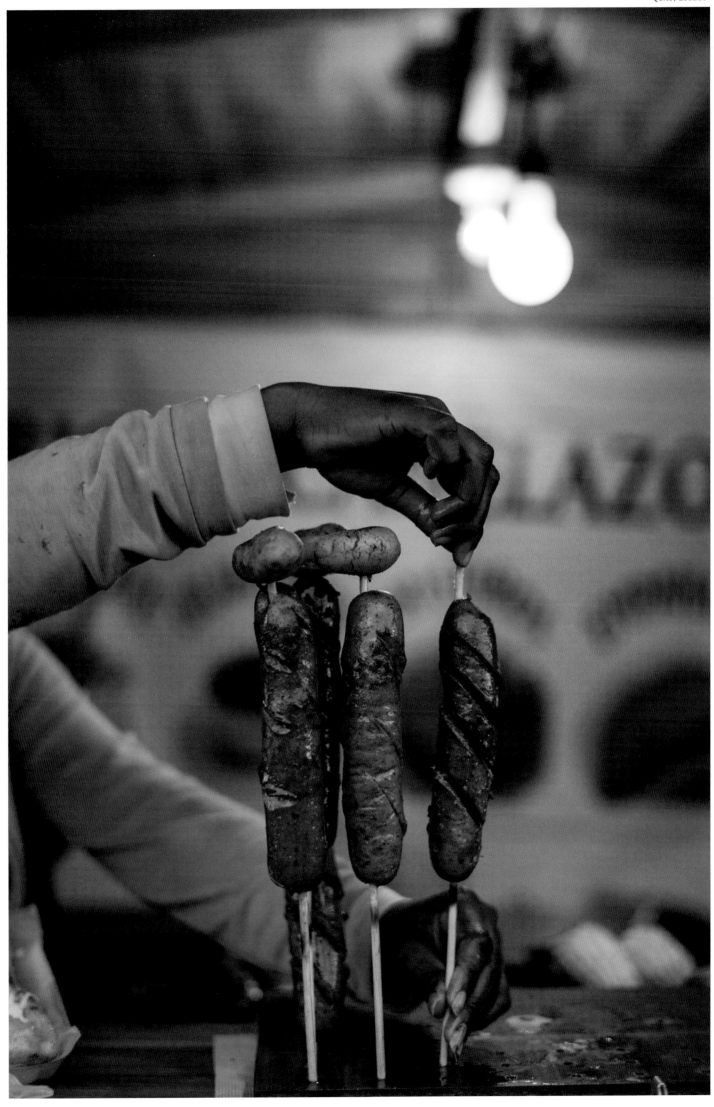

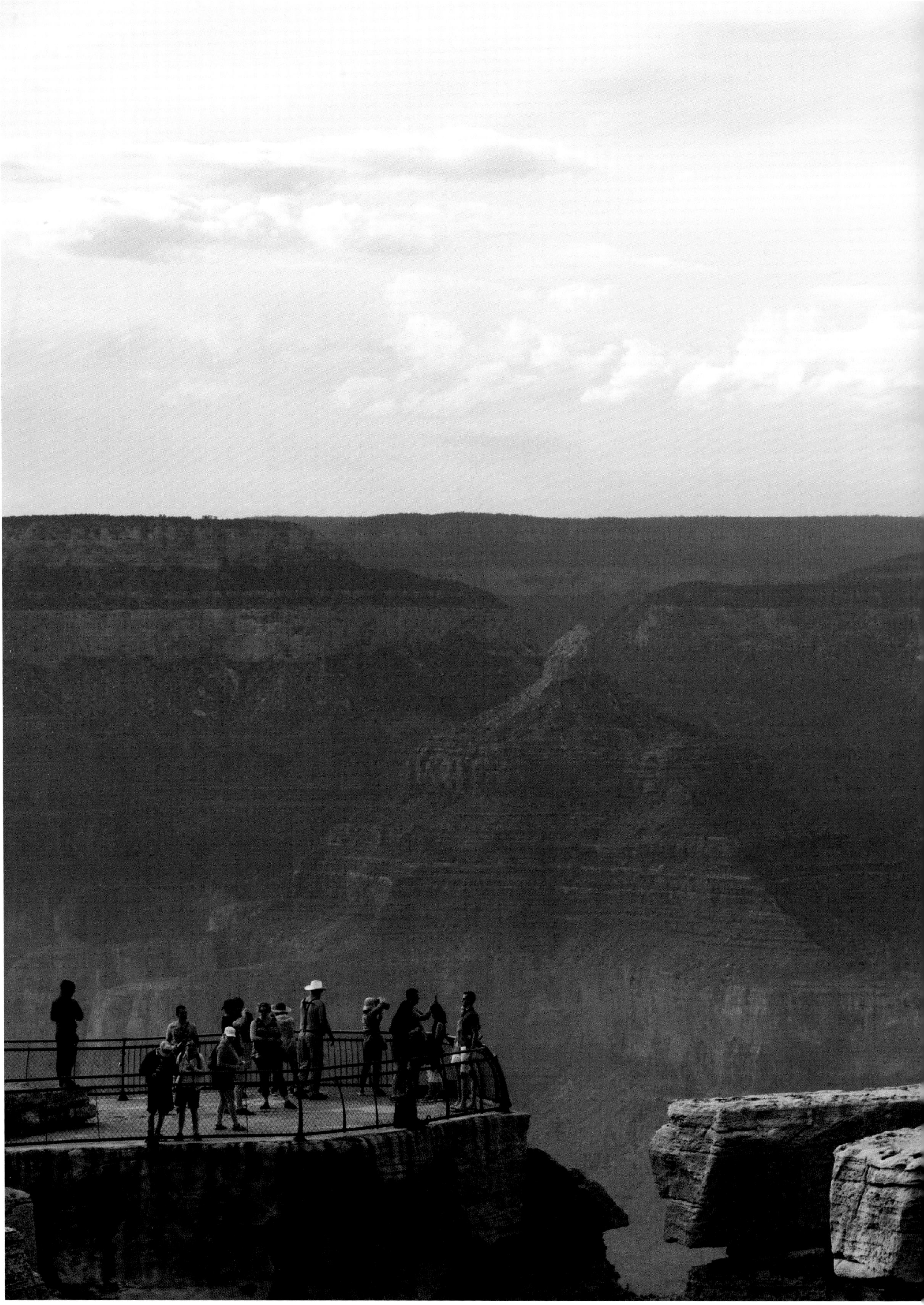

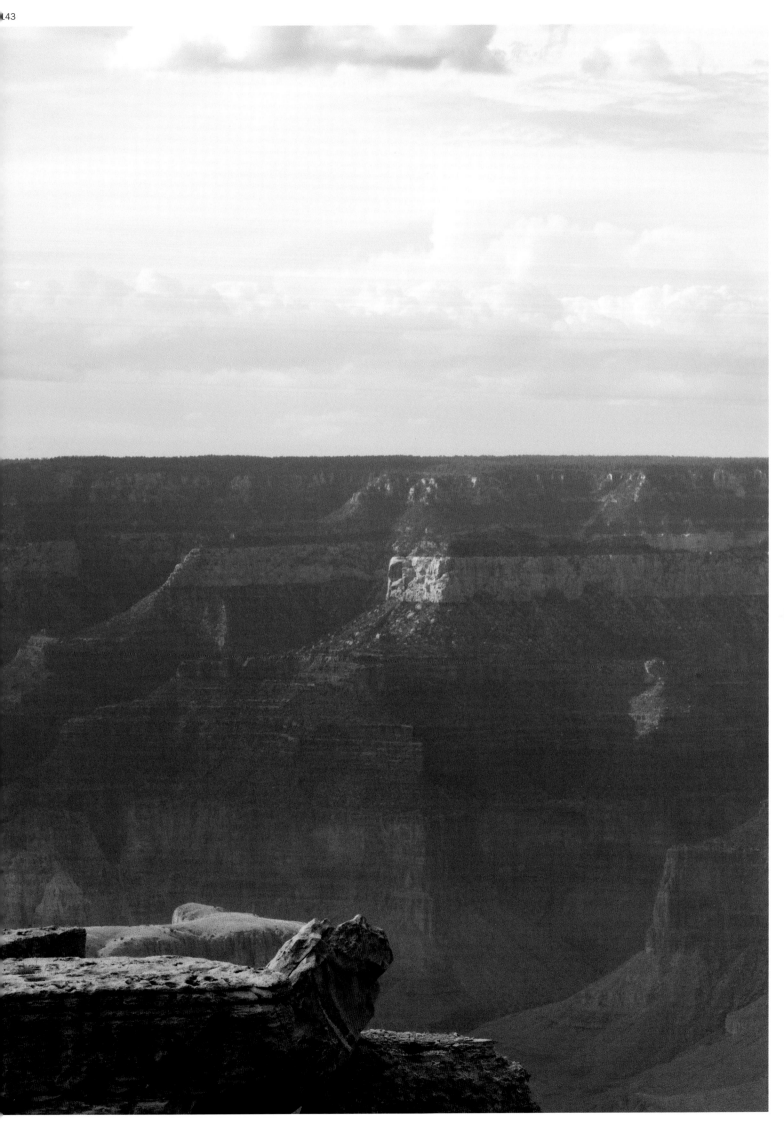

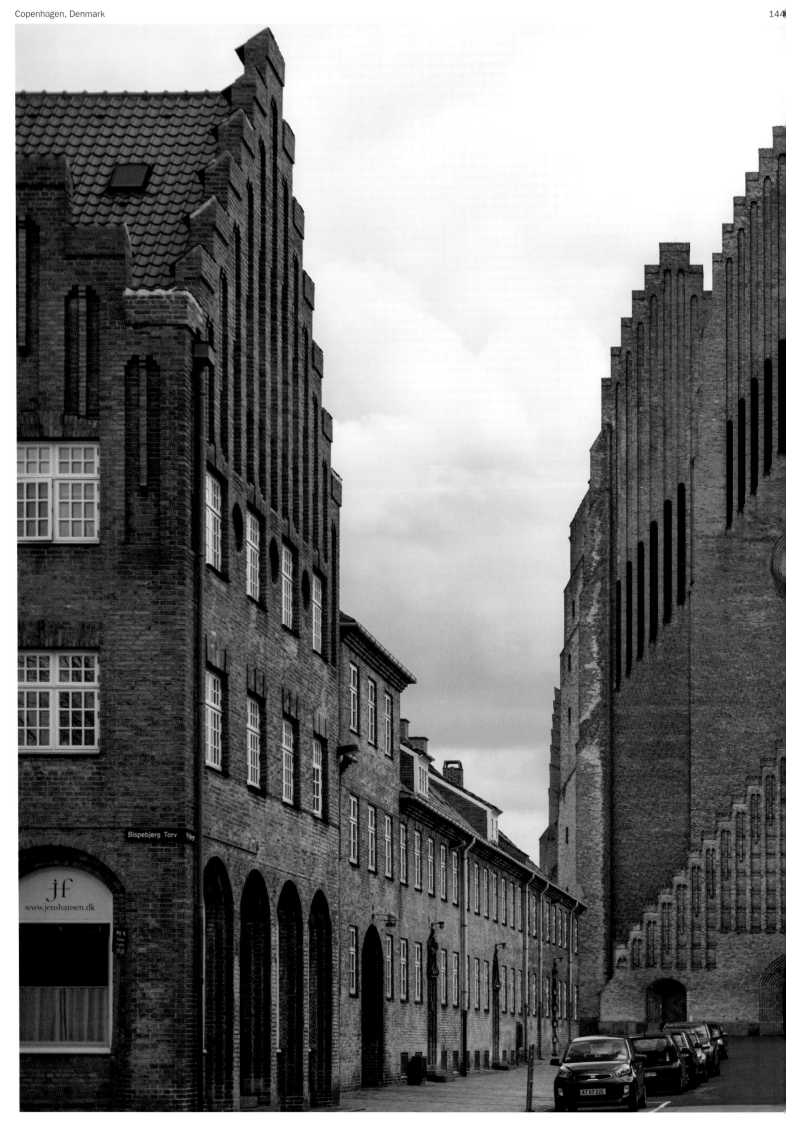

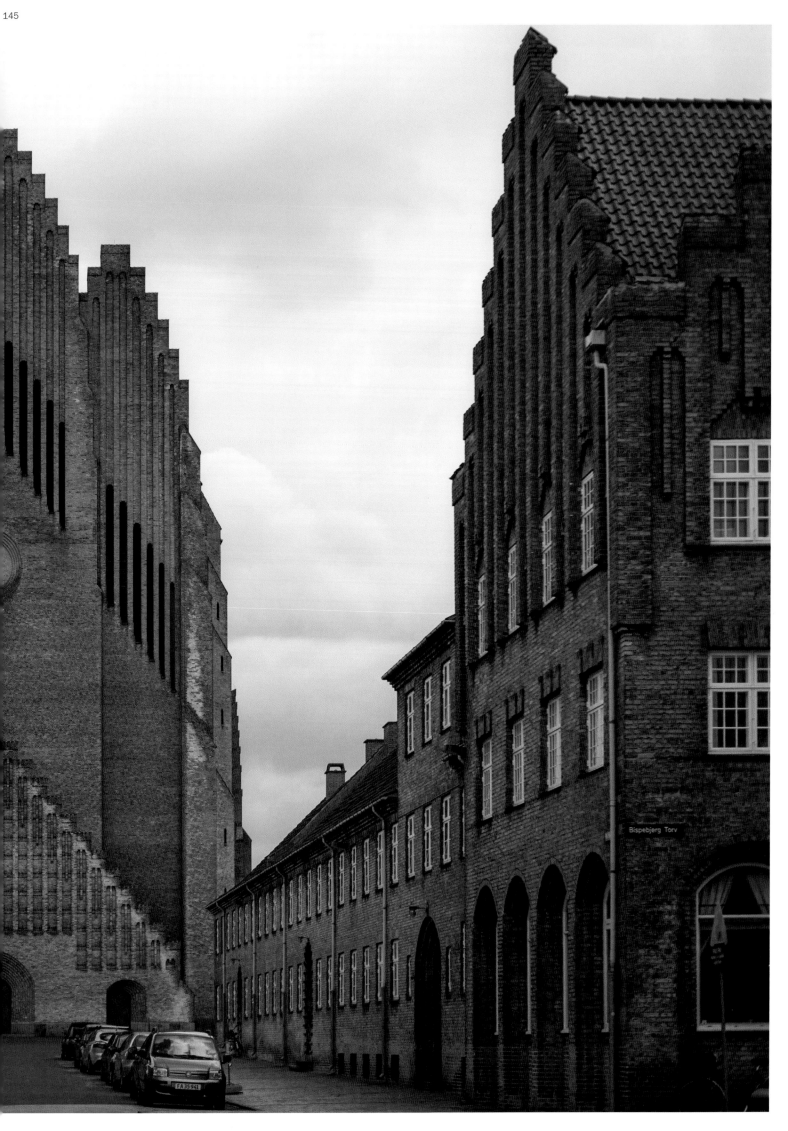

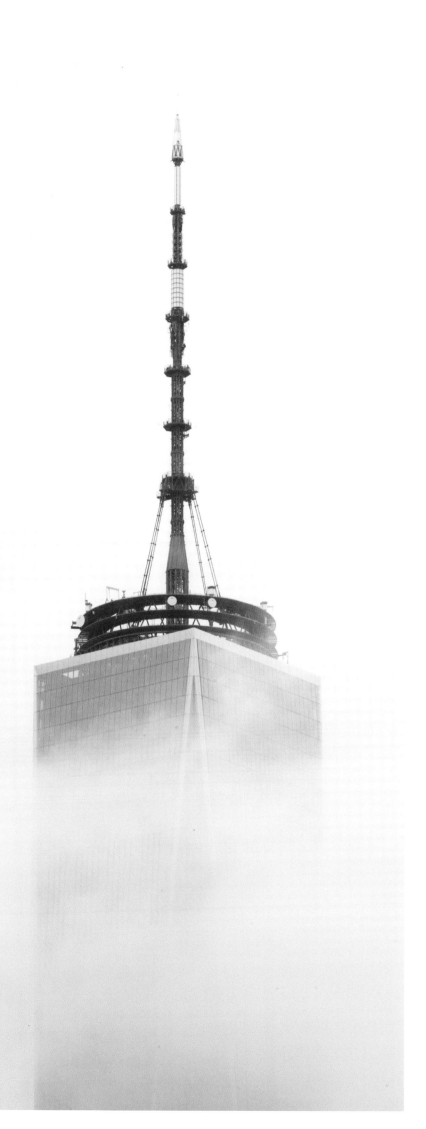

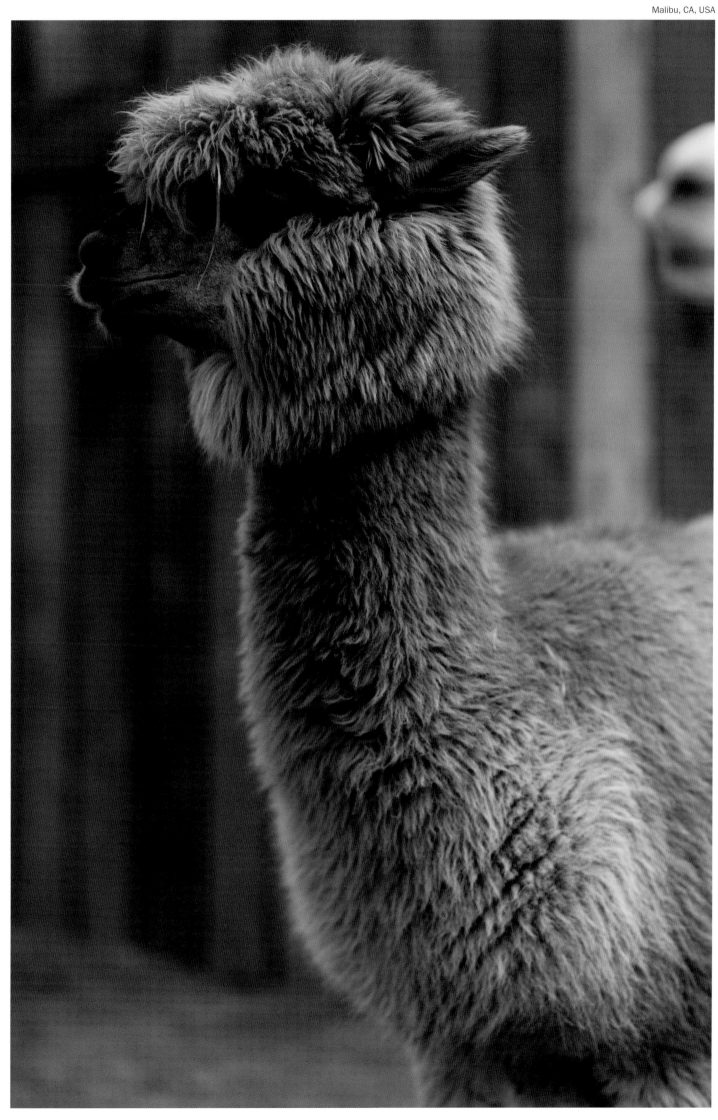

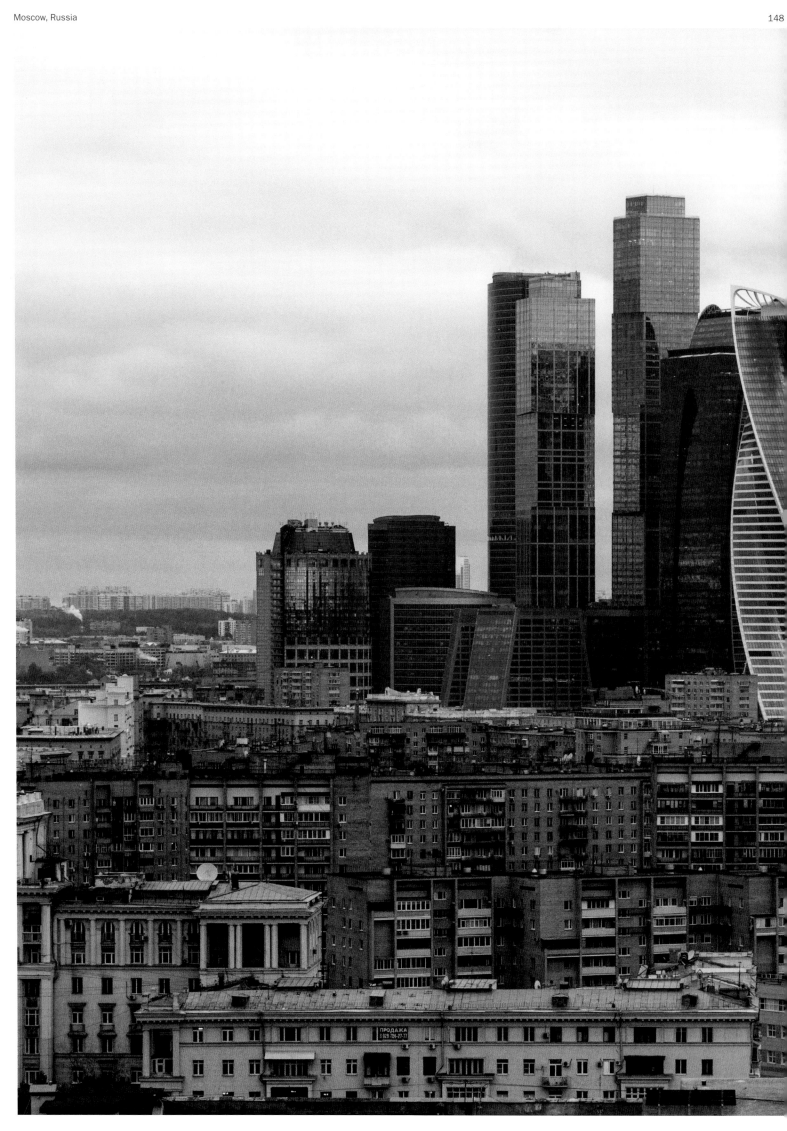

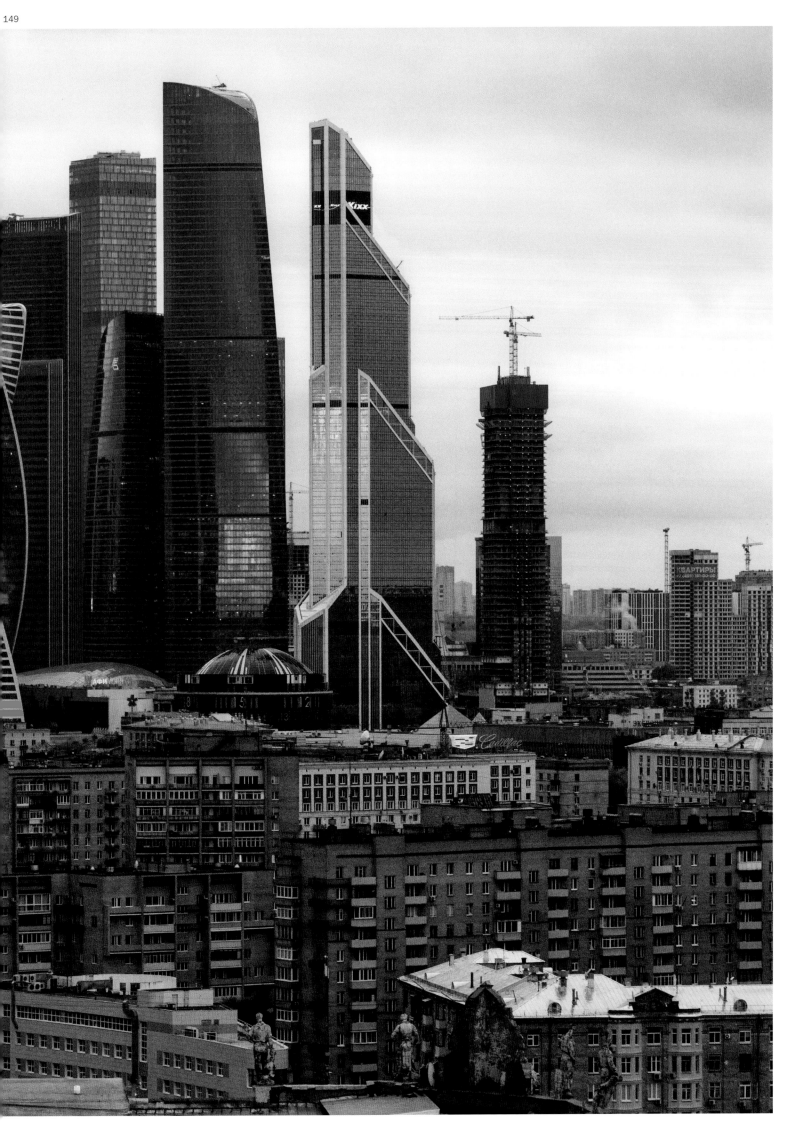

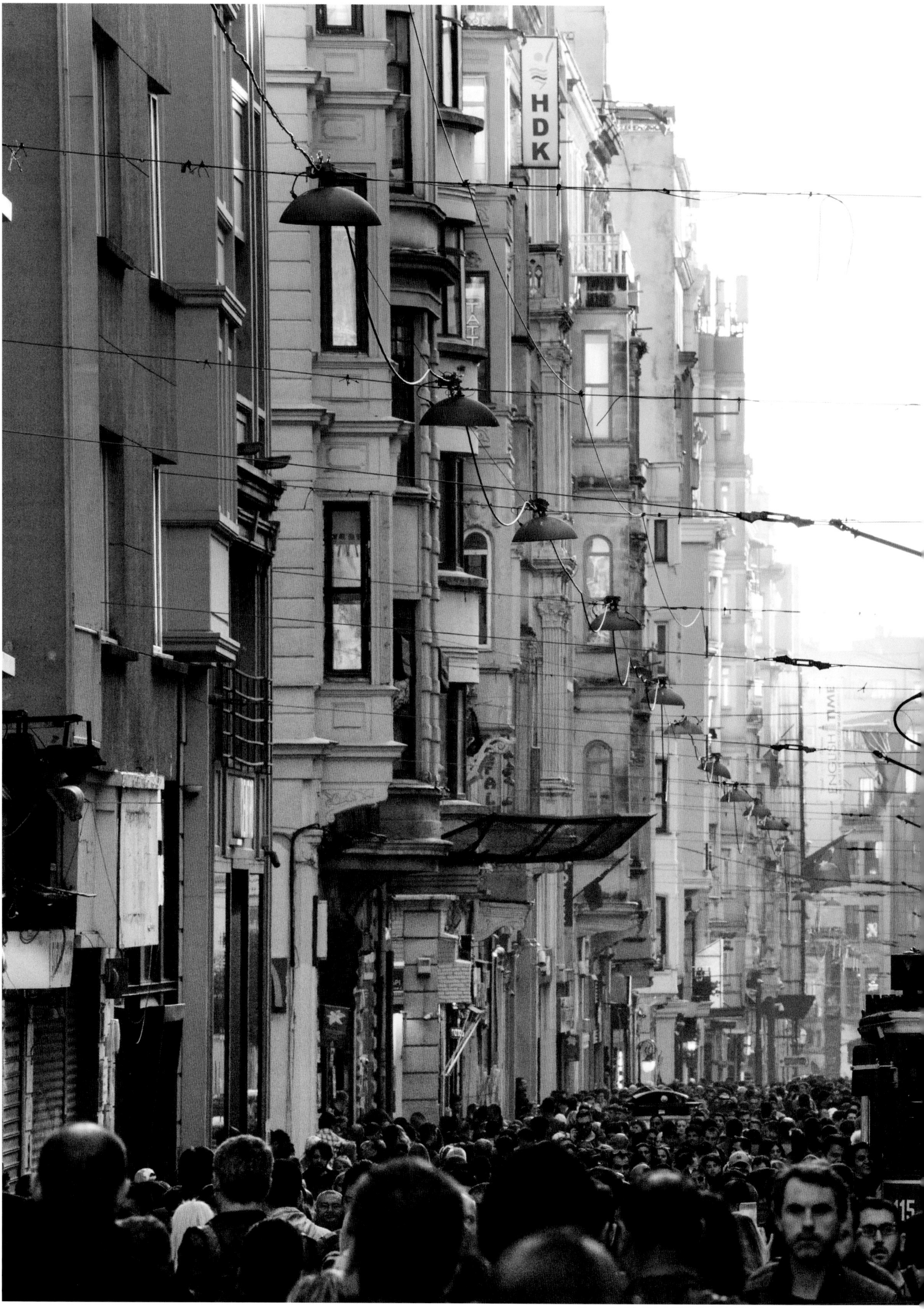
HDK

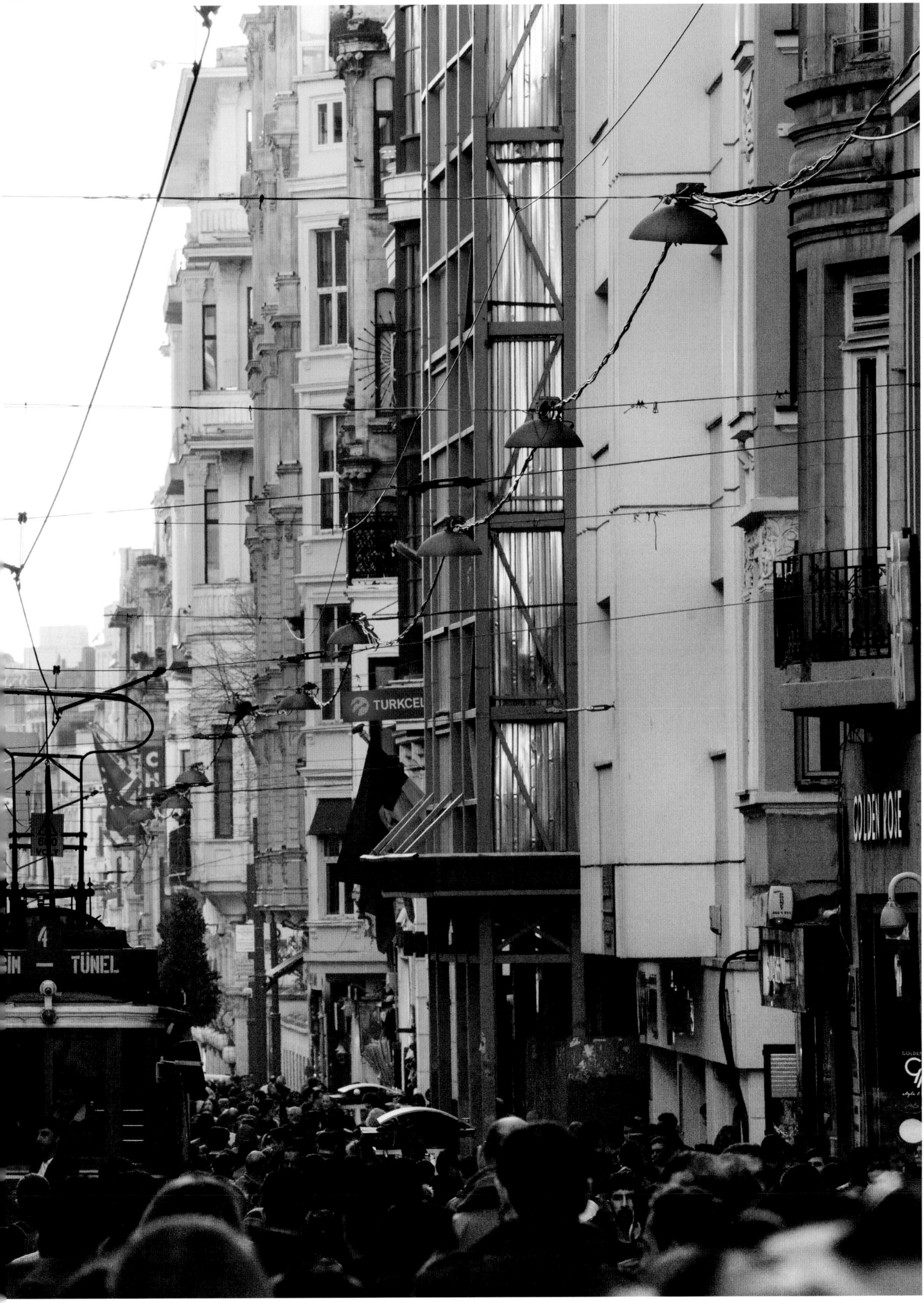
TURKCEL
İM — TÜNEL
GOLDEN ROSE

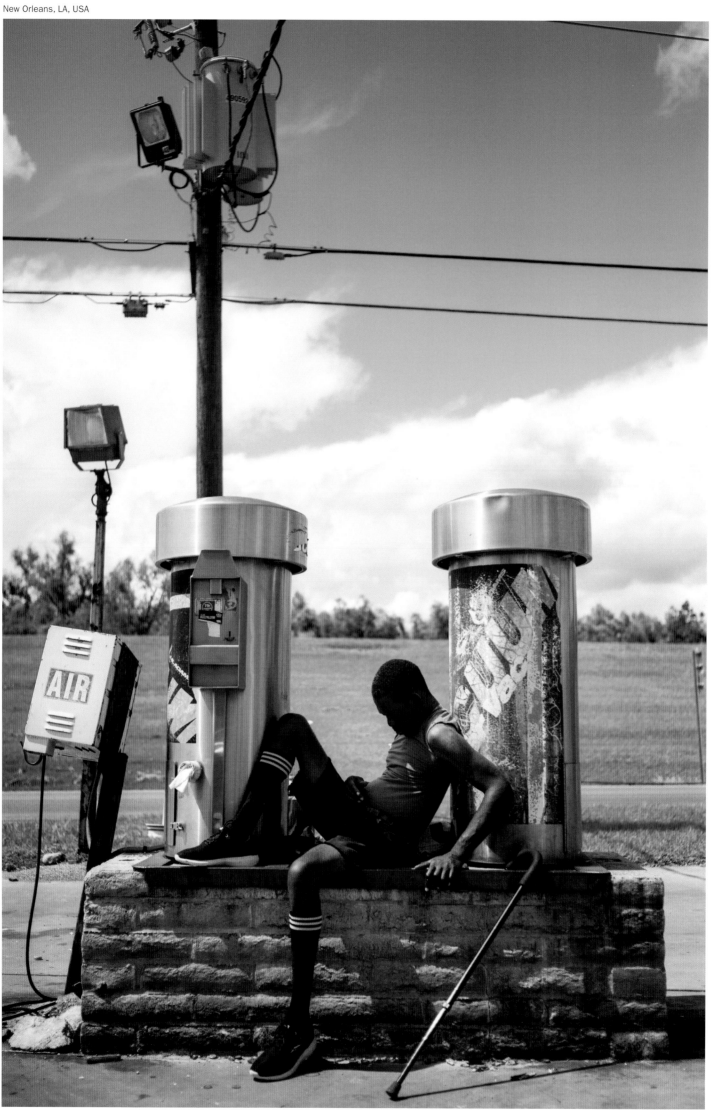

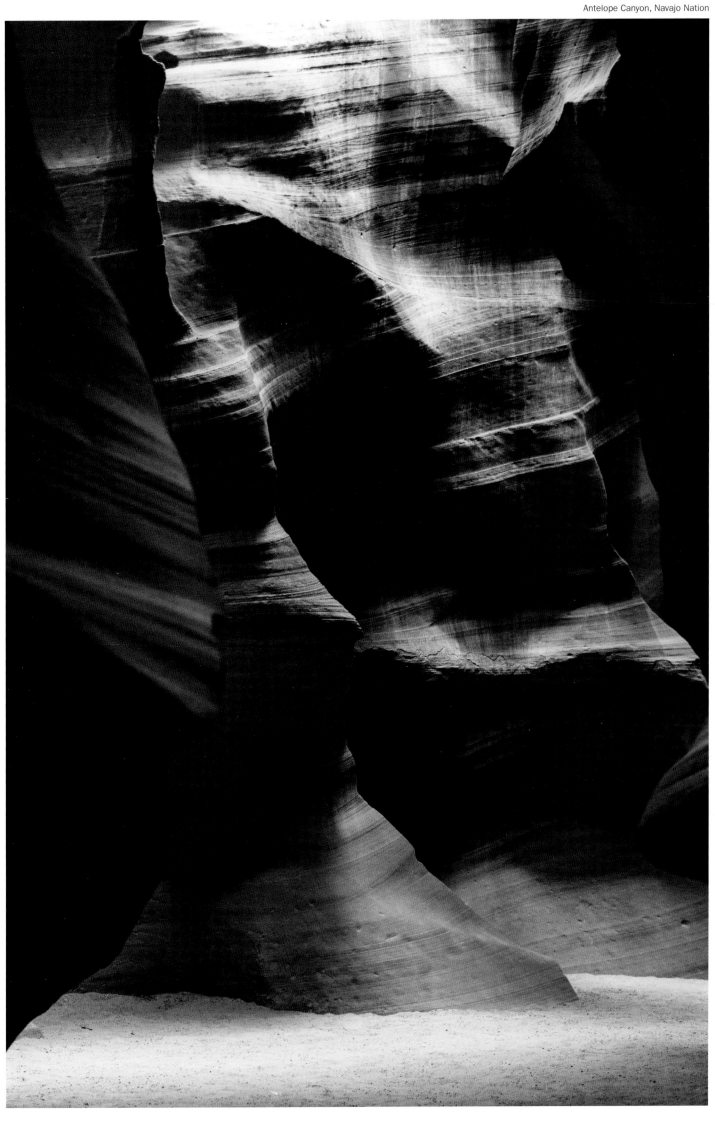

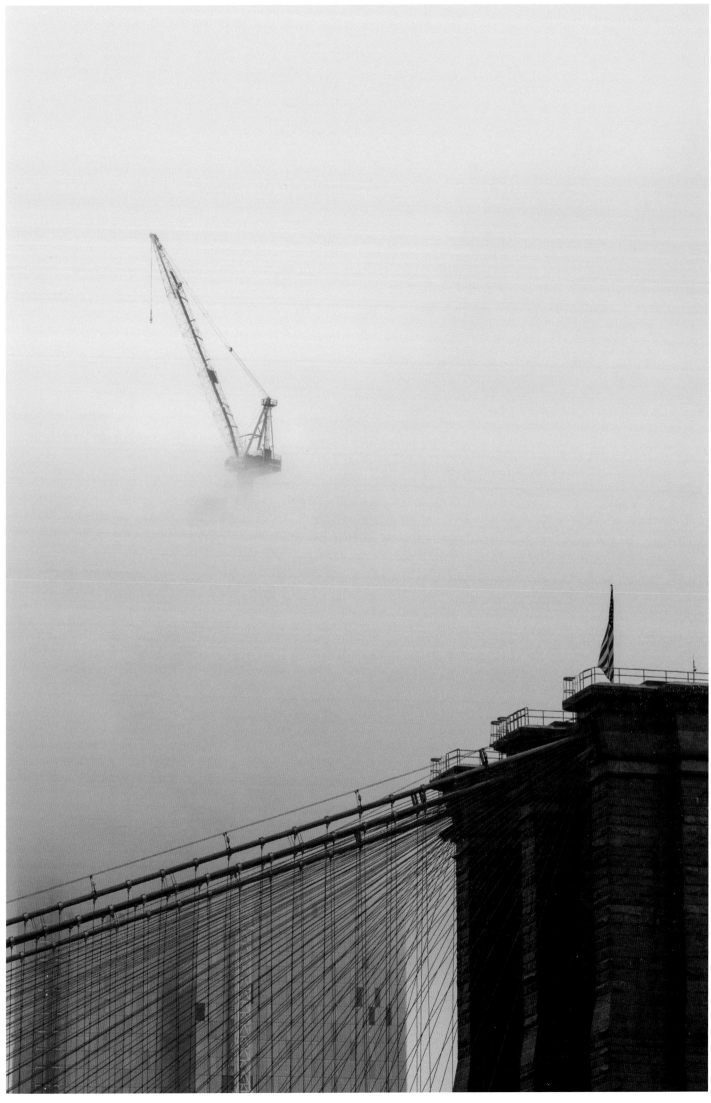

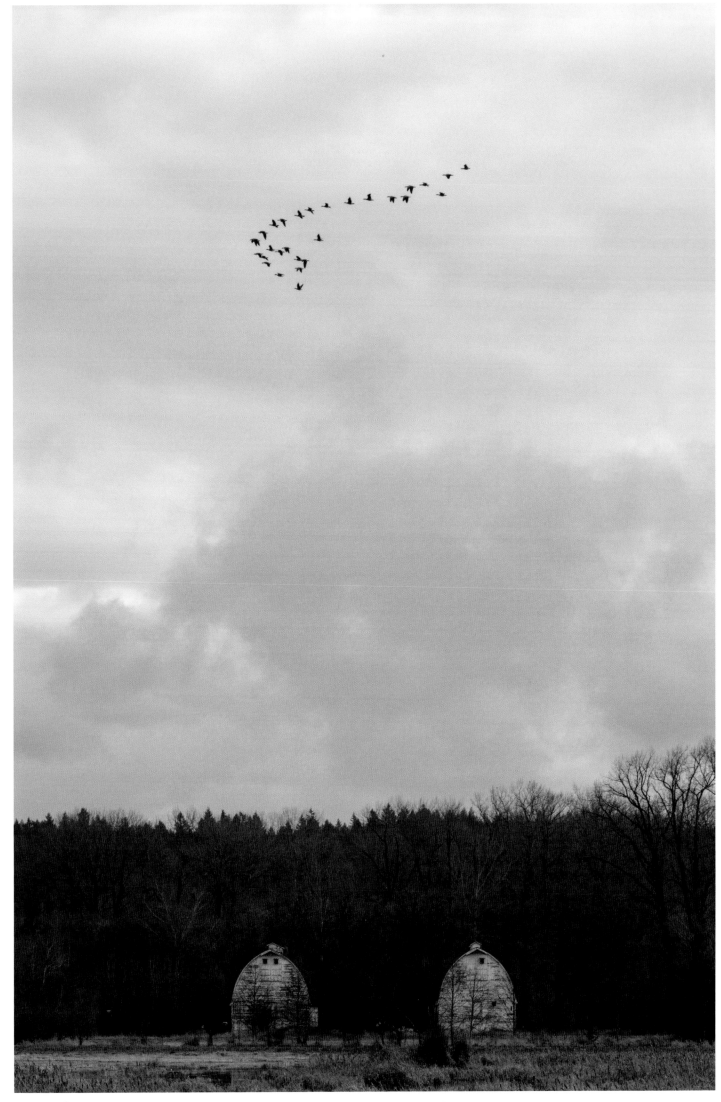

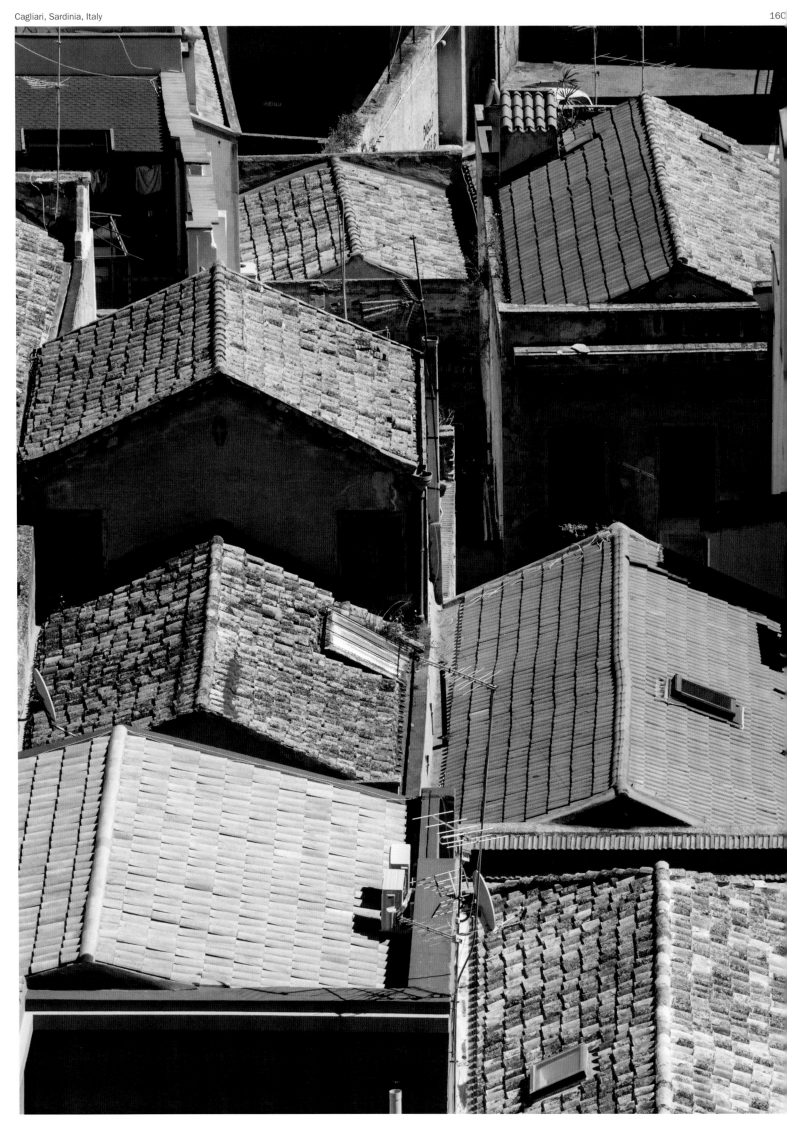

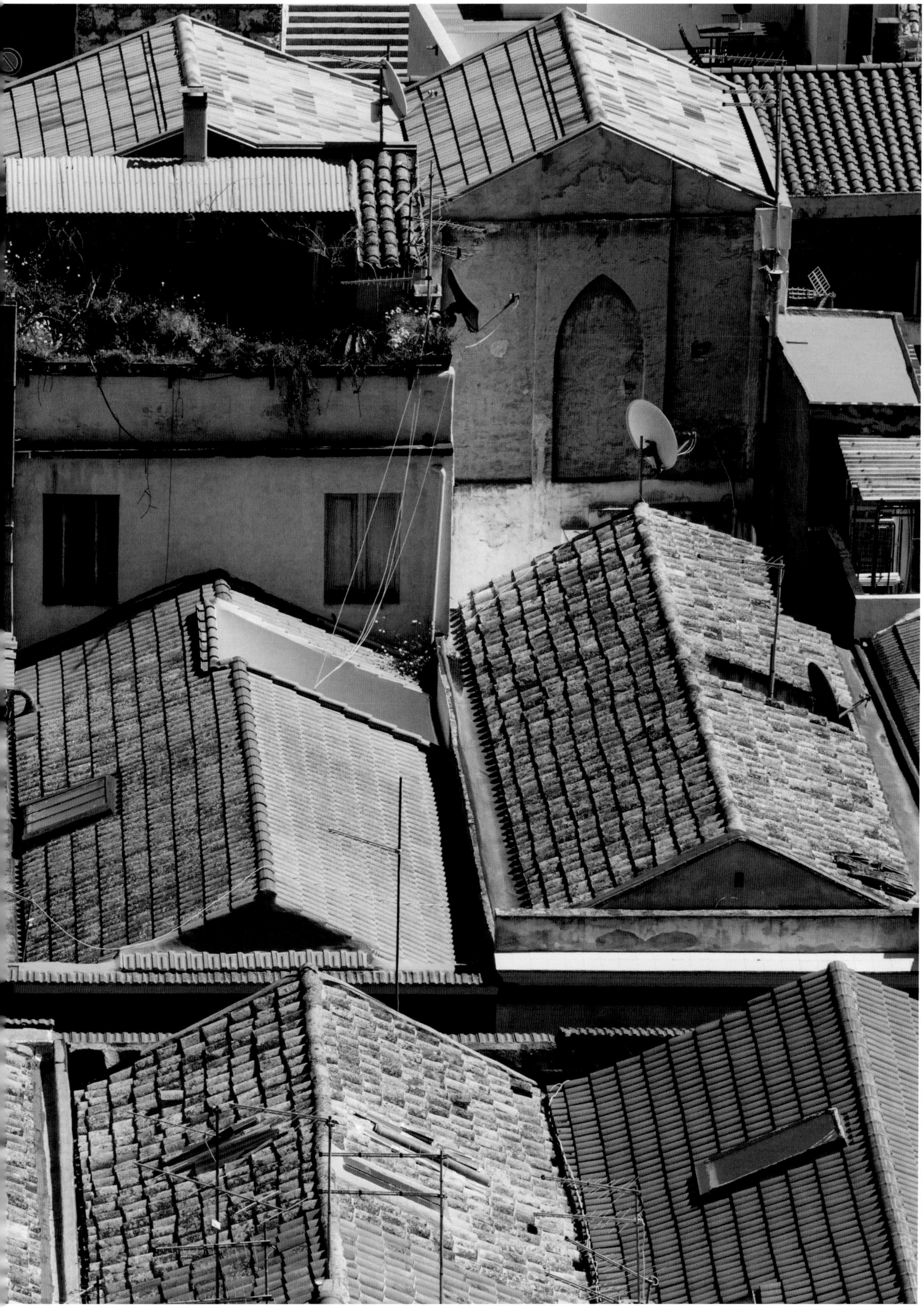

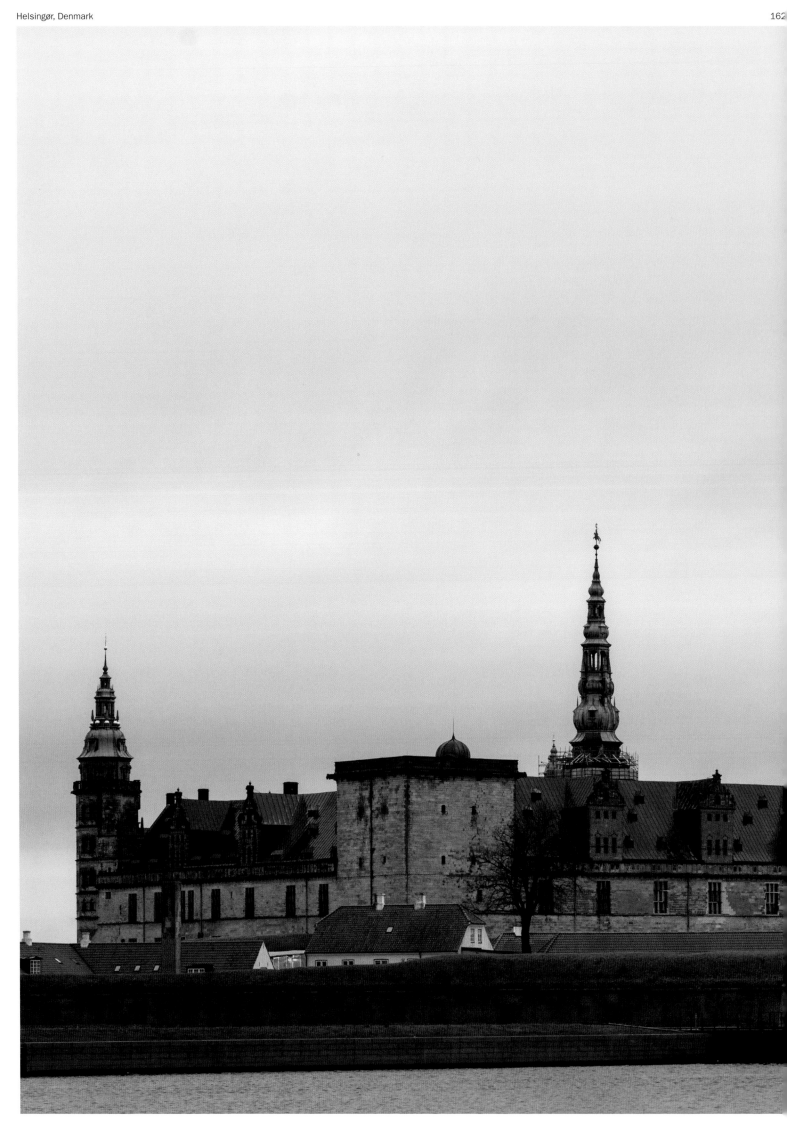

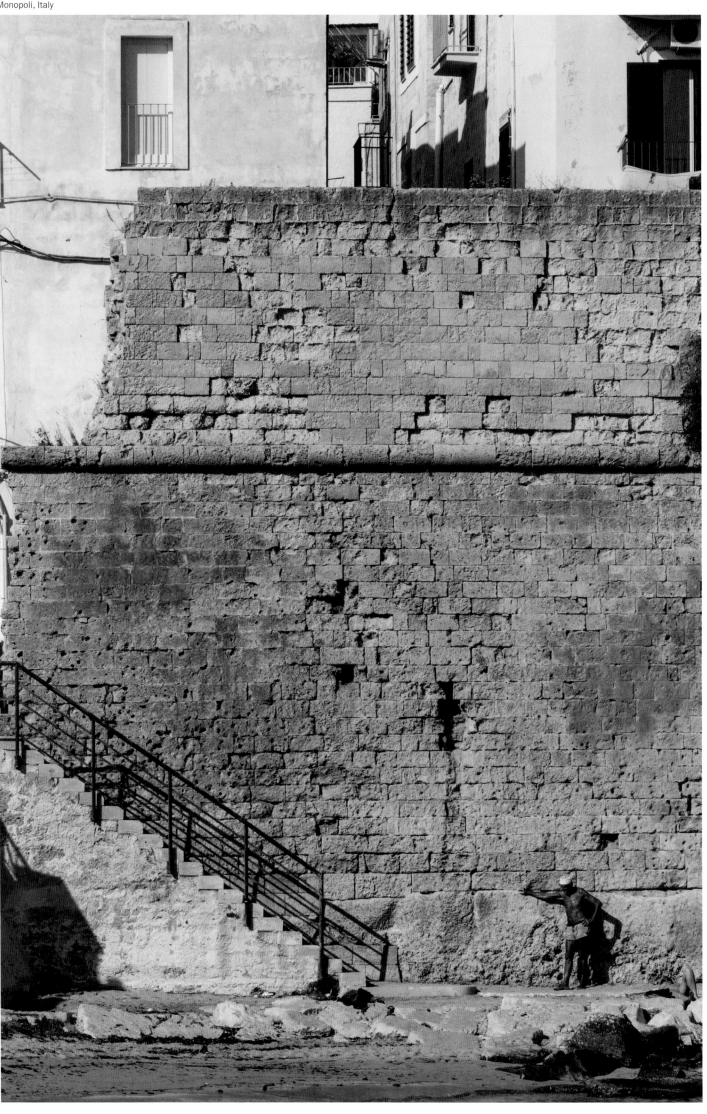

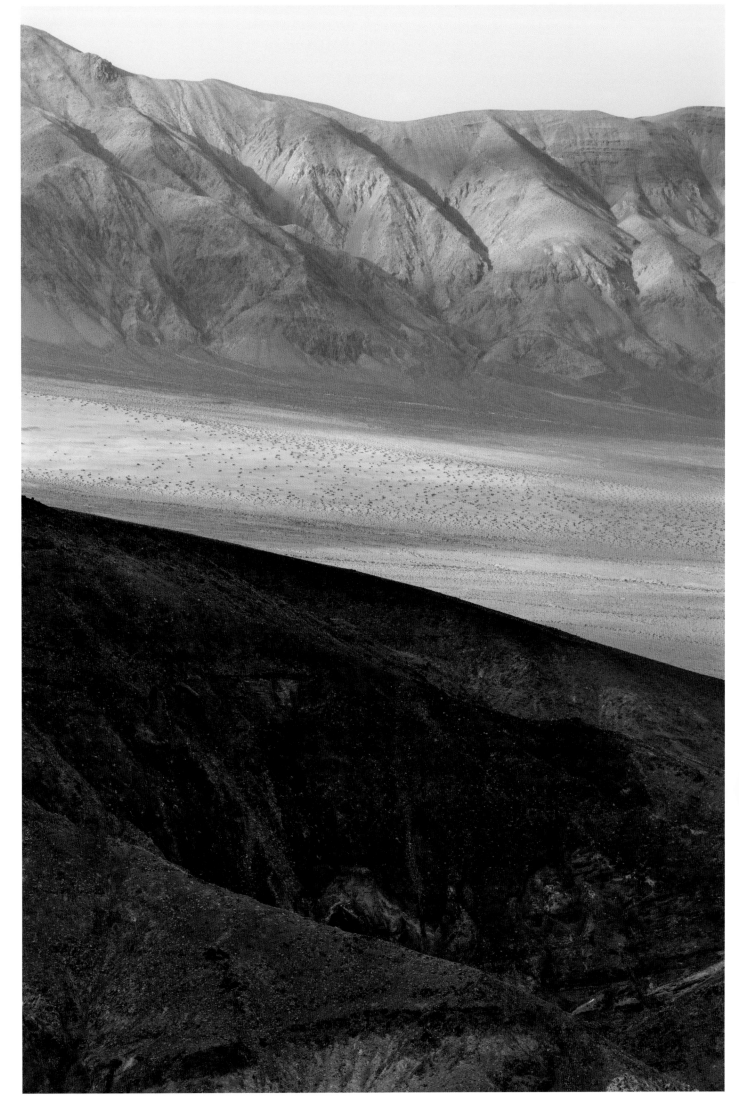

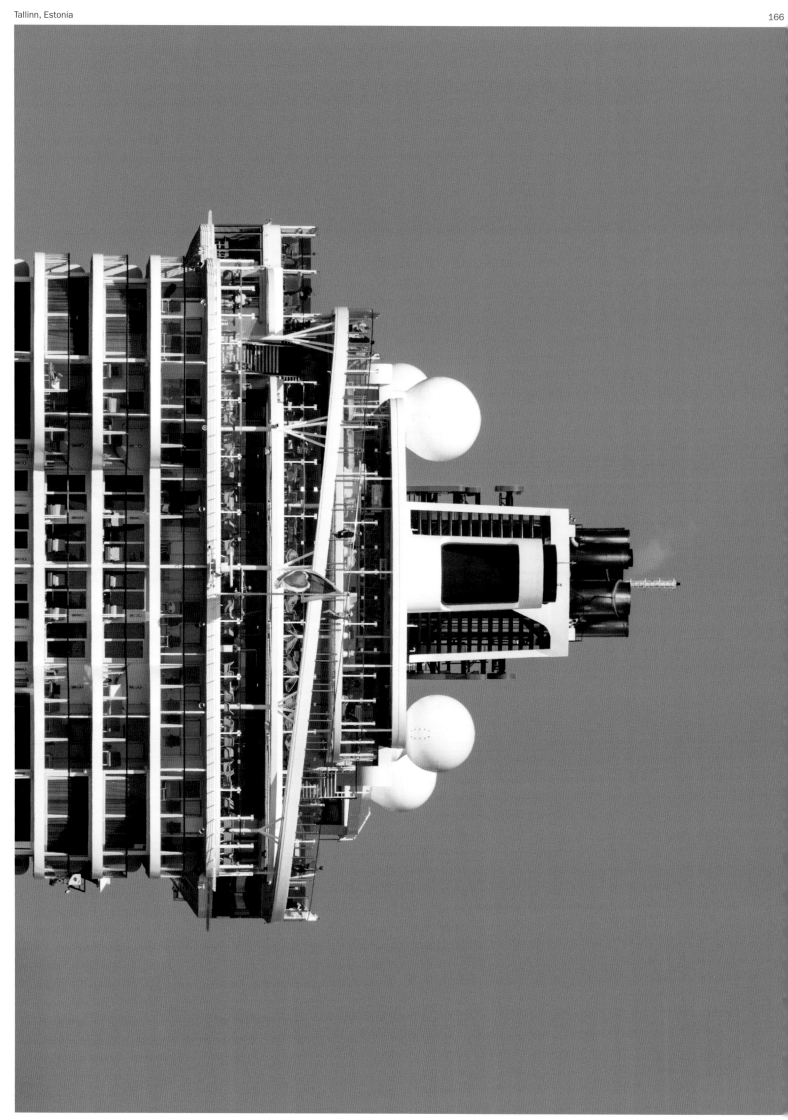

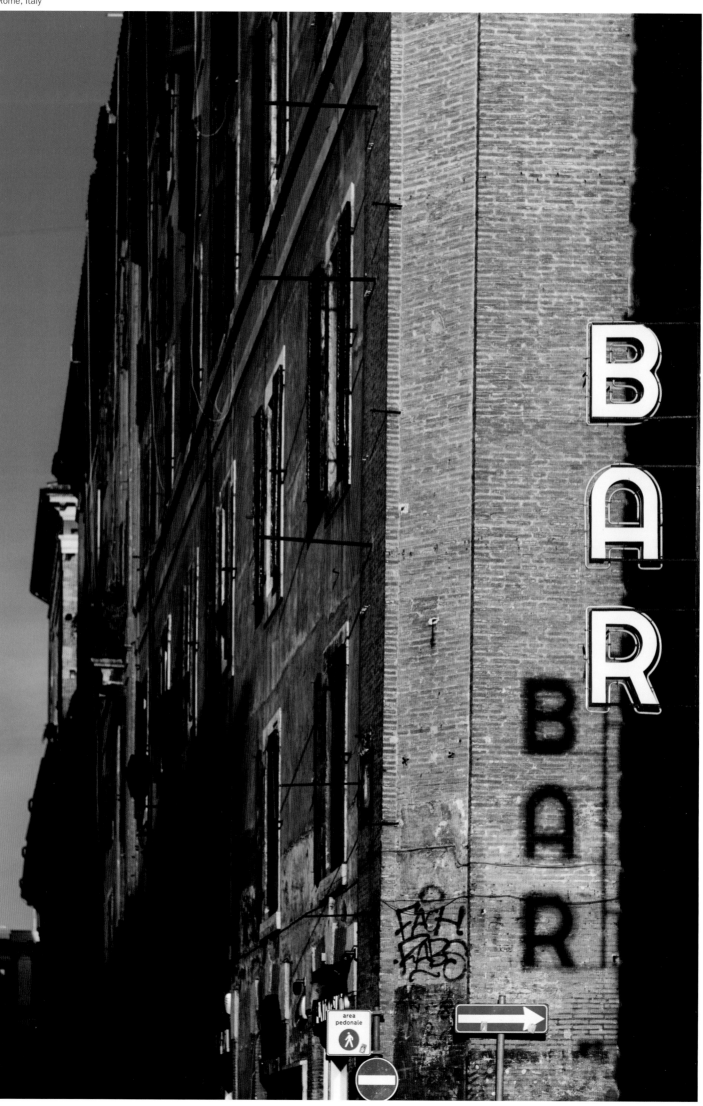

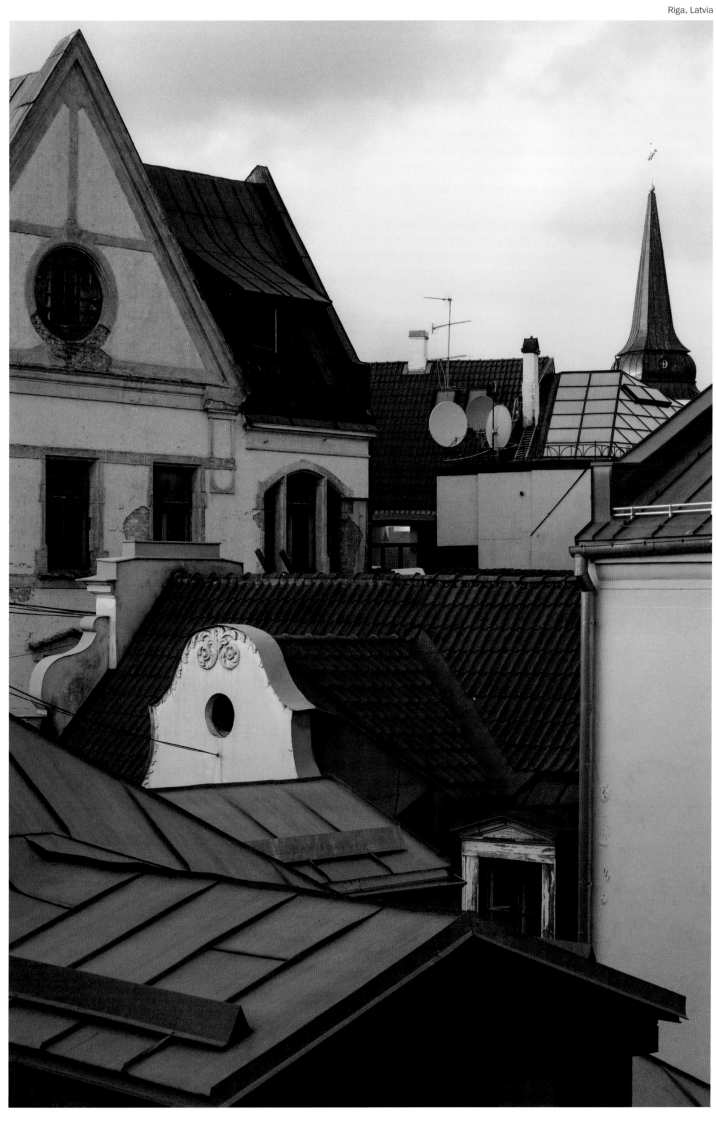

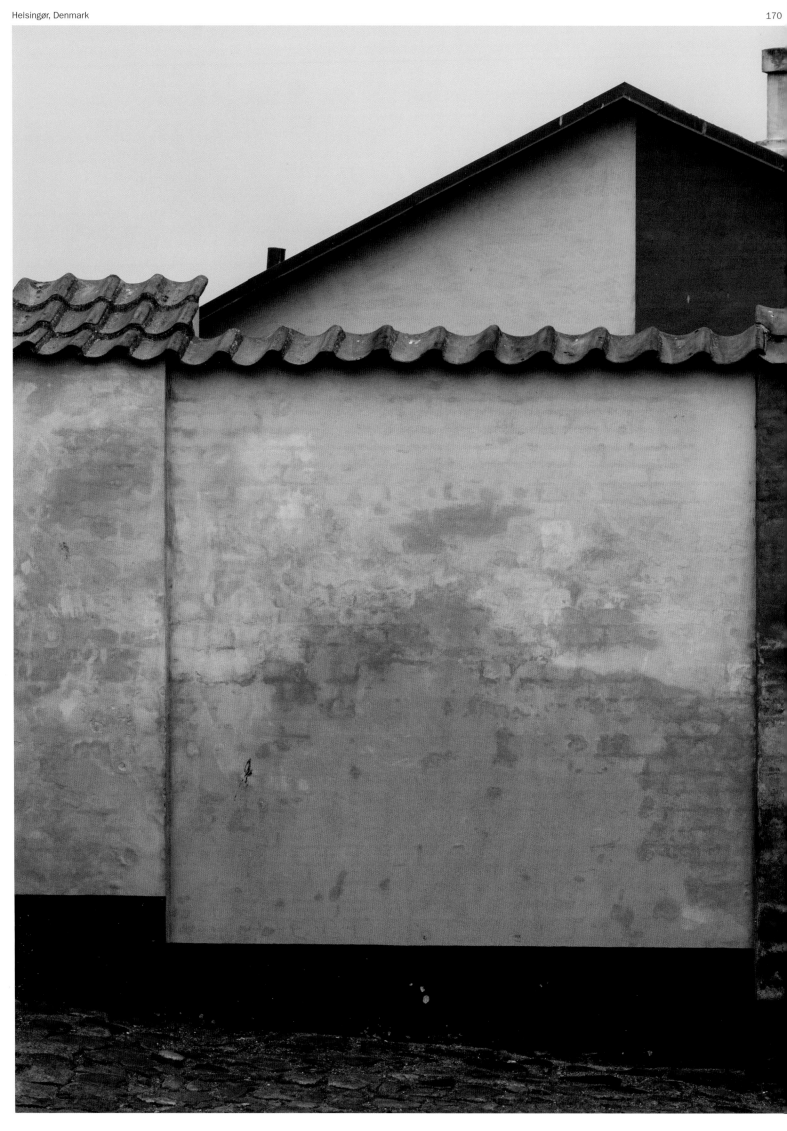

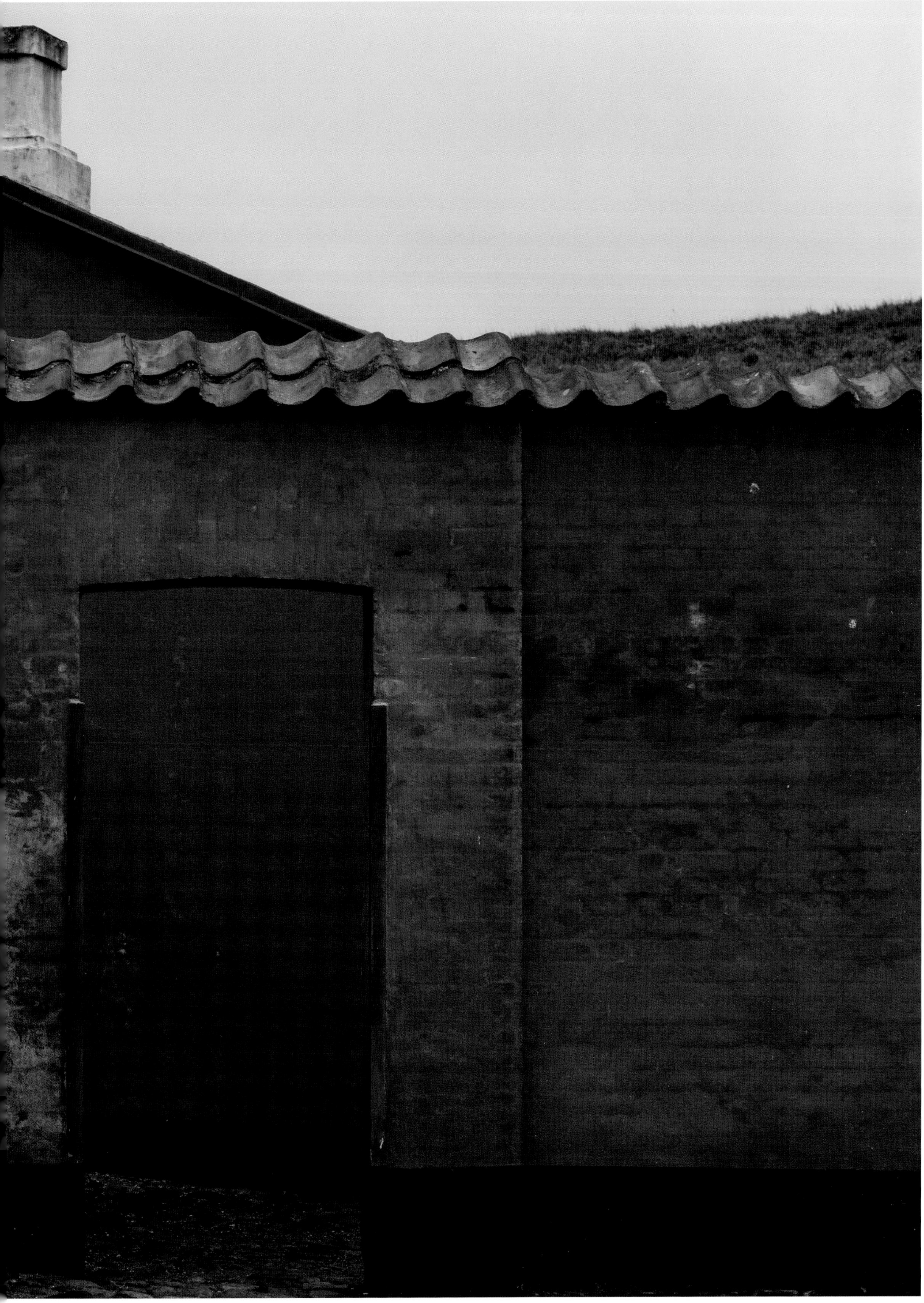

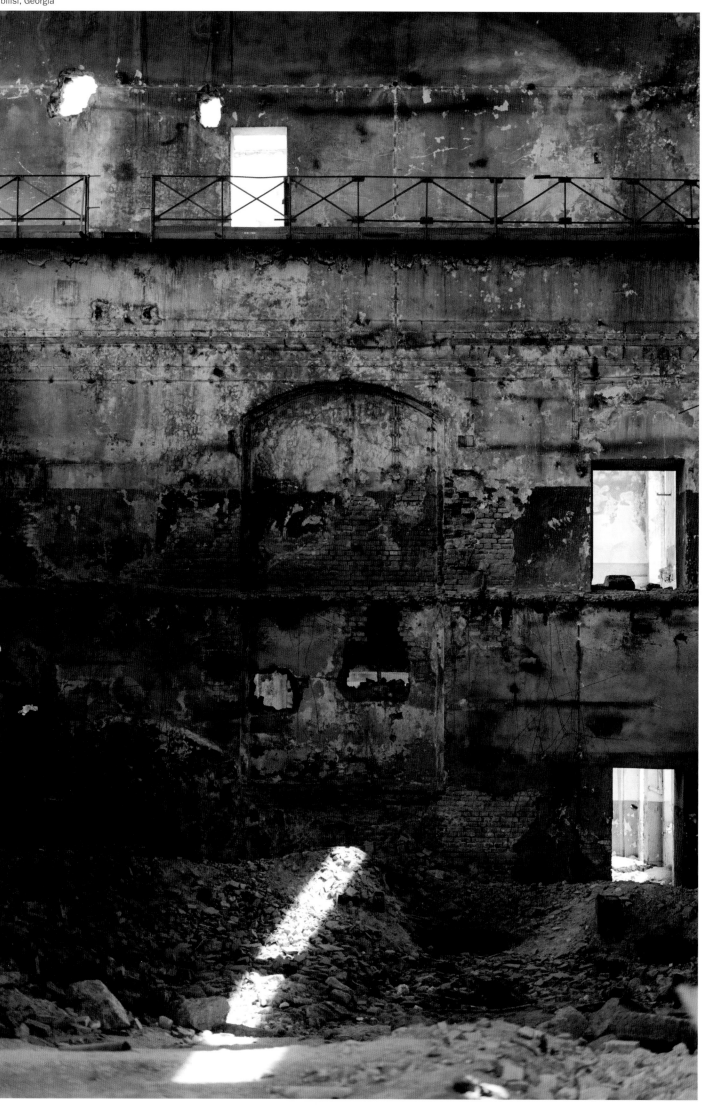

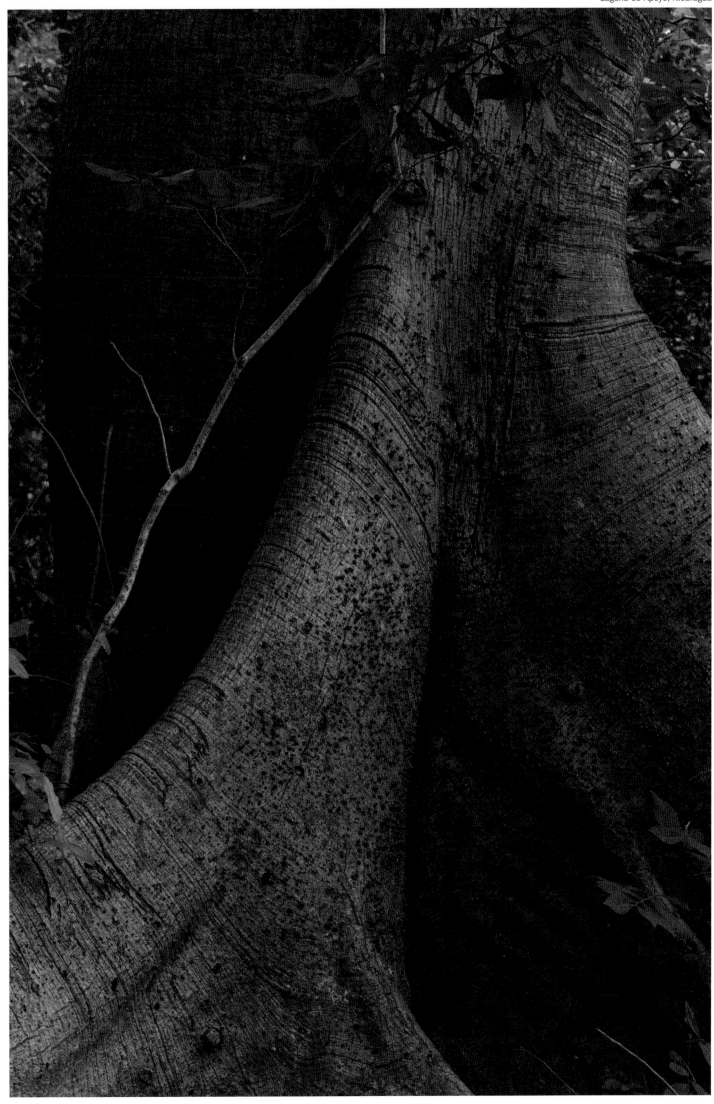

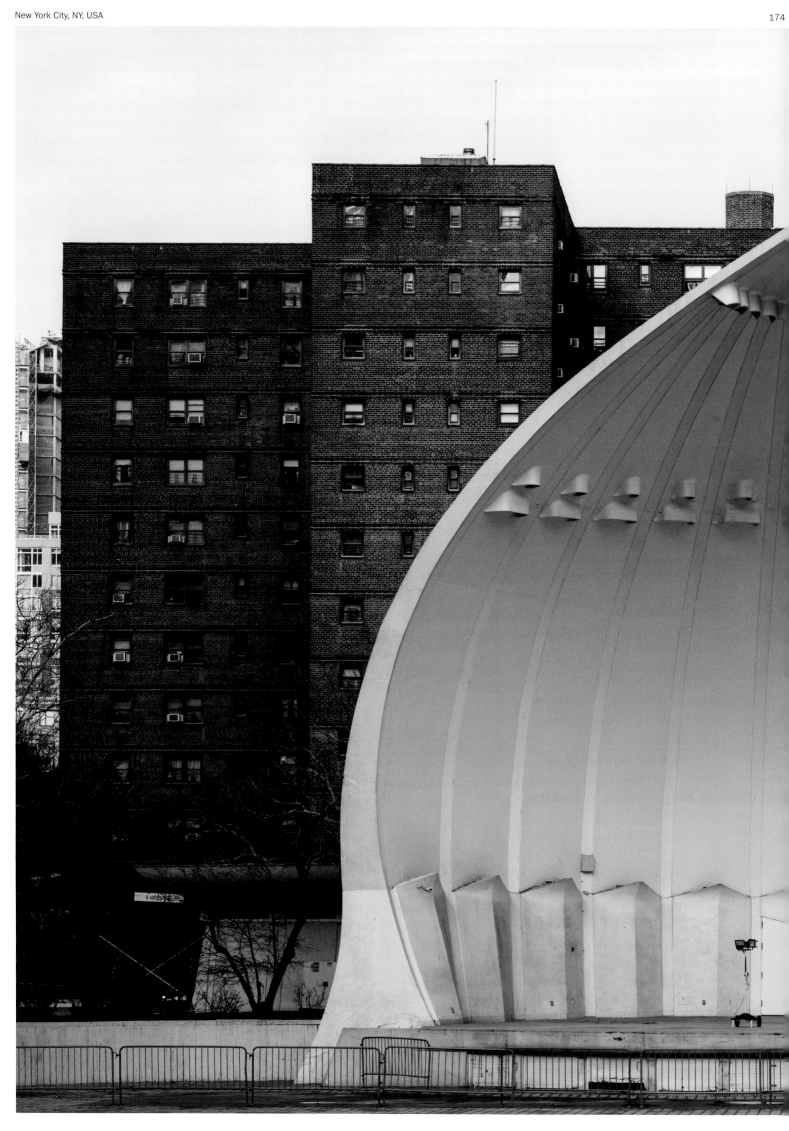

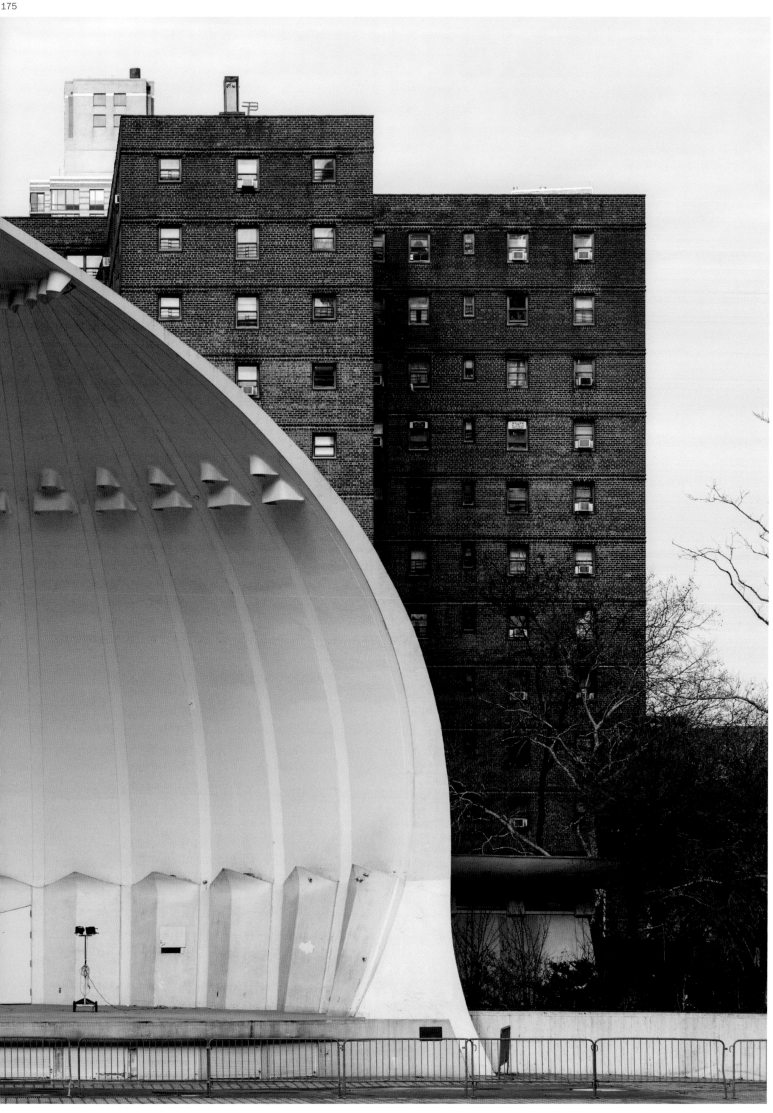

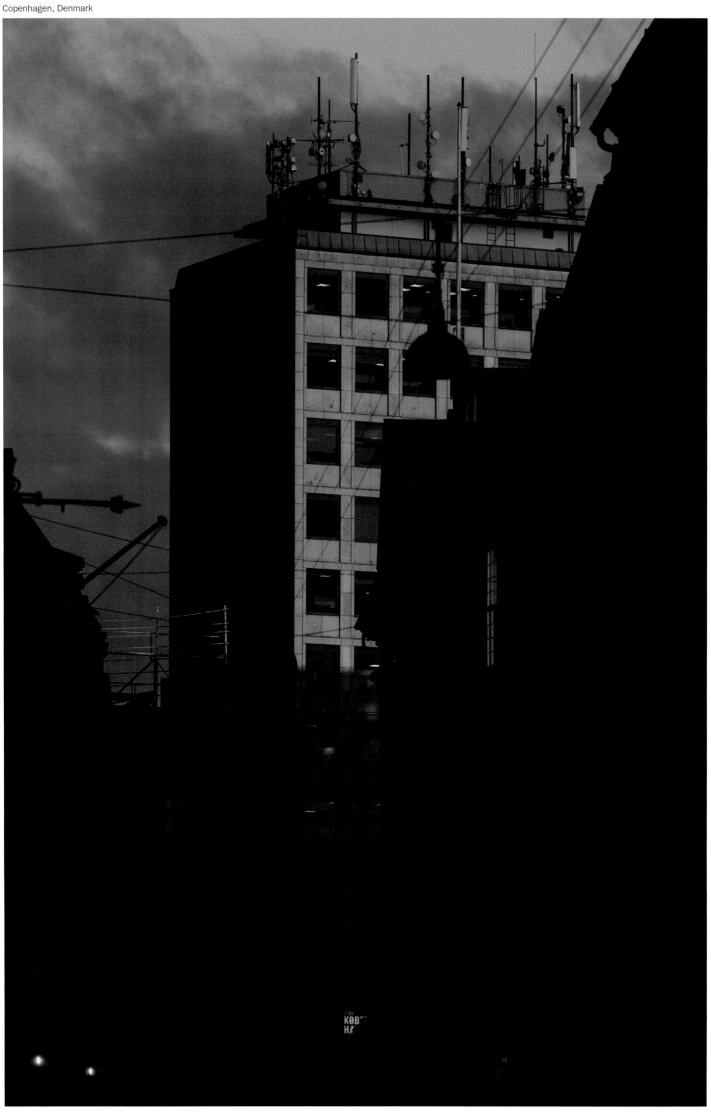

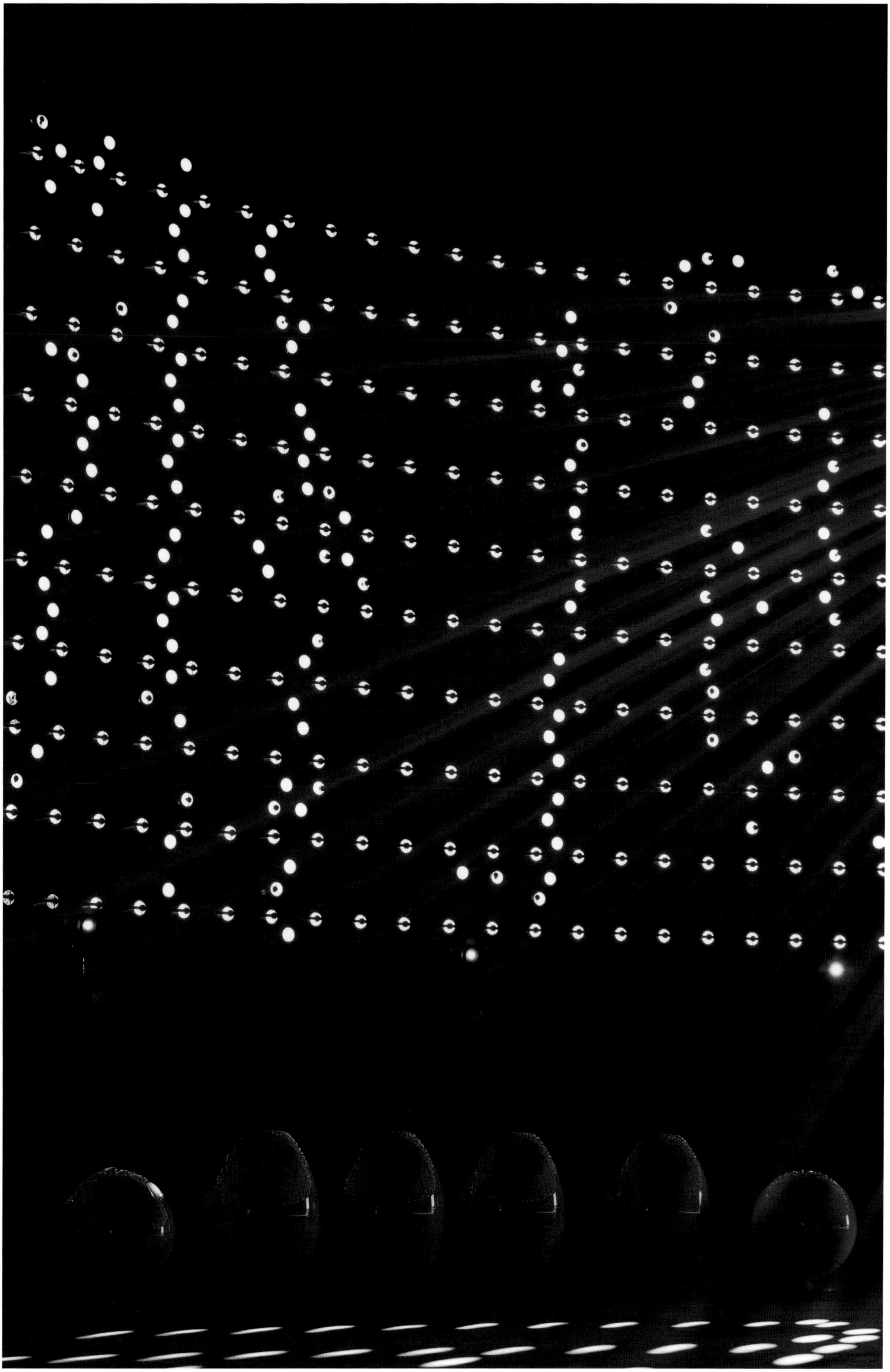

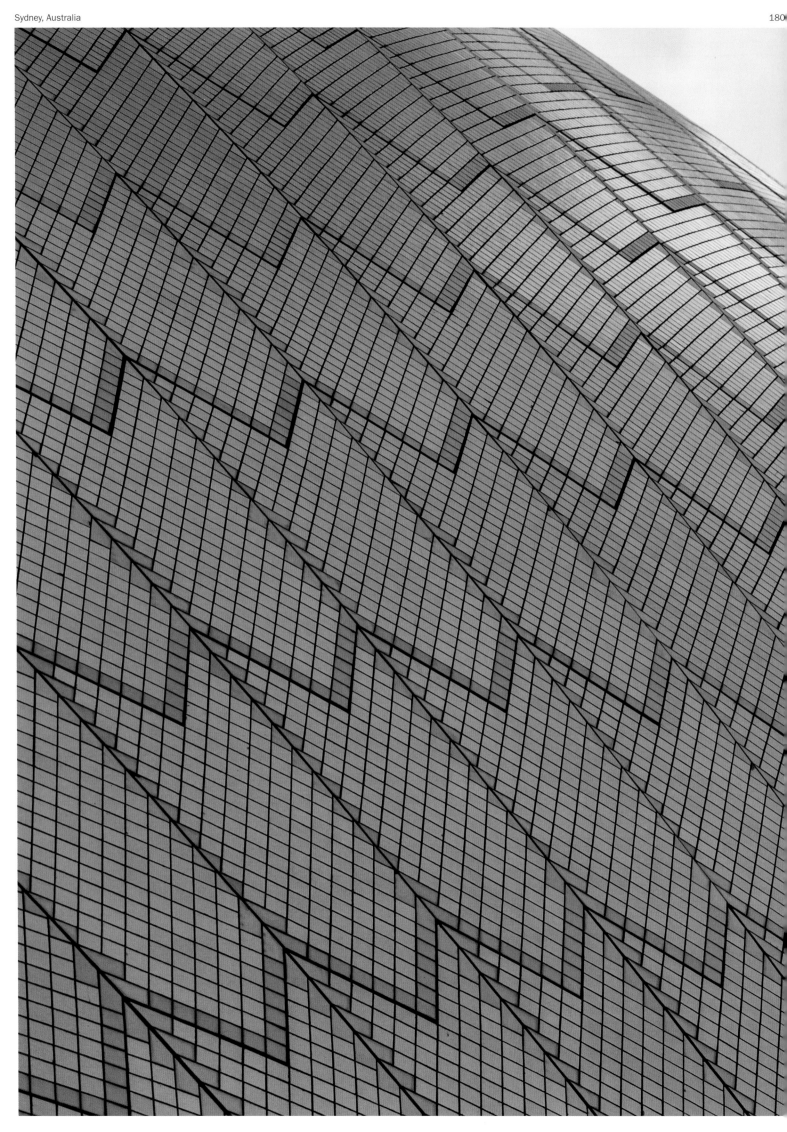

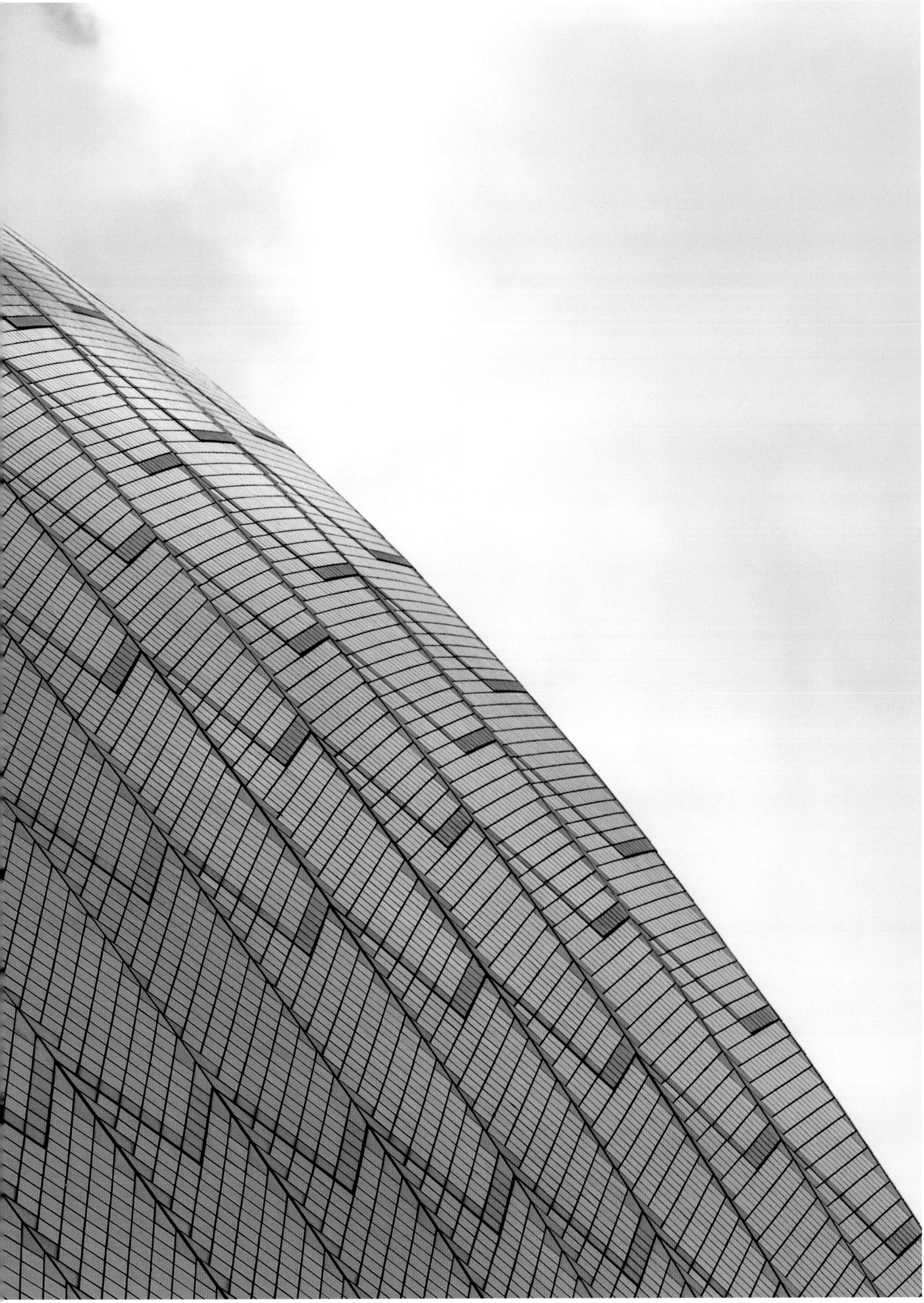

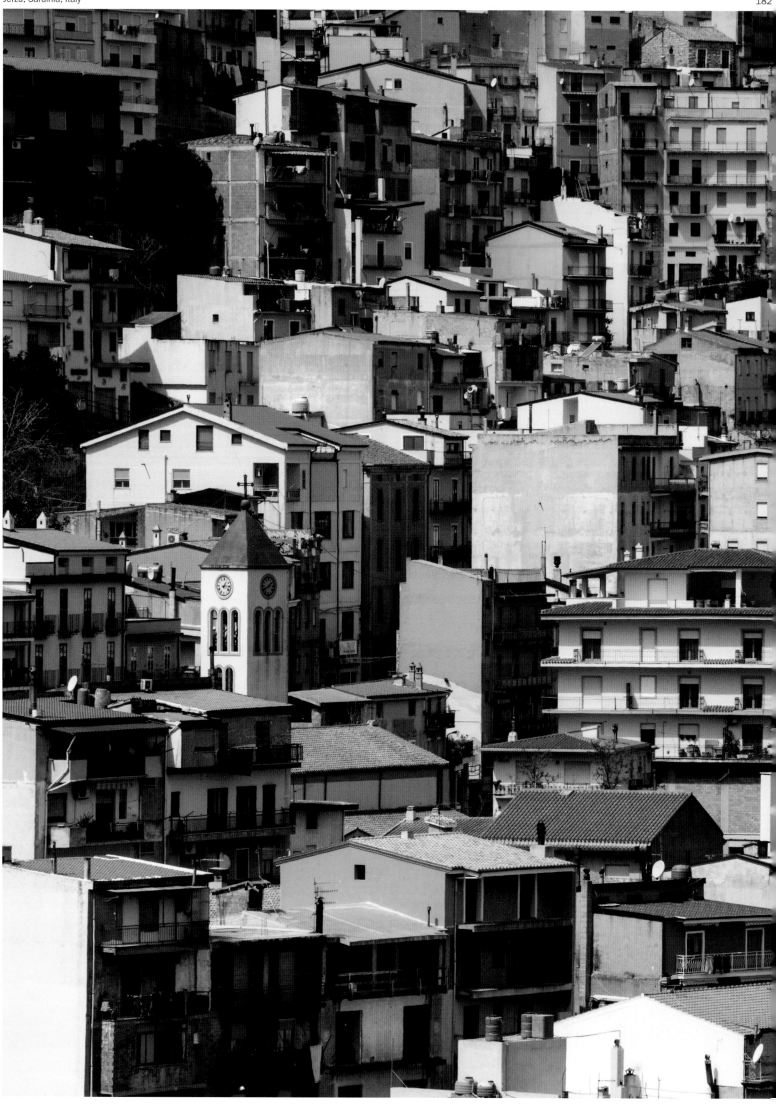

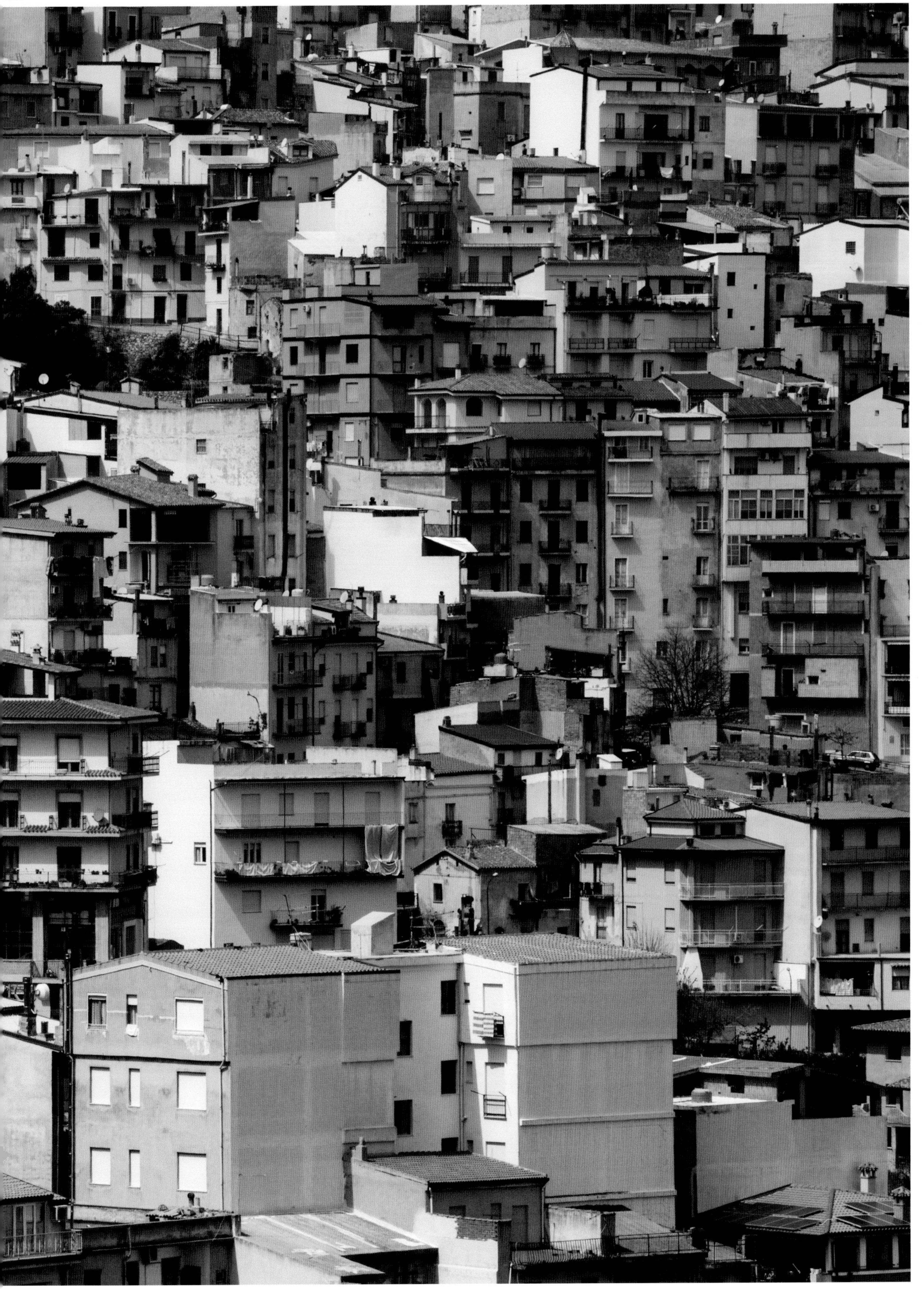

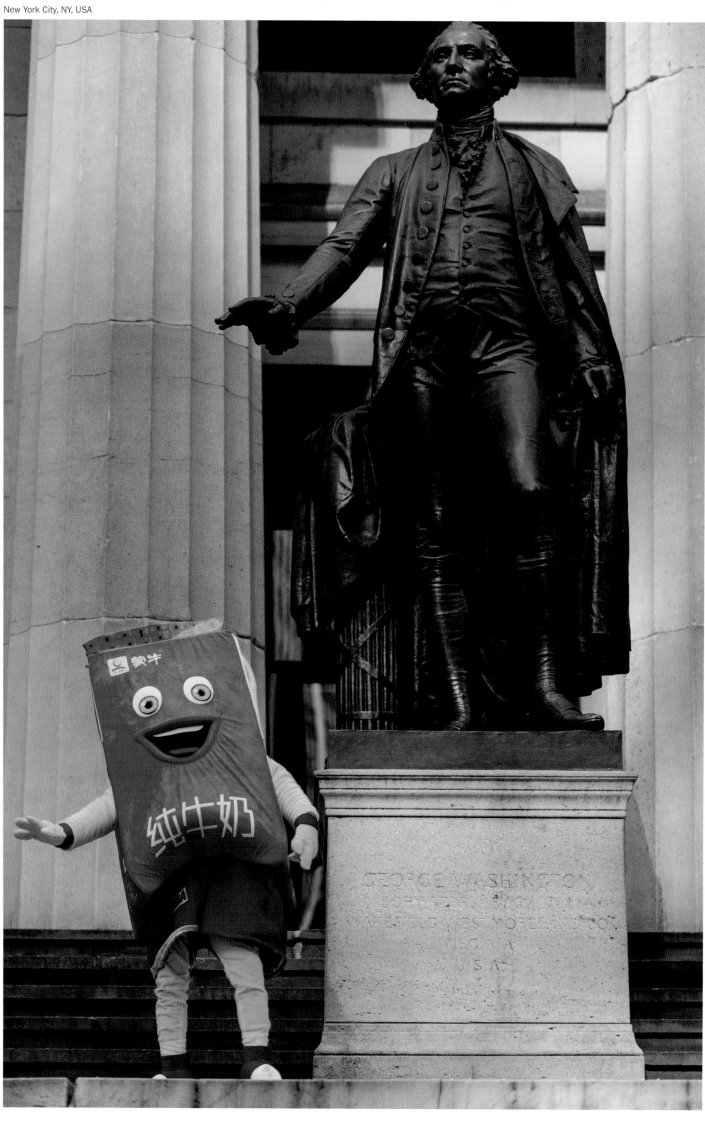

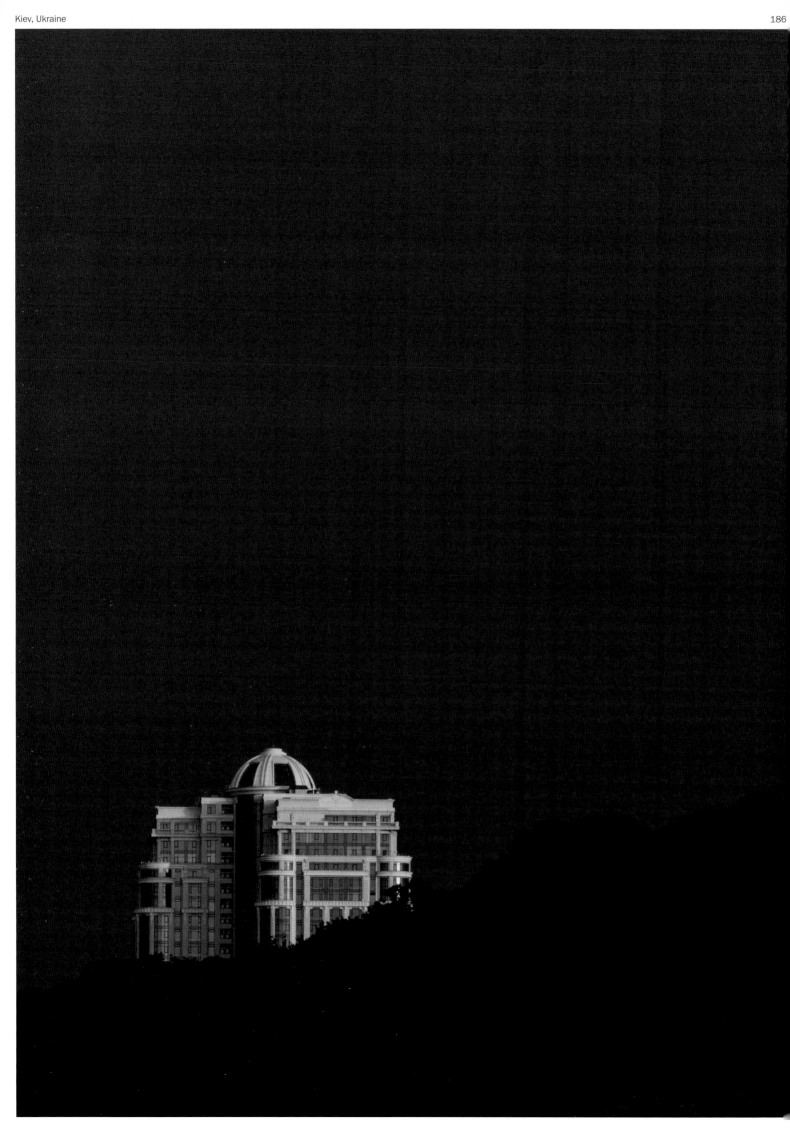

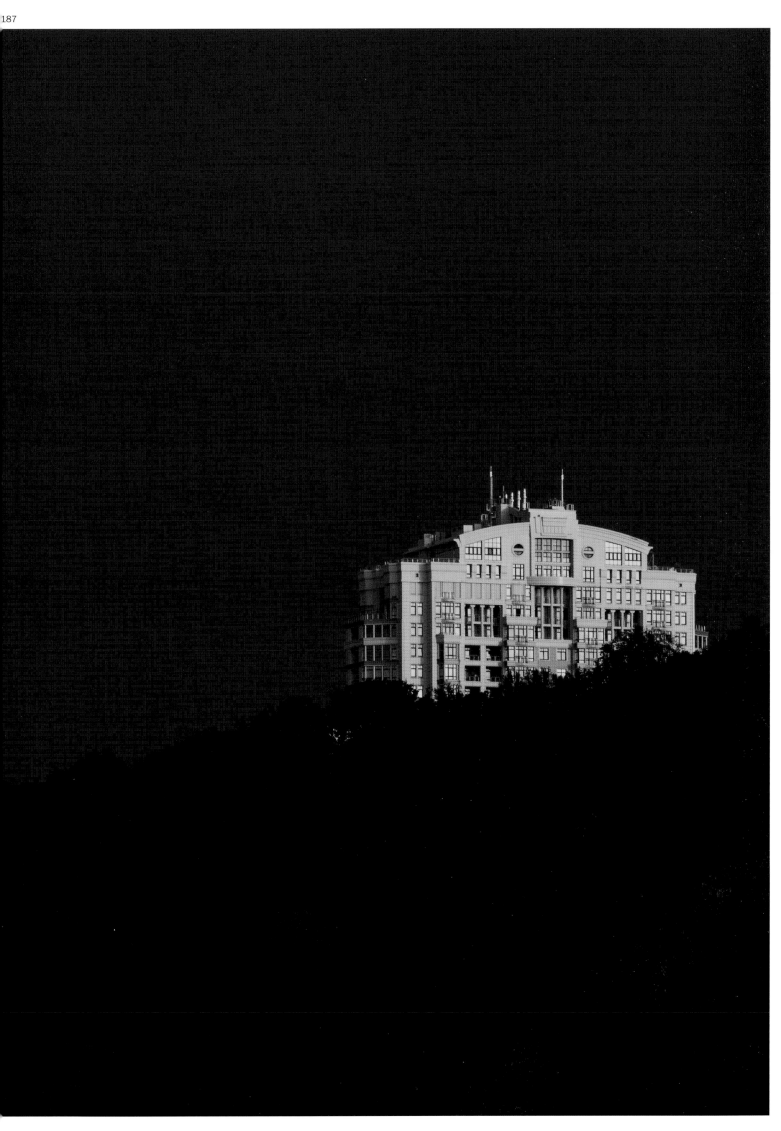

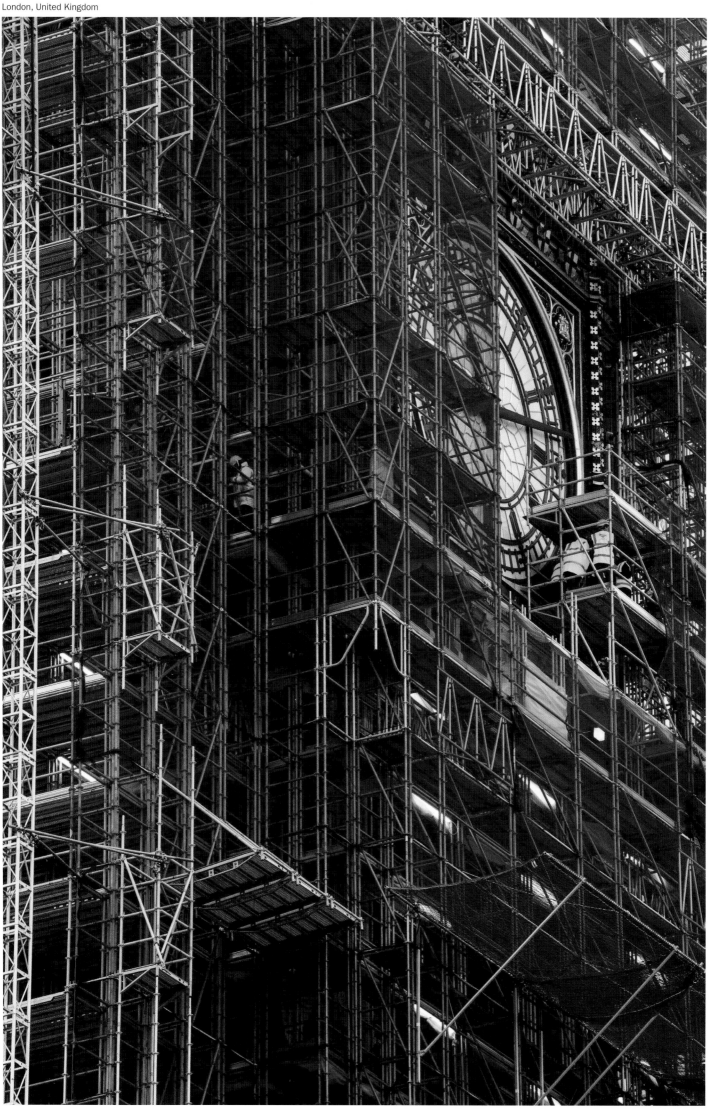

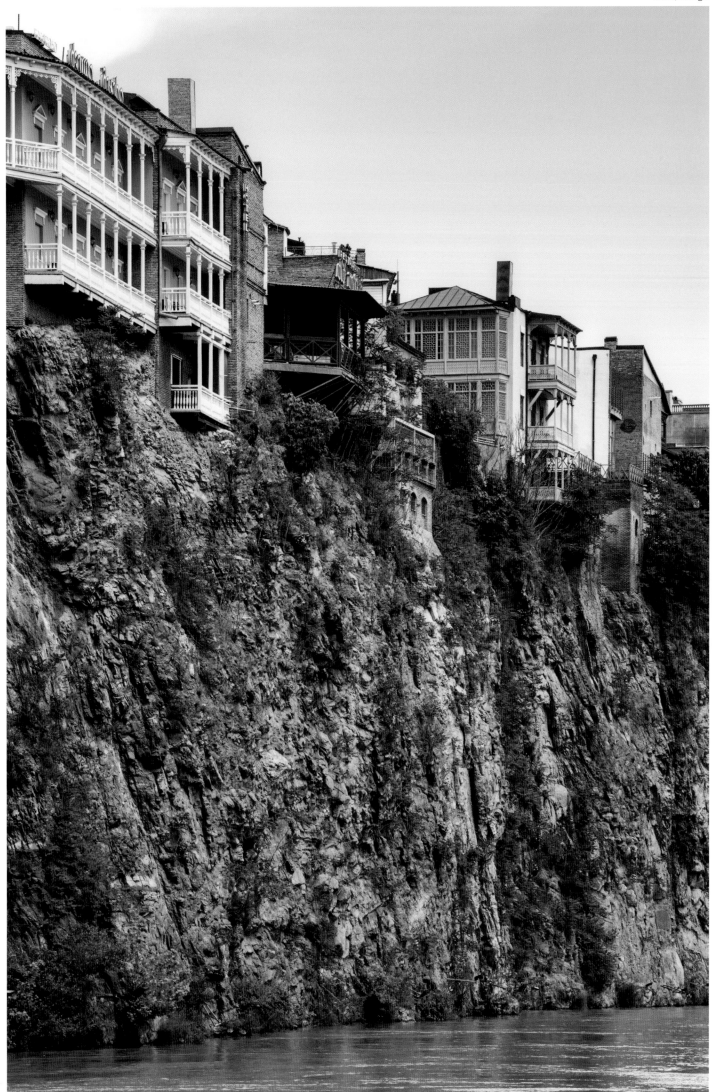

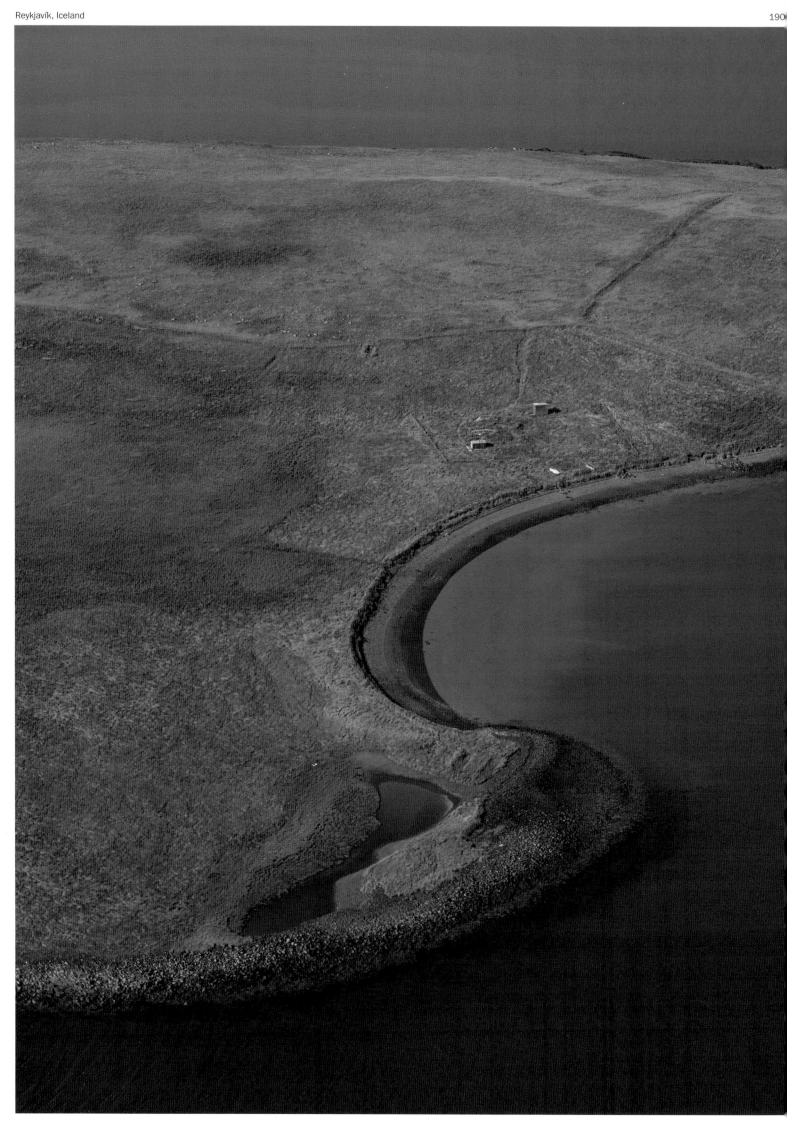

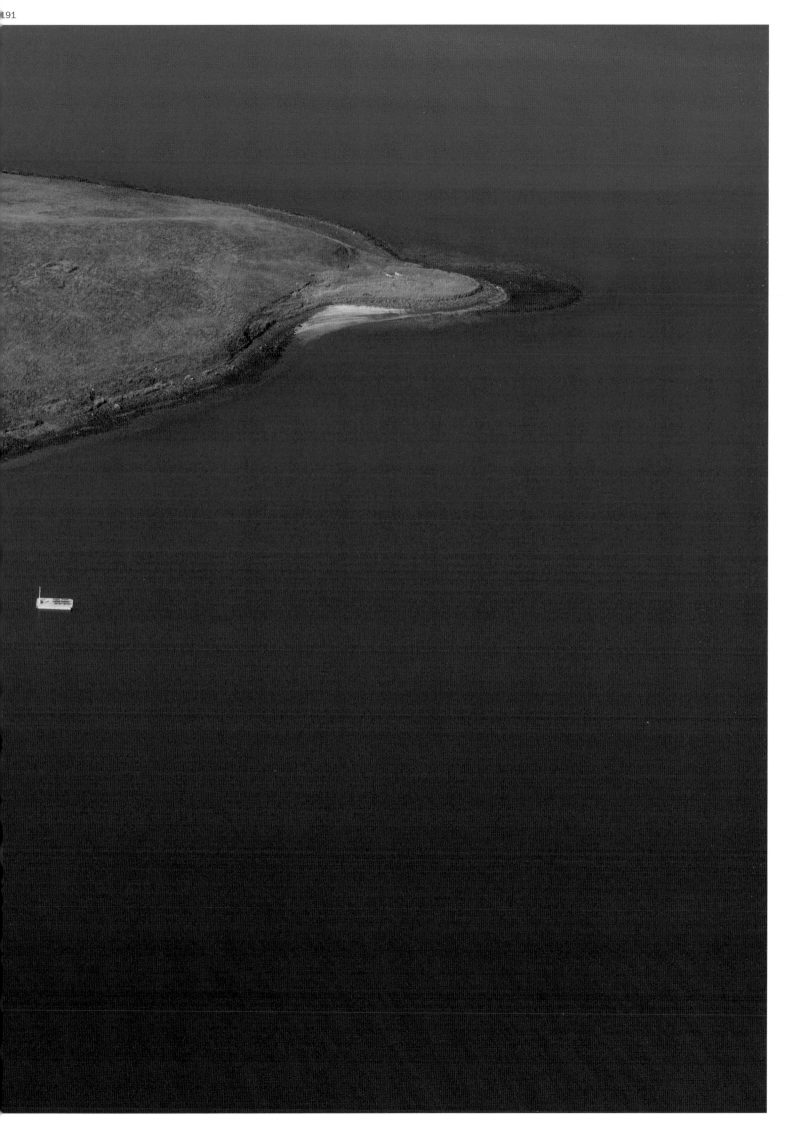

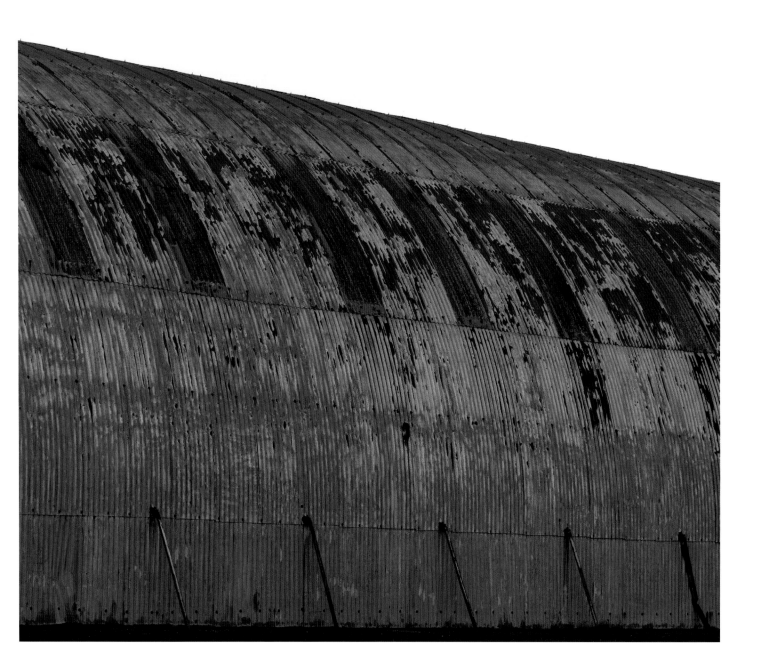

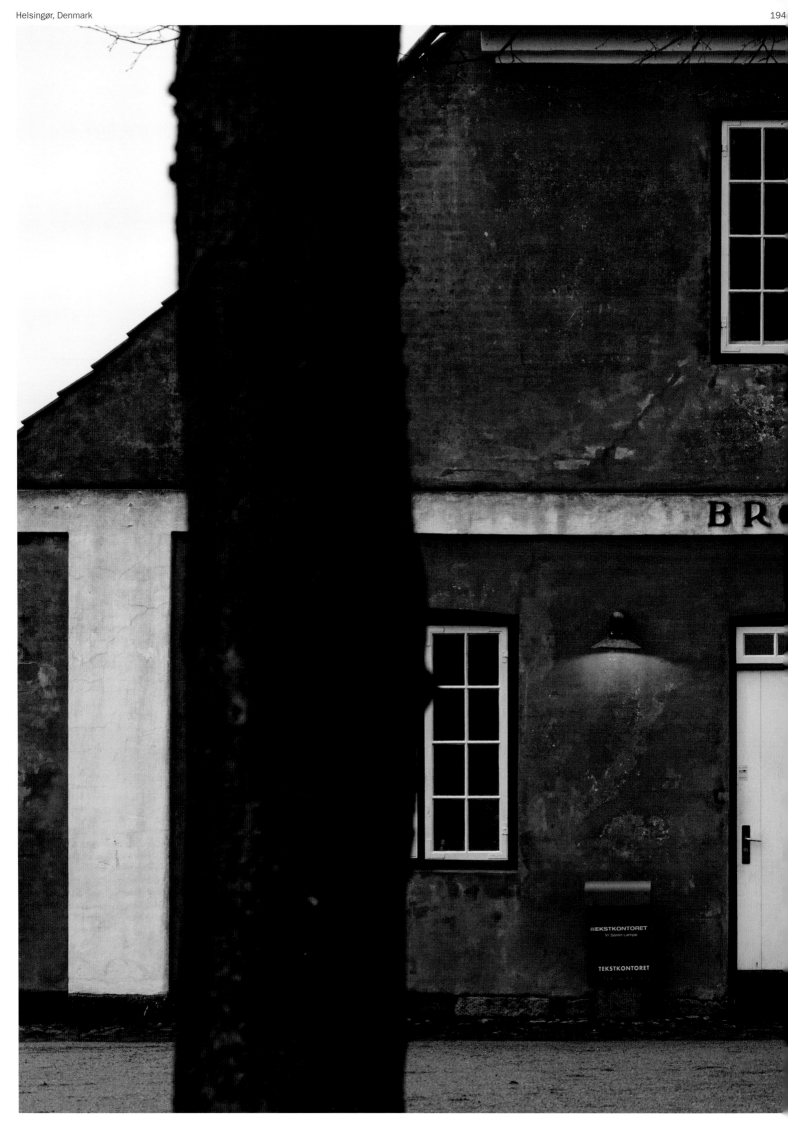

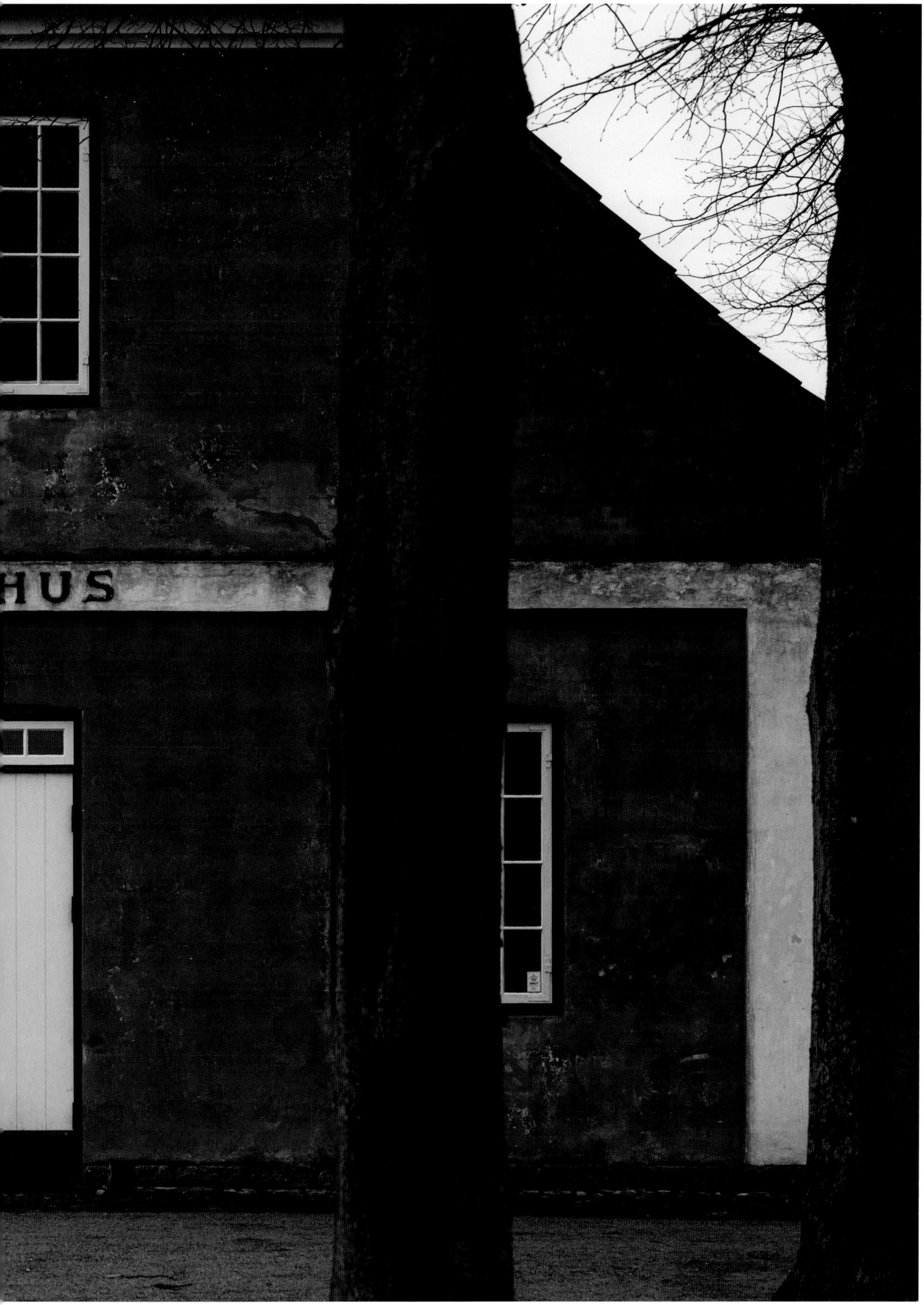
HUS

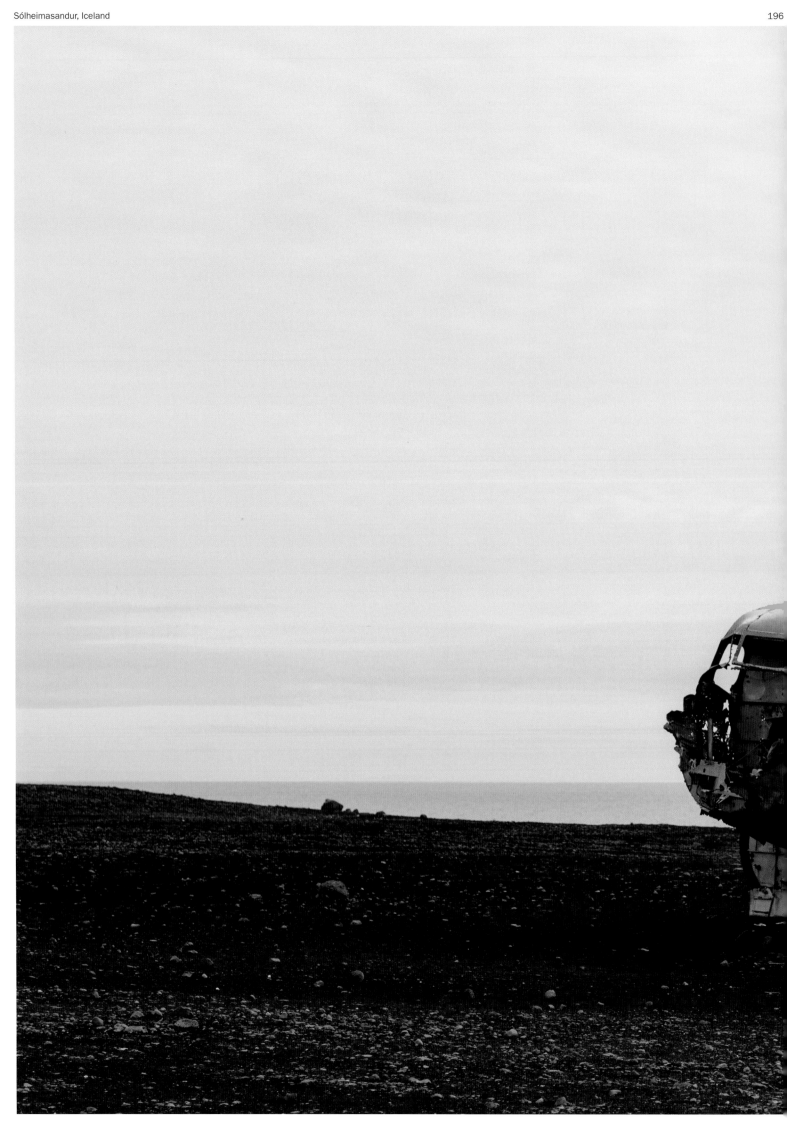

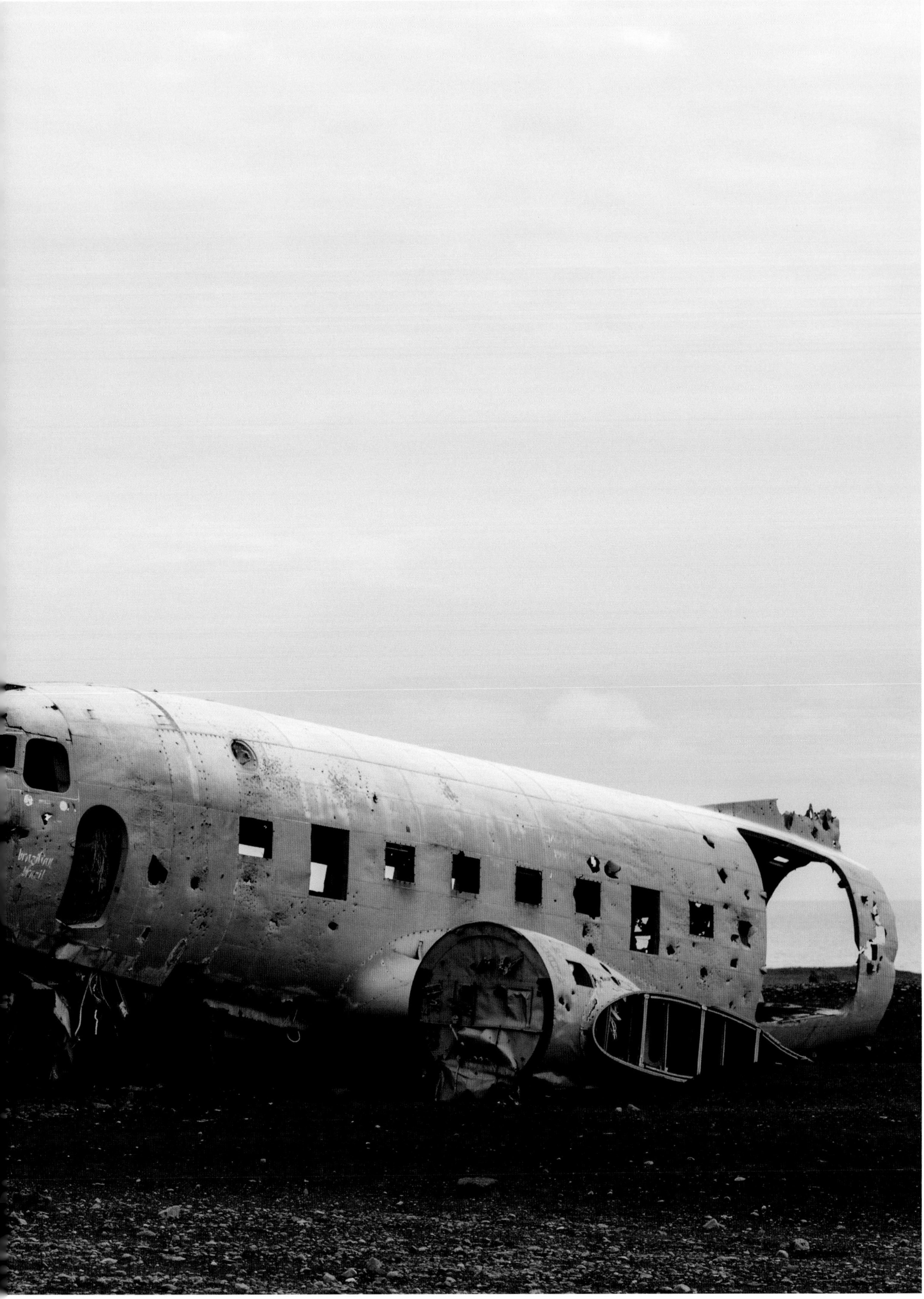

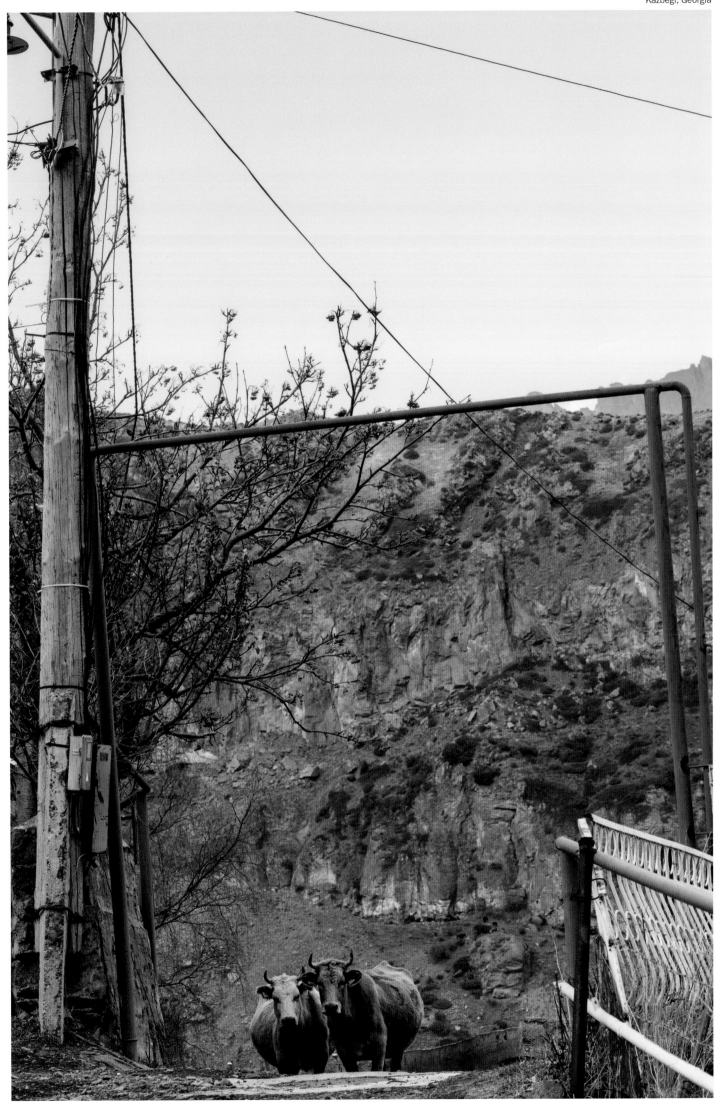

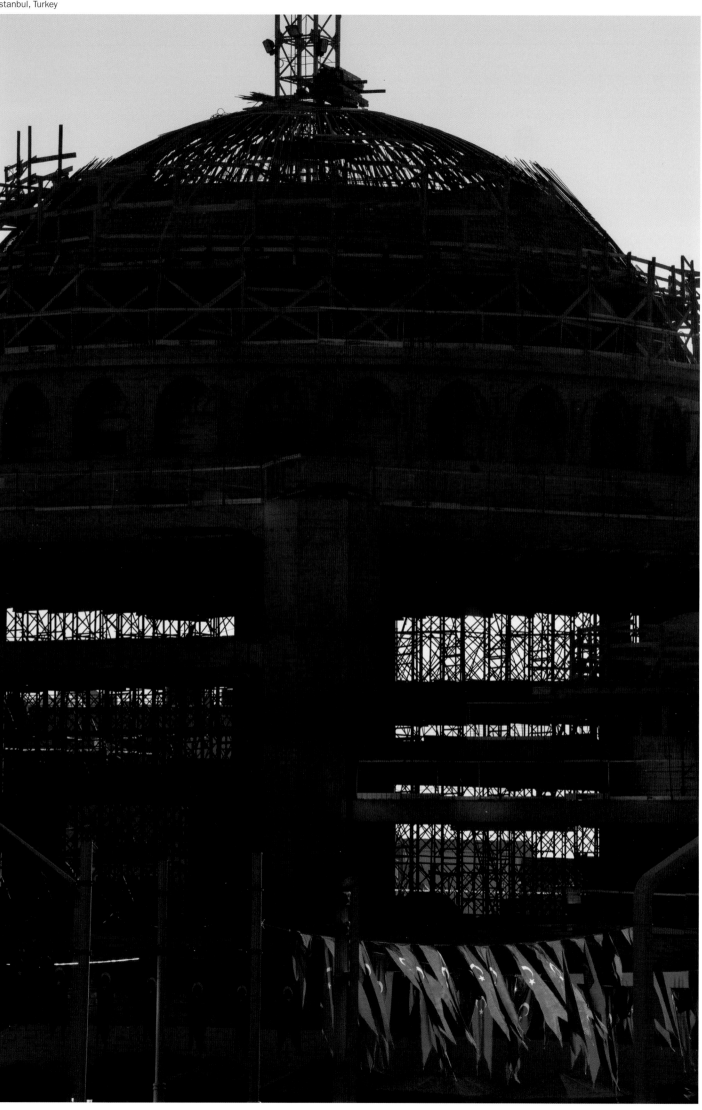

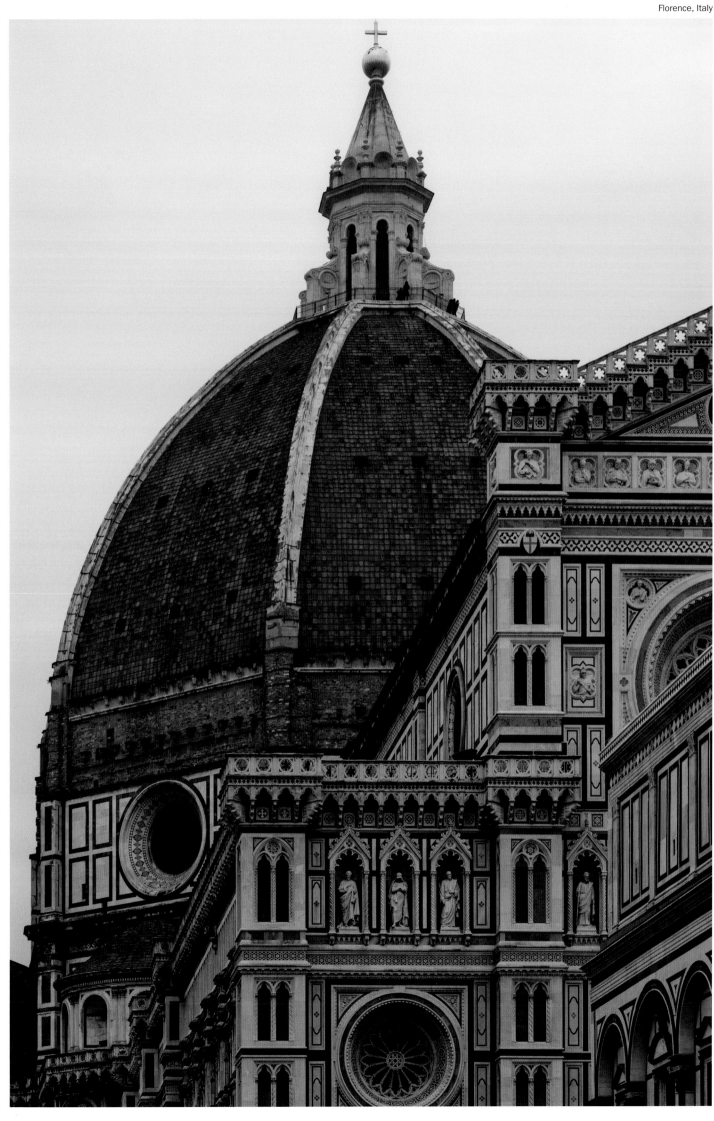

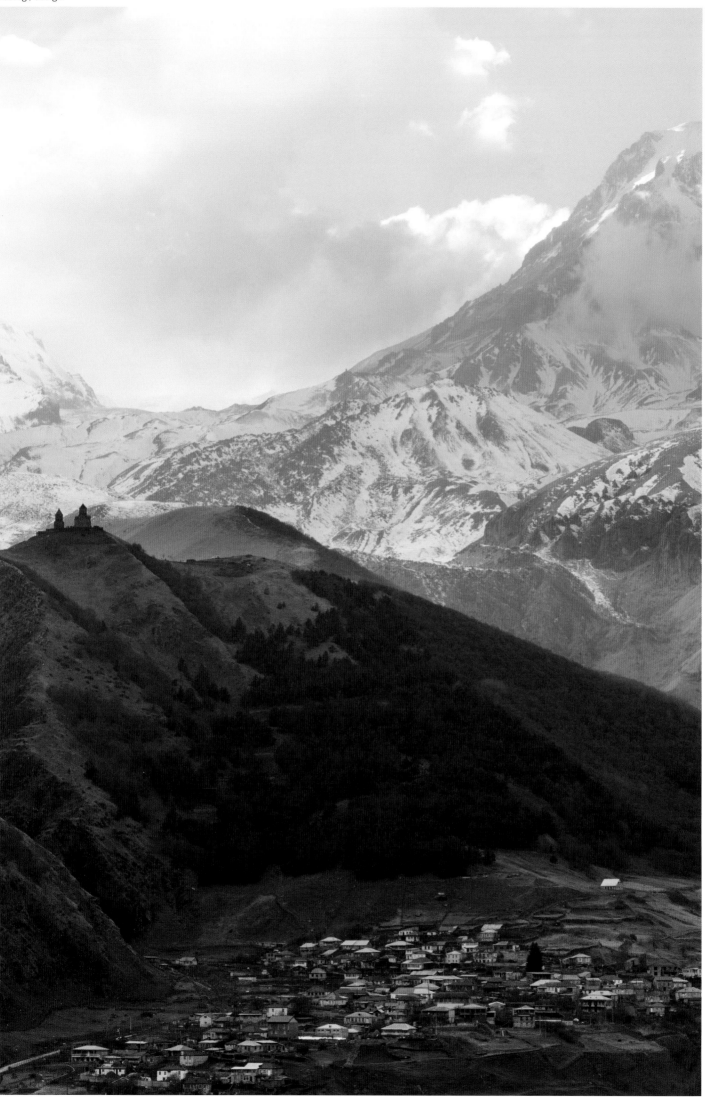

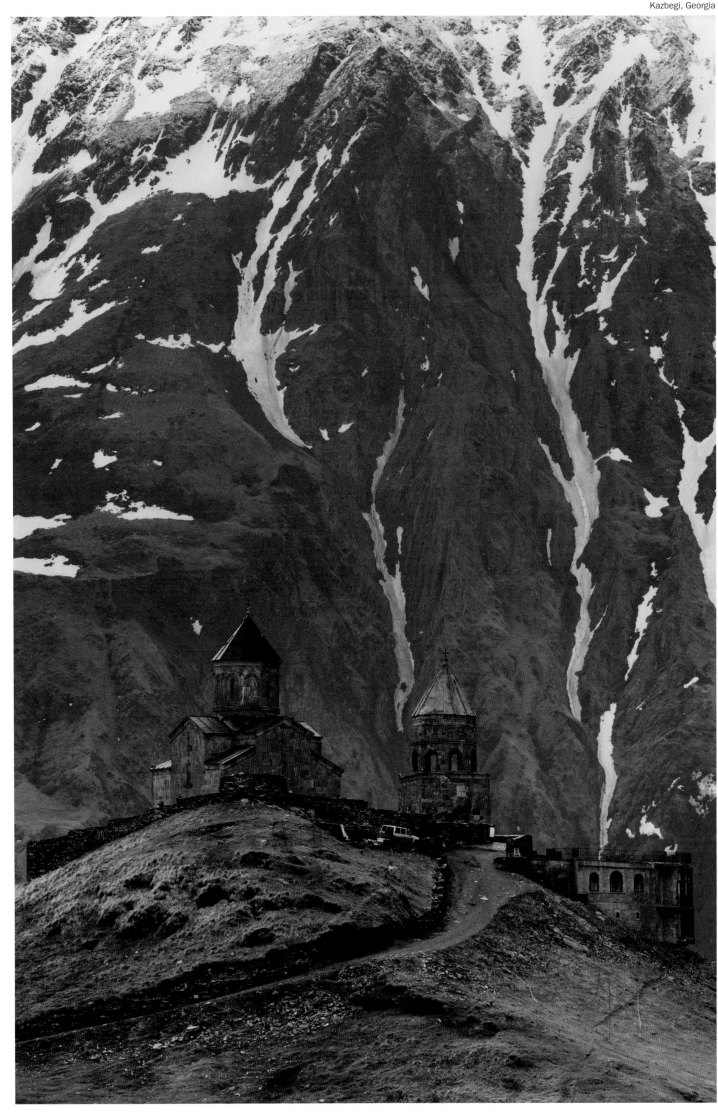

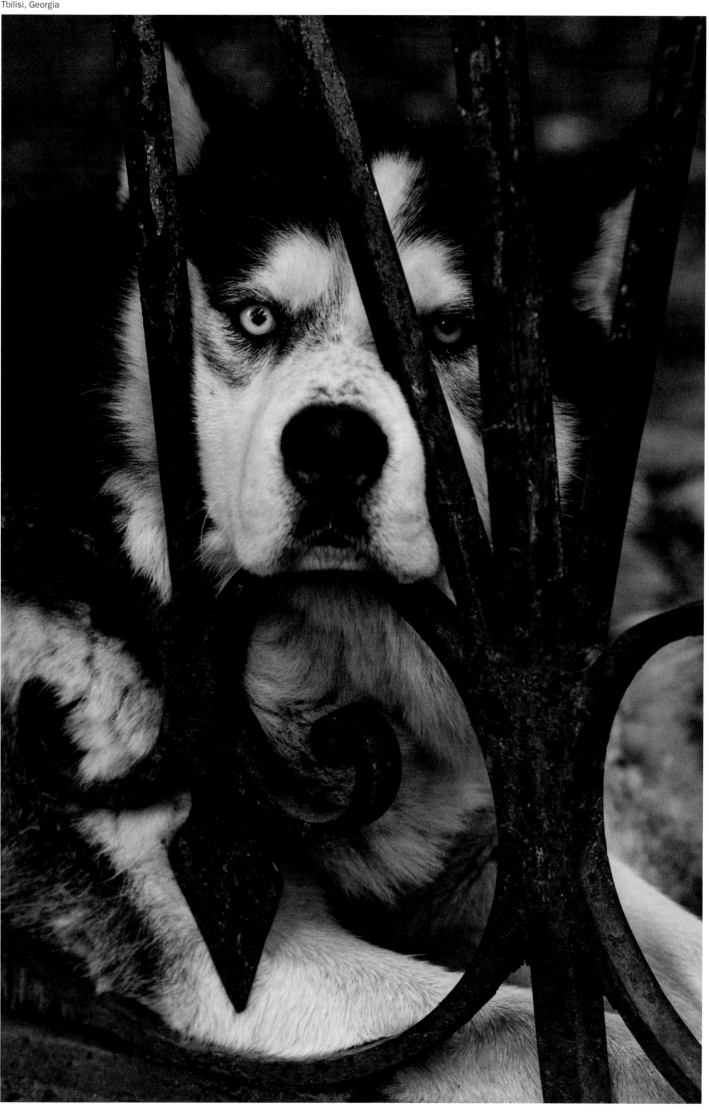

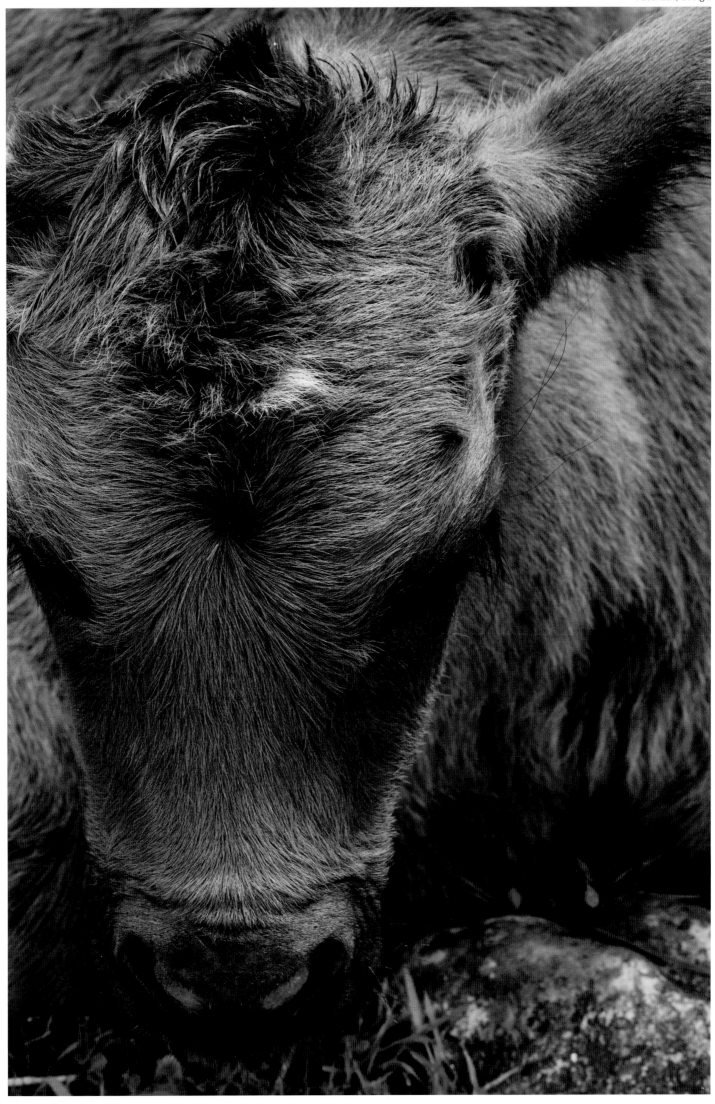

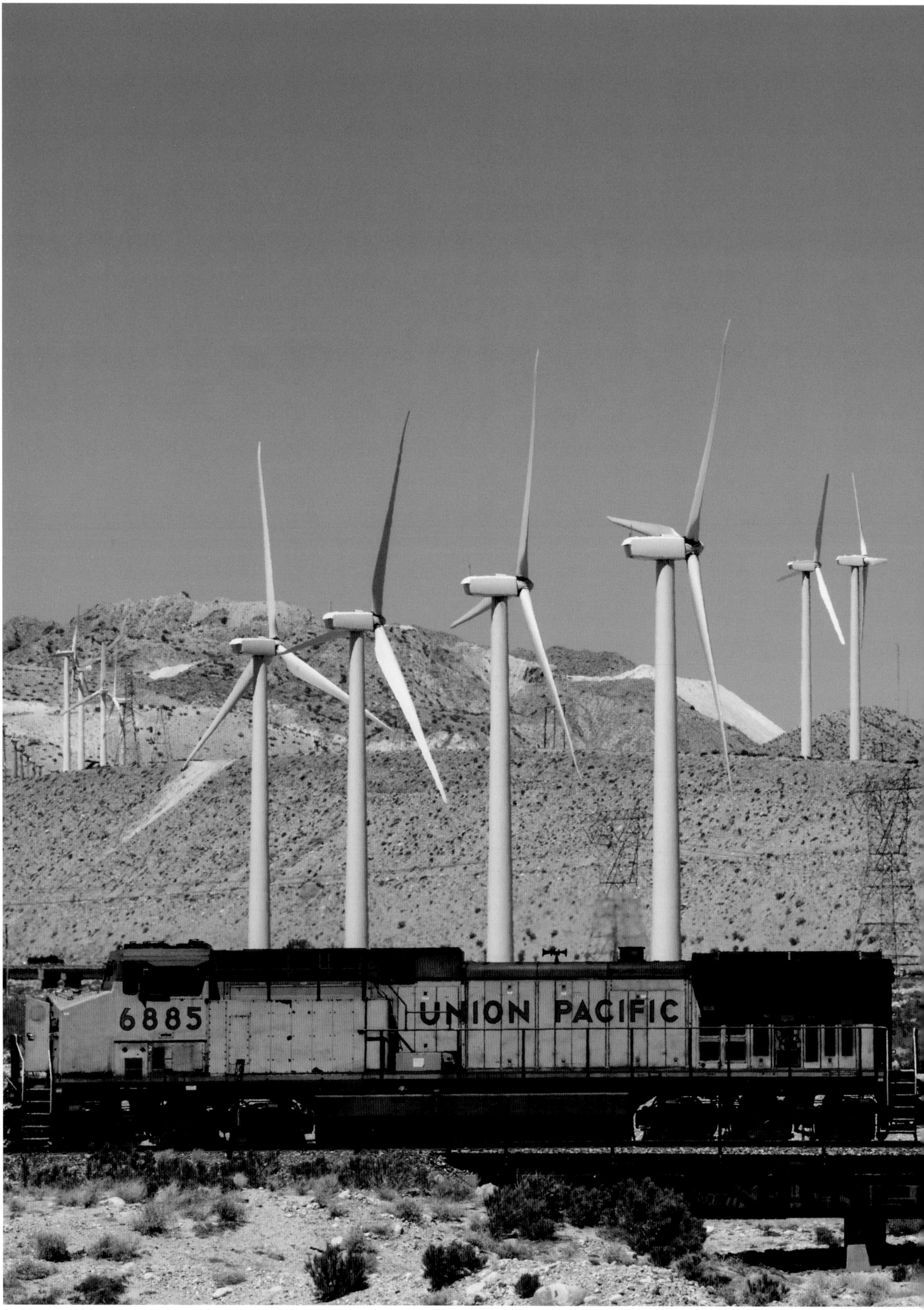
6885
UNION PACIFIC

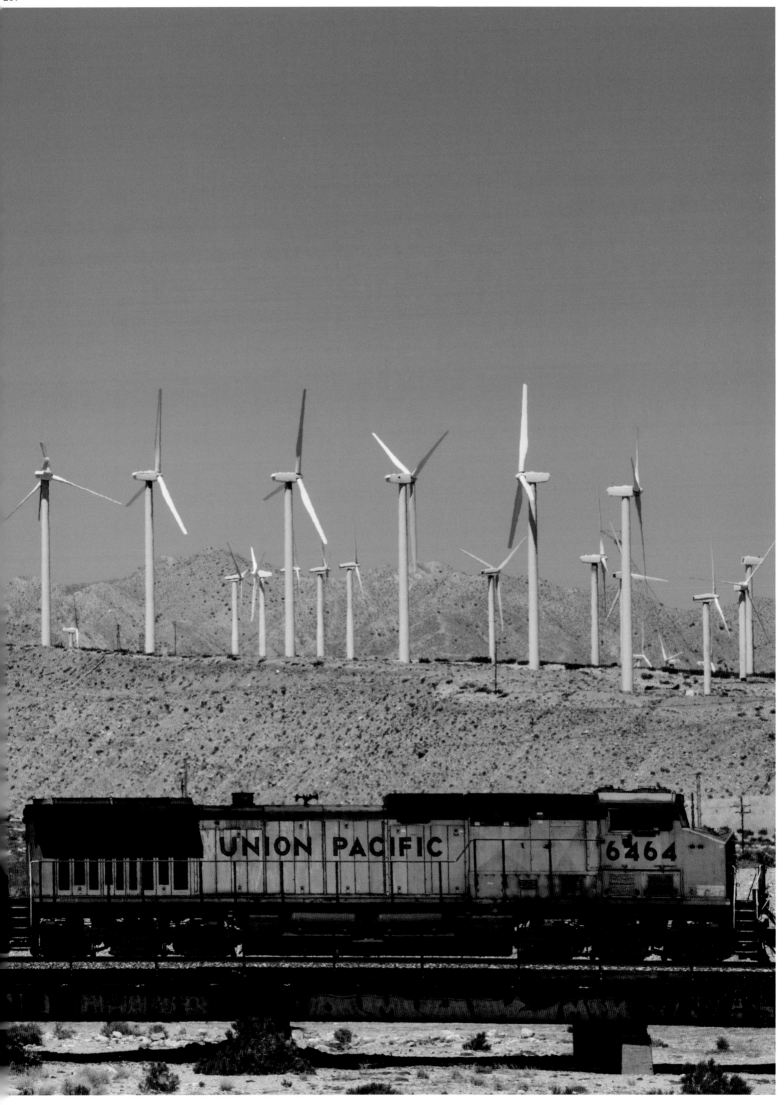

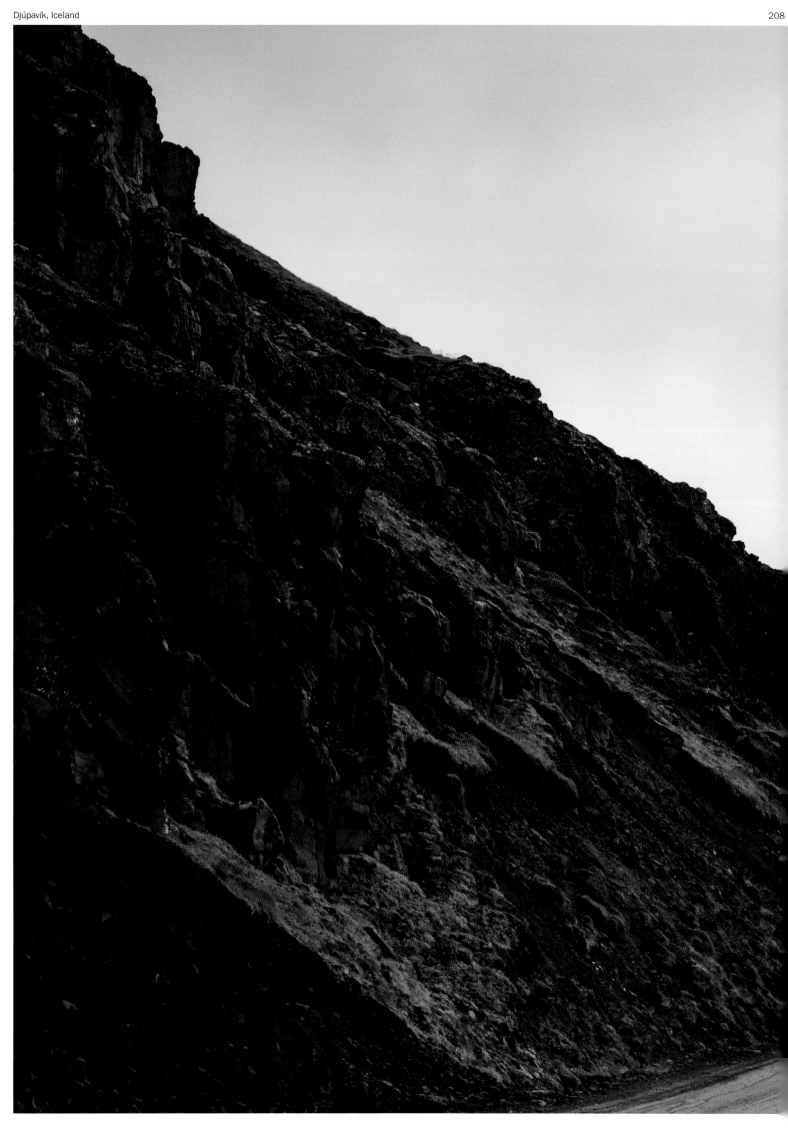

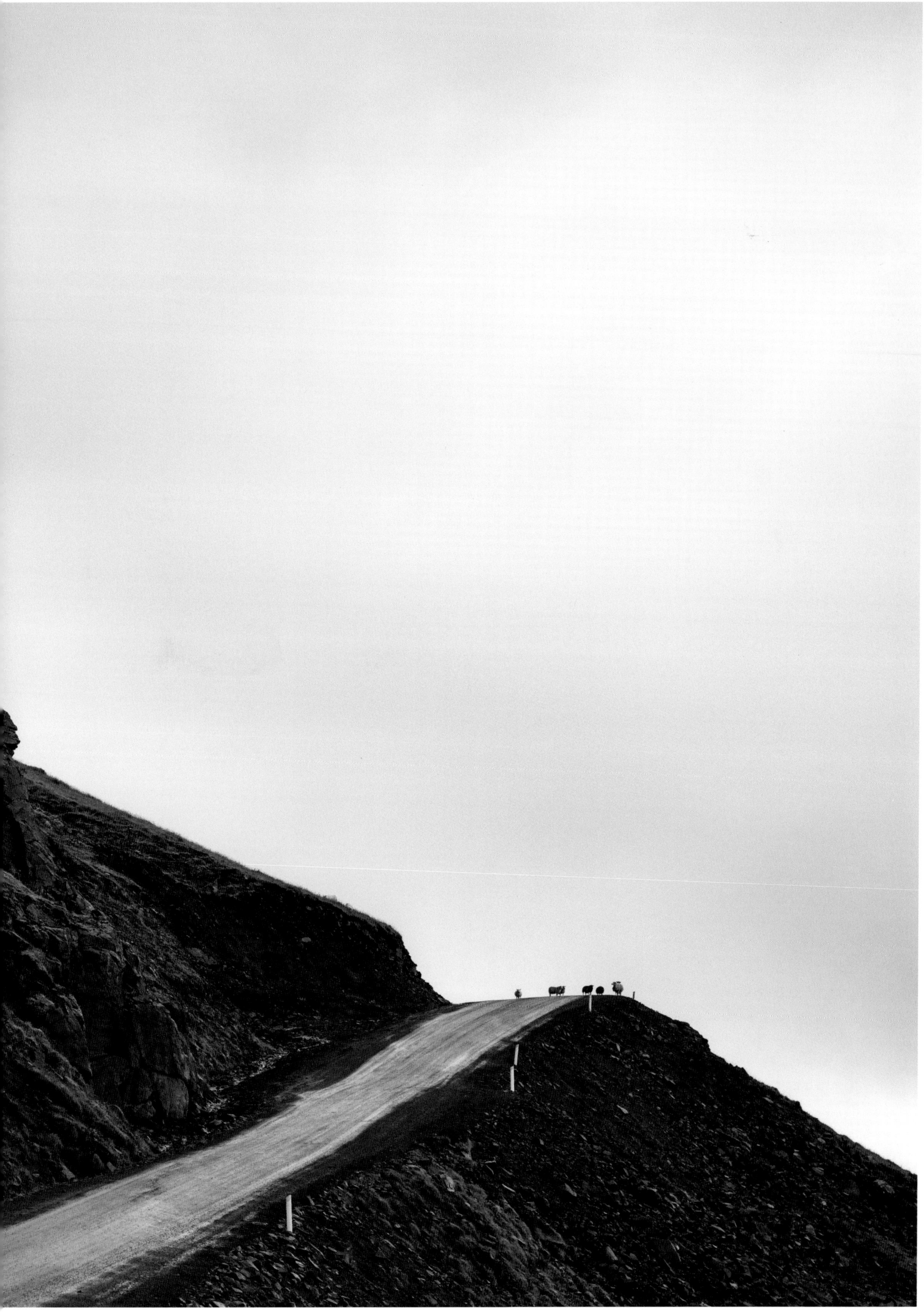

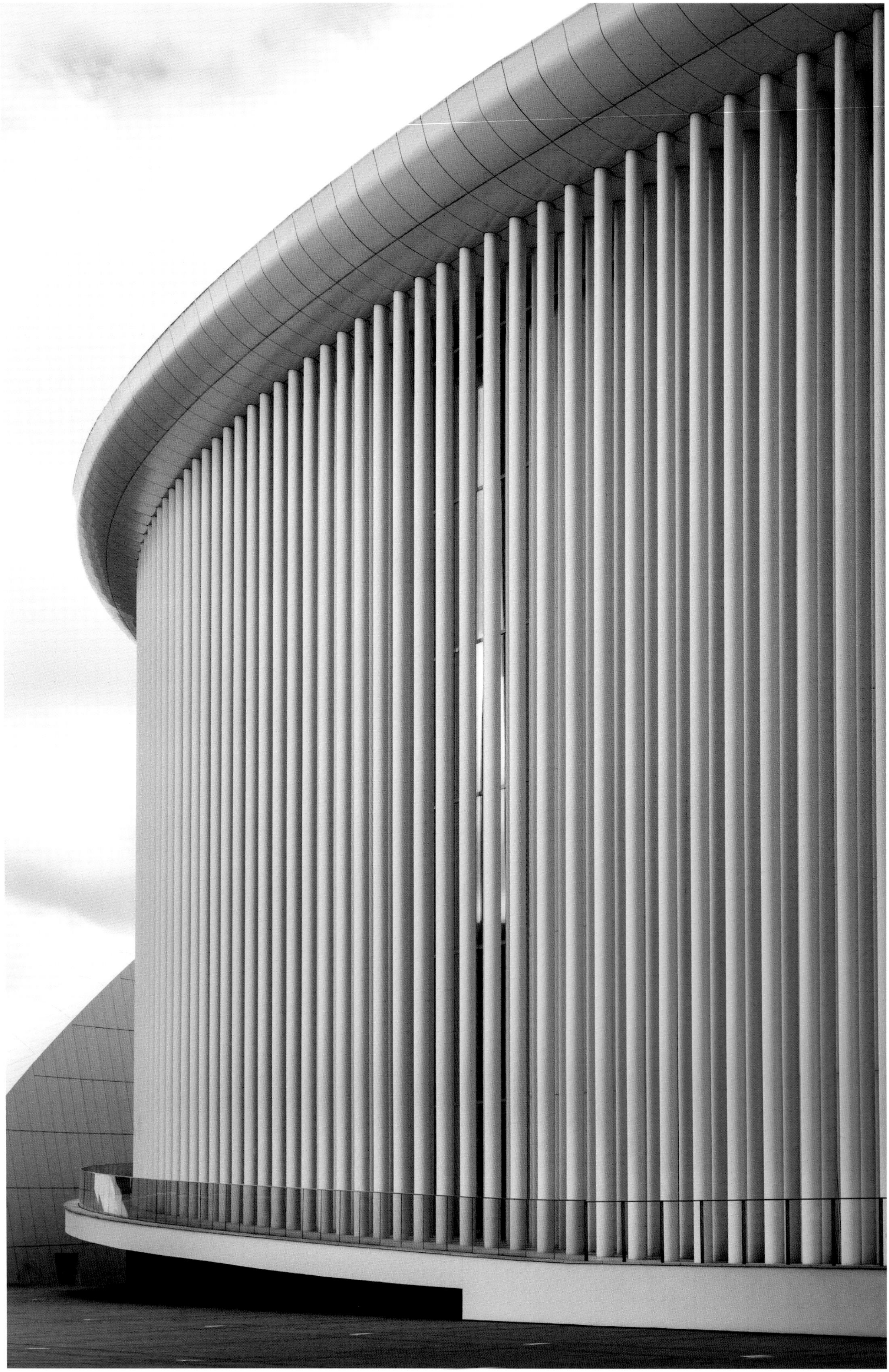

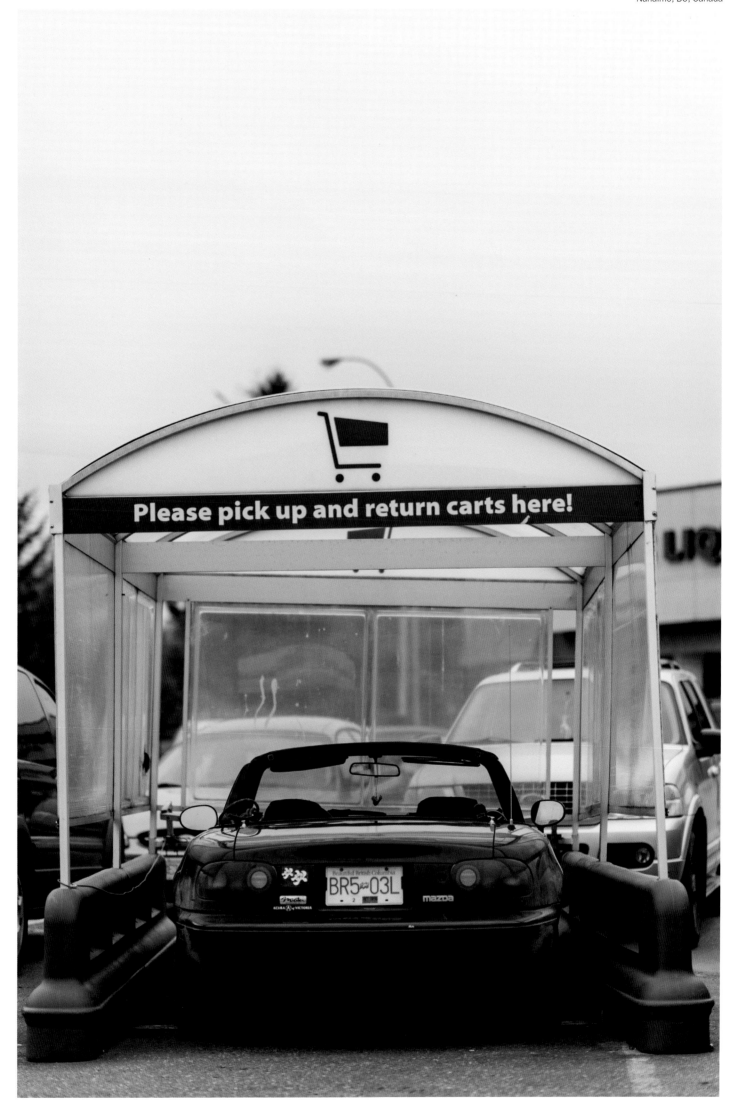

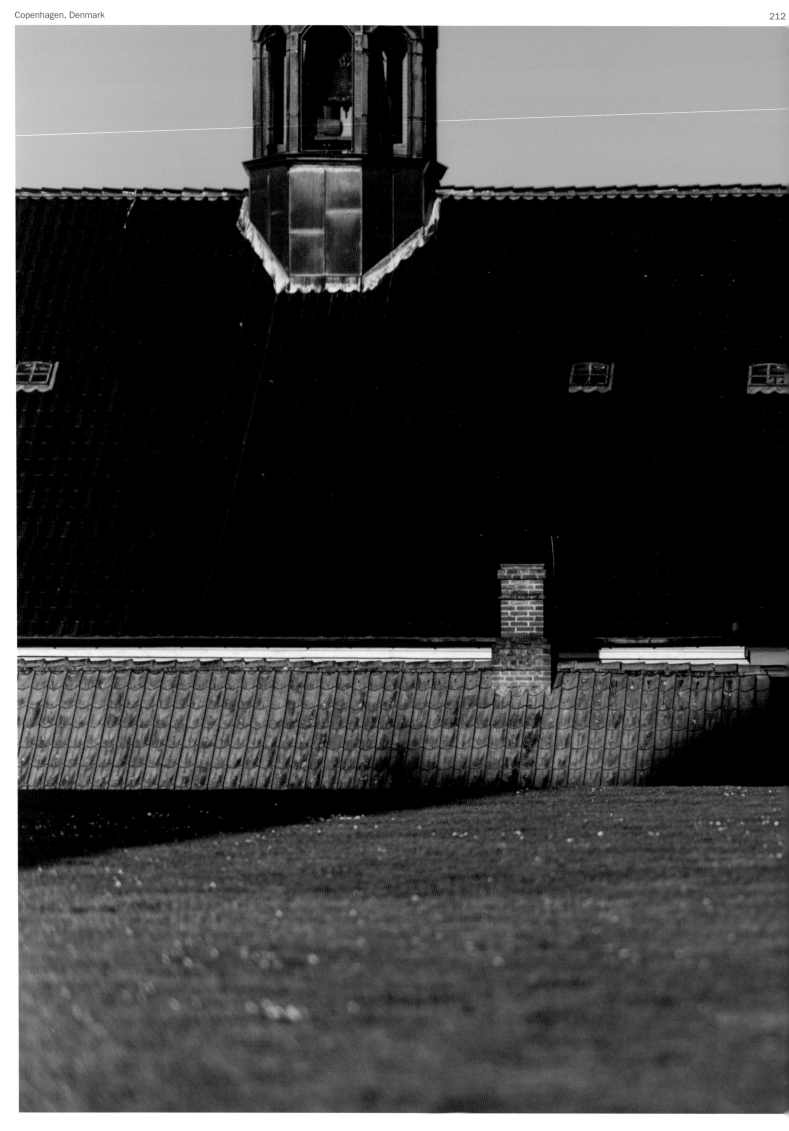

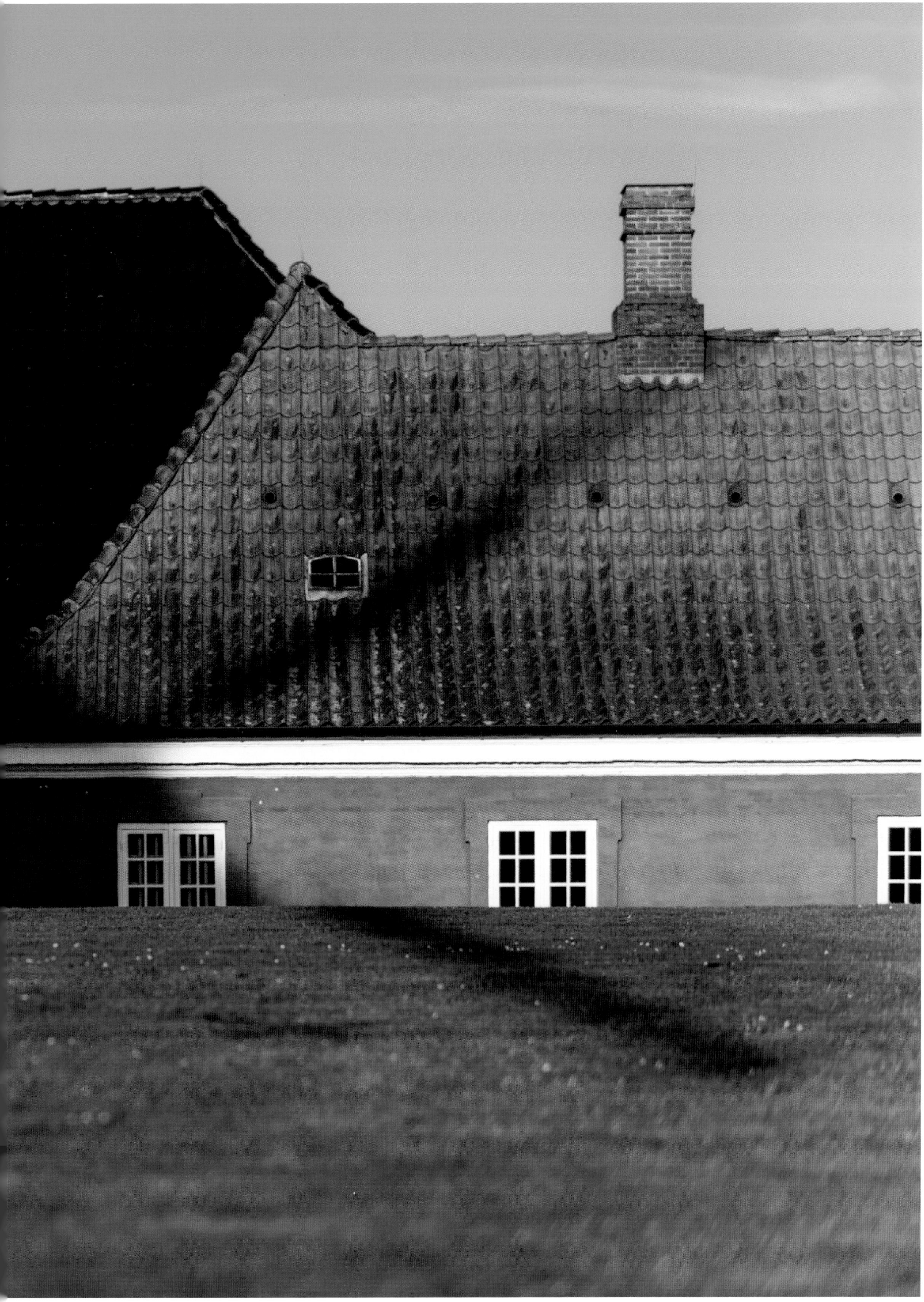

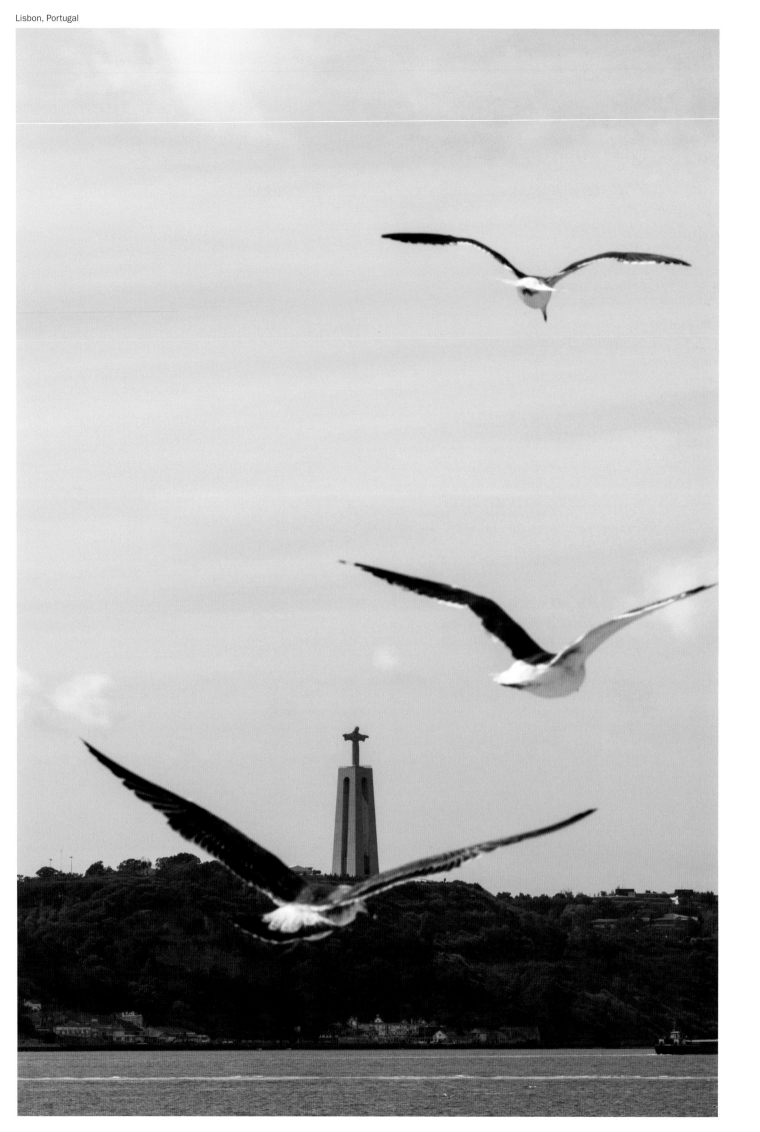

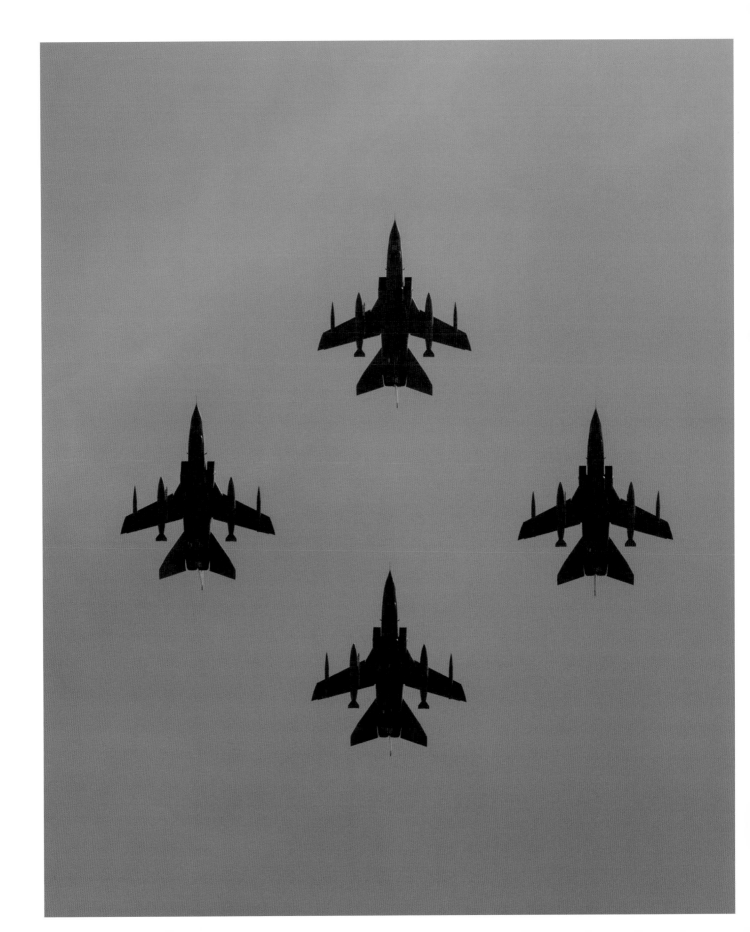

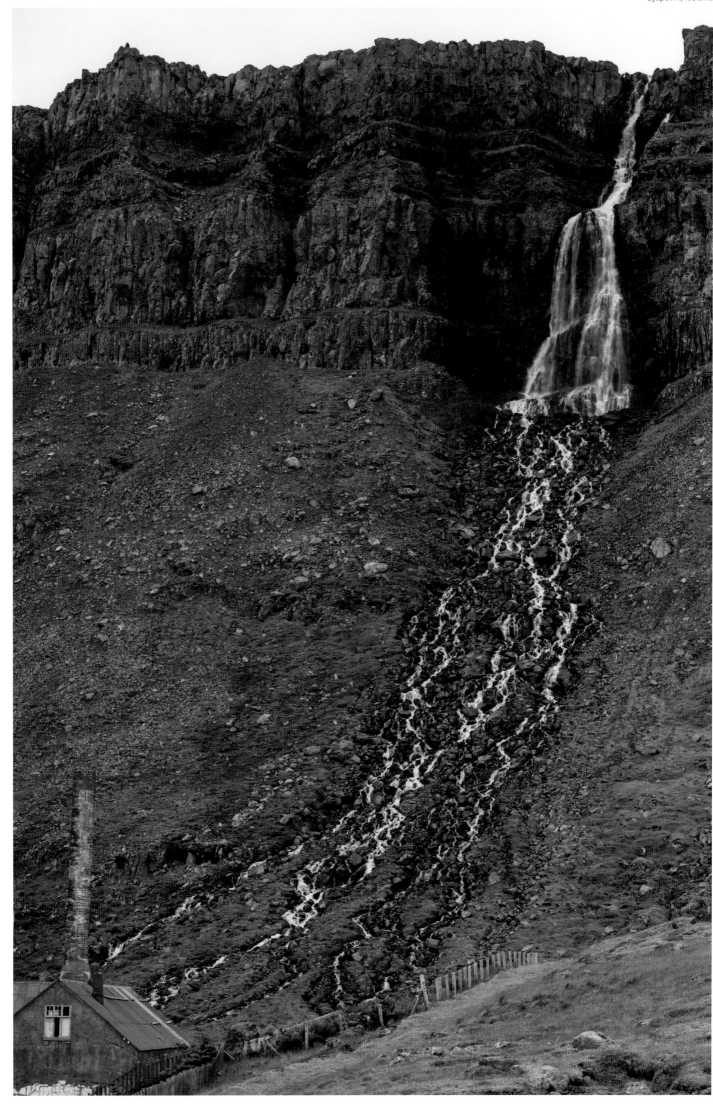

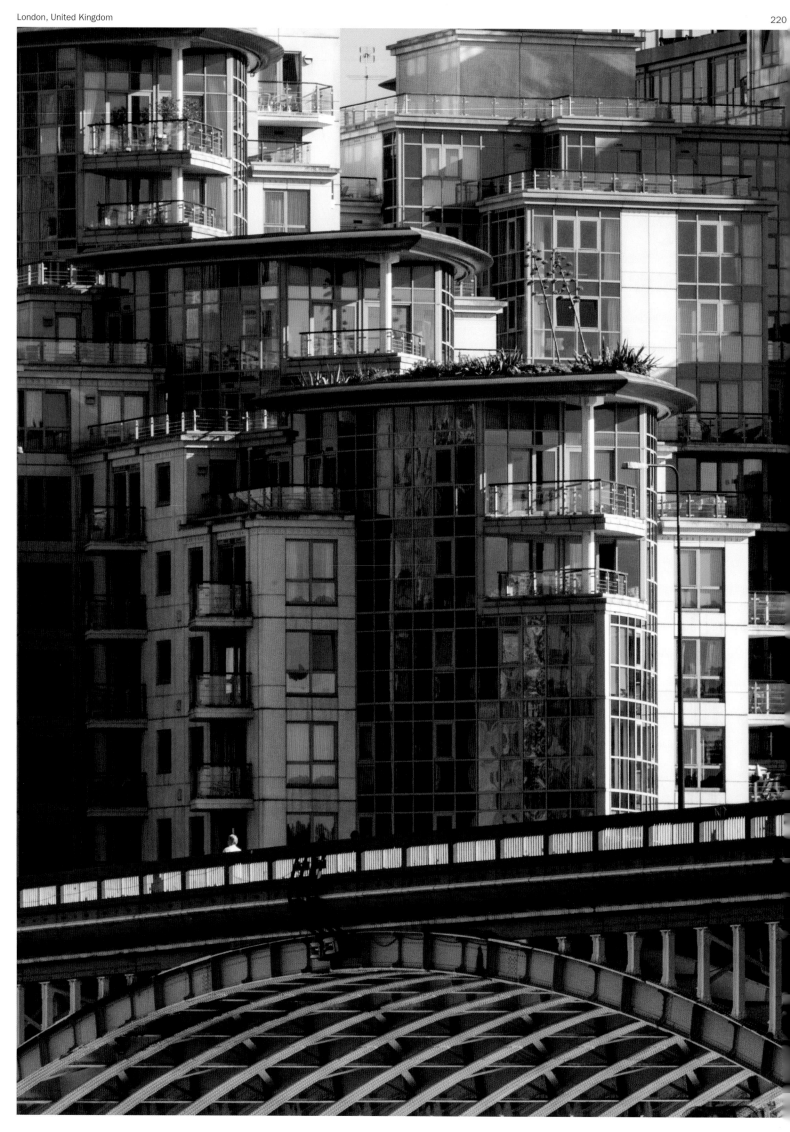

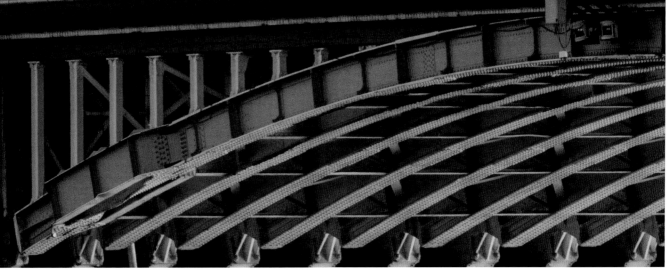

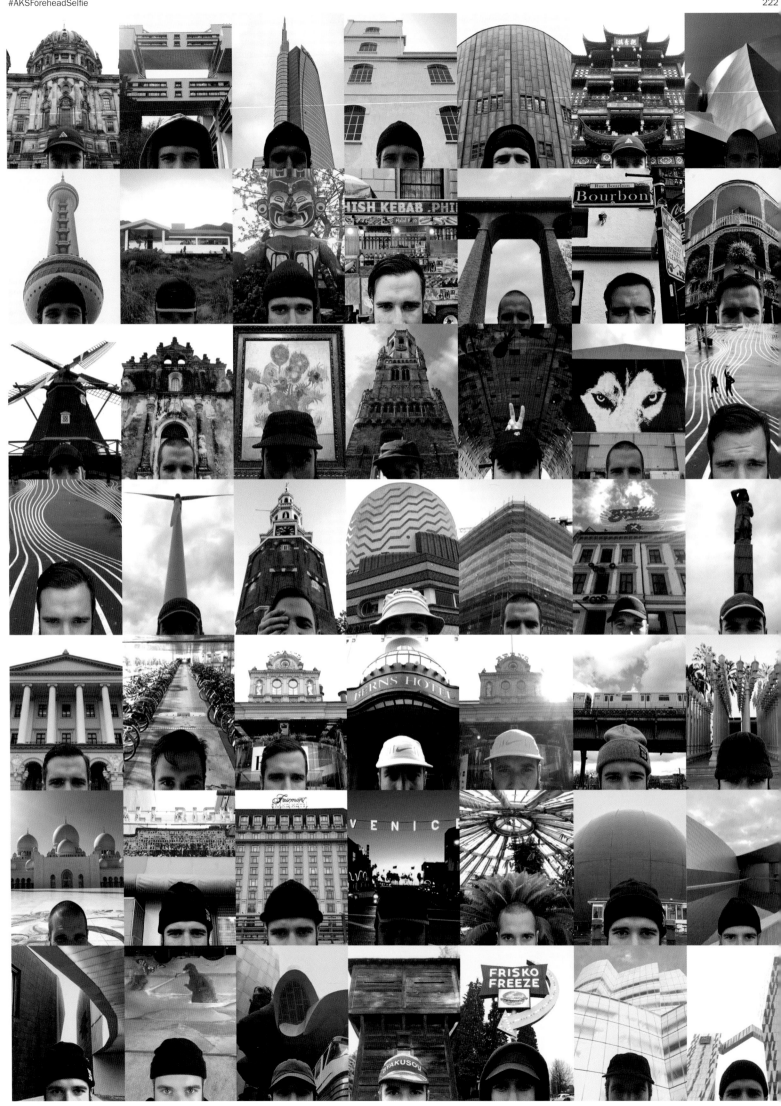

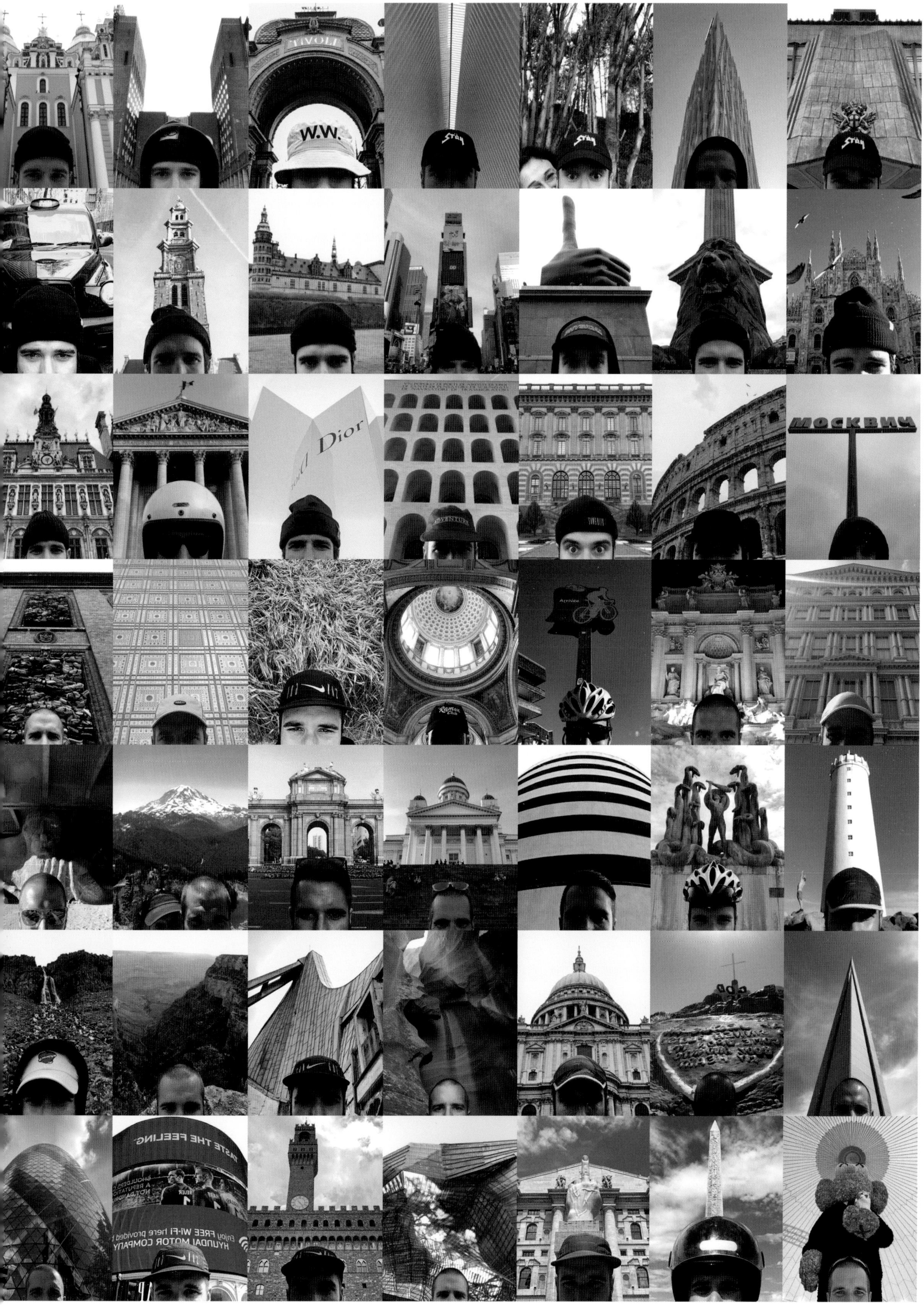
TIVOLI
W.W.
Dior
МОСКВИЧ
TASTE THE FEELING
HYUNDAI MOTOR COMPANY

**THANKS, MOM,
FOR THE TRAVEL GENE**

AND THANK YOU,
Cecilia Singley
Joe Harper
Errolson Hugh
Everyone who's touched
it at MENDO
And lastly, thanks for
everyone who's put up
with my jet jag.

ADAM KATZ SINDING
AdamKatzSinding.com
Studio@AdamKatzSinding.com
@aks

a **teNeues** | **MENDO** publication

© 2019 teNeues Media GmbH & Co. KG, Kempen
© 2019 MENDO *mendo.nl*
Photographs © 2019 Adam Katz Sinding
All rights reserved.

Edited and written by MENDO *mendo.nl*

Publisher: Gunifort Uwambaga, MENDO
Creative Director: Joost Albronda, MENDO
Copy: Mikel van den Boogaard, MENDO
Editorial Coordination: Christina Reuter, teNeues Media
Production: Dieter Haberzettl, teNeues Media
Color Separation: Jens Grundei
Copy Editing & Proofreading: Carla Sakamoto

Published by teNeues Publishing Group
teNeues Media GmbH & Co. KG
Am Selder 37, 47906 Kempen, Germany
Phone: +49-(0)2152-916-0
Fax: +49-(0)2152-916-111
e-mail: *books@teneues.com*

Press department: Andrea Rehn
Phone: +49-(0)2152-916-202
e-mail: *arehn@teneues.com*

teNeues Media GmbH & Co. KG
Munich Office
Pilotystraße 4 80538 Munich, Germany
Phone: +49-(0)89-443-8889-62
e-mail: *bkellner@teneues.com*

teNeues Media GmbH & Co. KG
Berlin Office
Kohlfurter Straße 41–43, 10999 Berlin, Germany
Phone: +49-(0)30-4195-3526-23
e-mail: *ajasper@teneues.com*

teNeues Publishing Company
350 7th Avenue, Suite 301, New York, NY 10001, USA
Phone: +1-212-627-9090
Fax: +1-212-627-9511

teNeues Publishing UK Ltd.
12 Ferndene Road, London SE24 0AQ, UK
Phone: +44-(0)20-3542-8997

teNeues France S.A.R.L.
39, rue des Billets, 18250 Henrichemont, France
Phone: +33-(0)2-4826-9348
Fax: +33-(0)1-7072-3482

www.teneues.com

ISBN 978-3-96171-199-4
Library of Congress Number: LoC 2019939879

Printed in the Czech Republic

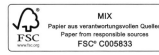

MIX
Papier aus verantwortungsvollen Quellen
Paper from responsible sources
FSC® C005833

teNeues Publishing Group
Kempen
Berlin
London
Munich
New York
Paris

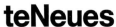

LIVE FROM F*CKING HVERARÖND
LIVE FROM F*CKING HOLON
LIVE FROM F*CKING PASANAURI
LIVE FROM F*CKING ACHKHOTI
LIVE FROM F*CKING DEATH VALLEY
LIVE FROM F*CKING MOUNT SAINT HELENS
LIVE FROM F*CKING HELSINKI
LIVE FROM F*CKING ZVARTNOTS
LIVE FROM F*CKING ROTTERDAM
LIVE FROM F*CKING DEAD SEA
LIVE FROM F*CKING TEL AVIV
LIVE FROM F*CKING CLALIAM BAY
LIVE FROM F*CKING PRAGUE
LIVE FROM F*CKING ANTELOPE CANYON
LIVE FROM F*CKING PISA
LIVE FROM F*CKING KLAMPENBORG
LIVE FROM F*CKING DYRHÓLAEY
LIVE FROM F*CKING ISTANBUL
LIVE FROM F*CKING QUITO
LIVE FROM F*CKING COPENHAGEN
LIVE FROM F*CKING MALIBU
LIVE FROM F*CKING MOSCOW
LIVE FROM F*CKING NEW ORLEANS
LIVE FROM F*CKING DUPONT
LIVE FROM F*CKING SHI SHI BEACH
LIVE FROM F*CKING CAGLIARI
LIVE FROM F*CKING HELSINGØR
LIVE FROM F*CKING MONOPOLI
LIVE FROM F*CKING RIGA
LIVE FROM F*CKING LAGUNA DE APOYO
LIVE FROM F*CKING JERZU
LIVE FROM F*CKING SÓLHEIMASANDUR
LIVE FROM F*CKING FLORENCE
LIVE FROM F*CKING PALM SPRINGS
LIVE FROM F*CKING LUXEMBOURG
LIVE FROM F*CKING NANAIMO
LIVE FROM F*CKING LISBON